SCIENCE
FUSiON

fusion [FYOO • zhuhn] a combination of two
or more things that releases energy

This Write-In Student Edition belongs to

Belsabel Semere 6

Teacher/Room

Ms. Hansrote 5th room 12

 HOUGHTON MIFFLIN HARCOURT

HOUGHTON MIFFLIN HARCOURT

Front Cover: *crab* ©Mark Webb/Alamy; *Great Basin National Park* ©Frans Lanting/Corbis; *tree frog* ©DLILLC/Corbis; *beaker* ©Gregor Schuster/Getty Images; *rowers* ©Stockbyte/Getty Images.

Back Cover: *Giant's Causeway* ©Rod McLean/Alamy; *digital screen* ©Michael Melford/Stone/Getty Images; *mountain biker* ©Jerome Prevost/TempSport/Corbis; *gecko* ©Pete Orelup/Getty Images.

Printed in the United States of America

ISBN 978-0-547-71937-5

19 20 21   0877   22 21 20 19
4500785625   CDEFG

Consulting Authors

Michael A. DiSpezio
Global Educator
North Falmouth, Massachusetts

Marjorie Frank
*Science Writer and Content-Area Reading
    Specialist*
Brooklyn, New York

Michael Heithaus
*Director, School of Environment and Society
Associate Professor, Department of Biological
    Sciences*
Florida International University
North Miami, Florida

Donna Ogle
Professor of Reading and Language
National-Louis University
Chicago, Illinois

Program Advisors

Paul D. Asimow
*Professor of Geology and
    Geochemistry*
California Institute of Technology
Pasadena, California

Bobby Jeanpierre
*Associate Professor of Science
    Education*
University of Central Florida
Orlando, Florida

Gerald H. Krockover
*Professor of Earth and Atmospheric
    Science Education*
Purdue University
West Lafayette, Indiana

Rose Pringle
Associate Professor
School of Teaching and Learning
College of Education
University of Florida
Gainesville, Florida

Carolyn Staudt
Curriculum Designer for Technology
KidSolve, Inc.
The Concord Consortium
Concord, Massachusetts

Larry Stookey
Science Department
Antigo High School
Antigo, Wisconsin

Carol J. Valenta
*Associate Director of the Museum and
    Senior Vice President*
Saint Louis Science Center
St. Louis, Missouri

Barry A. Van Deman
President and CEO
Museum of Life and Science
Durham, North Carolina

Power Up with Science Fusion!

Your program fuses . . .

e-Learning & Virtual Labs

Labs & Explorations

Write-In Student Edition

. . . to generate new science energy for today's science learner— *you.*

Write-In Student Edition

Be an active reader and make this book your own!

Write your ideas, answer questions, make notes, and record activity results right on these pages.

Learn science concepts and skills by interacting with every page.

Pushes and pulls

Gravity
Gravity pu... force that k... on the roa...

...uses objects
object... stop moving

Active Re... As you read these t... ...ges, draw circles around two words tha... ...e types of forces.

...hat have you pus... ...r pulled ...ay? Maybe you p...ed open a ...d on your shoes... ...ush or a ...ce. Suppose you wa... ...change ...omething is moving. A... ...an object's speed or dire...

Many ...rces act on you. Gravity is a for... that pulls o...jects down to Earth. Gr... keeps you on the ground o... Friction is a fo... against the direc... slow things down...

Labs & Activities

Science is all about doing.

Ask questions and test your ideas.

Draw conclusions and share what you learn.

How Does Drought Affect Plants?

A drought happens when a place gets much less rainfall than normal. What happens to plants when their environment changes and they do not get the usual amount of water?

Materials
5 plastic cups
black marker
125 seeds
potting soil
water
measuring cup

1. Label the cups A through E.

2. Fill each cup with moist potting soil. Plant 25 seeds in each cup.

3. Water the cups according to the following schedule:
- Cup A—50 mL of water each day
- Cup B—25 mL of water each day
- Cup C—50 mL of water every other day
- Cup D—50 mL of water once a week
- Cup E—no water

4. Make a hypothesis how the seeds in the different cups will grow.

5. Place the cups on a sunny windowsill. Observe the cups for two weeks.

Exciting investigations for every lesson.

e-Learning & Virtual Labs

Digital lessons and virtual labs provide e-learning options for every lesson of *ScienceFusion*.

What Are Organs and Body Systems?

Unit 2 Lesson 1 : What Objects Are Part of the Solar >

The "Oddball Planets"

On your own or with a group, explore science concepts in a digital world.

360° of Inquiry

Contents

LIFE SCIENCE

© Houghton Mifflin Harcourt Publishing Company   (b) ©David Noton/Alamy Images

© Houghton Mifflin Harcourt Publishing Company   (b) ©Martin Shields/Alamy Images

PHYSICAL SCIENCE

© Houghton Mifflin Harcourt Publishing Company   (t) ©Getty Images/Digital Vision

Changes to Earth's Surface

Big Idea

Earth's surface is constantly changing.

I Wonder Why

Canyon de Chelly is a deep sandstone canyon in the high desert of Northern Arizona. Why did it get this way? *Turn the page to find out.*

Here's why The action of wind and water over time, along with the slow rising of the surface of Earth, cut Canyon de Chelly into the sandstone rock of Northern Arizona.

In this unit, you will explore the Big Idea, the Essential Questions, and the Investigations on the Inquiry Flipchart.

Levels of Inquiry Key ■ DIRECTED ■ GUIDED ■ INDEPENDENT

Track Your Progress

Big Idea Earth's surface is constantly changing.

Essential Questions

Now I Get the Big Idea!

Science Notebook

Before you begin each lesson, be sure to write your thoughts about the Essential Question.

Essential Question

How Do Weathering and Erosion Shape Earth's Surface?

Engage Your Brain!

Find the answer to the following question in this lesson and record it here.

How do you think this arch formed?

_____

_____

_____

Active Reading

Lesson Vocabulary

List the terms. As you learn about each one, make notes in the Interactive Glossary.

_____

_____

_____

_____

Cause and Effect

Some ideas in this lesson are connected by a cause-and-effect relationship. Why something happens is a cause. What happens as a result of something else is an effect. Active readers look for effects by asking themselves, What happened? They look for causes by asking why it happened.

What can Break a Boulder?

When you think of rocks, words like *hard* and *solid* may come to mind. You may think rocks can't ever break, but that's not true. Rocks can be cracked and crushed by mere wind and rain.

Active Reading As you read these pages, underline all of the different things that can cause a rock to break down.

The roots of this tree broke apart the rock.

When it rains, water can get into the cracks of rocks.

When water freezes, it expands. This widens the cracks.

When water freezes again, it pushes the cracks in the rocks even wider. When this happens many times, the rock breaks apart.

The process of rock breaking apart is called **weathering**. Many different things can cause weathering. Gravity can cause rocks to fall down a cliff and break rocks below. Flowing water can cause rocks to tumble and scrape against rocks in the riverbed. Sand blown by wind can scrape against rocks.

Living things can also cause weathering. A tree's roots can grow in a small crack in a rock. As the roots grow, it can push the rock apart until the rock breaks. Animals may dig up rocks, causing the rocks to be exposed to wind and rain.

Chemicals in water and rain that flow through and around rocks can also cause weathering. These chemicals can combine with the rock and change it so that it crumbles and wears away. Look at the statues on this page. Chemical weathering has already changed one of the statues.

WEATHERED

How Will Weathering Change What This Statue Looks Like?

Describe how this statue may look in the future.

old, dirty, it will have mold

Rocks on the Move

Don't rocks just sit around in the sun all day?
No! Rocks can move—find out how.

Weathering is the beginning of a series of changes that often occur to rocks on Earth's surface. The same wind and water that can cause weathering also can carry the broken bits of rock away. The process of moving weathered rock from one place to another is called **erosion** [uh•ROH•zhuhn].

1

1 The erosion of rock is caused by many different natural processes. Moving water is one of the most common causes of erosion. The fast-moving water in this stream can shift or move large rocks near the top of the mountain. Together with gravity, water can cause the rocks to move downhill.

2

2 The water pulls the larger pieces of weathered rock along the river's bottom. As the water slows down, it has less energy. It cannot move the largest rocks and pebbles. These are left behind as the water moves on. The dropping of weathered rock by wind or moving water is known as **deposition** [dep•uh•ZISH•uhn].

What Happens Next?

These pictures show the Yangtze River before and after a dam was built across the river. How do you think the dam affects the movement of sediment?

the dam made it more wide then before

BEFORE

AFTER

③

As the water in a river continues to slow down, more bits of weathered rock are dropped. This happens because slow-moving water has less energy than fast-moving water. So, slow-moving water can carry only very small pieces of rock, such as sand and silt. These bits of rock are called **sediment**.

③

④

When rivers reach the ocean, they slow down even more. As they slow down, much of the remaining sediment in the water is dropped. Over time, the sediment piles up near the mouth of the river. It forms a landform called a *delta*.

④

Blowing in the Wind

The wind is just moving air, so what can it do? A lot—wind can pick up and move sand and other sediment.

Active Reading As you read the text, circle three effects the wind has on Earth's surface.

A landform is a natural land shape or feature. Weathering and erosion by wind change landforms. Wind can carry particles of sediment from place to place. When the wind deposits a lot of sand in one area, *sand dunes* form. Sand dunes are often found near sandy beaches, but dunes also form far from oceans. The dunes of some deserts span thousands of kilometers.

The shape of a sand dune constantly changes. Wind sweeps up one side of a dune and lifts sand from its surface. Then, gravity pulls the sand down the other slope.

An entire hill of sand gradually advances in this way.

Blowing sediment can also cause changes to other landforms. Particles carried by wind collide with exposed rock and cause weathering. Exposed rock can slowly erode, leaving interesting shapes. Mushroom rocks and arches are formed by water but shaped by the wind. Over time, they become thinner and more fragile. Eventually, gravity pulls these formations to the ground.

▶ Draw an arrow on the dunes to show the direction in which the wind is blowing. Explain how this relates to the direction of the dune's movement.

the hill give me

Namibia, Africa

The dunes of the Namib Desert can move up to 10 m (33 ft) each year.

Wall Arch

BEFORE

AFTER

▶ Write a sentence that explains what shaped Wall Arch. Then name three processes that caused it to collapse.

_____

_____

_____

_____

_____

_____

Utah, United States

Until its collapse in 2008, Wall Arch's opening was 22 m (72 ft) high and 10 m (33 ft) wide.

Ice Carvings

Can you imagine an ice cube the size of a city?
Some chunks of ice are even larger than that!

Active Reading As you read the text, **underline** two landforms caused by glaciers.

Huge sheets of ice are called glaciers. Glaciers are found in very cold places. Because glaciers are made of solid ice, you may think they do not move. But gravity pulls glaciers downhill. The ice flows like a very slow river. As a glacier flows, it picks up the rocks and soil beneath it. A glacier can pick up rocks as big as school buses!

▶ Think of two ways gravity helps glaciers shape landforms.

_____

_____

_____

_____

Glaciers formed the Great Lakes in North America.

Glacier Bay, Alaska

A glacier can make grooves in rock. A little bit of ice can weather rock, too. Water seeps into tiny cracks and expands as it freezes. This widens the cracks until the rock breaks.

CARVED BY ICE!

As a glacier moves forward, it pushes boulders against the ground below. They can carve deep grooves into rock. When a glacier begins to melt, the rocks and sediment it carried downhill drop out. The dropped-off sediment forms different land features, including hills called *moraines* [muh•RAYNES].

Many glaciers, such as the one at Glacier Bay, Alaska, are still frozen today. In the distant past, though, much more of Earth's surface was covered with glaciers. A huge glacier once covered most of Canada and the northern United States. The ice cut deep grooves that filled with fresh water as the glacier melted. This formed the Great Lakes. The largest, Lake Superior, is more than 400 m deep in some places!

Do the Math!
Analyze Data

As a glacier's front edge moves downhill, it is said to be advancing. A glacier that melts faster than its front edge advances is said to be retreating. Look at the data on the diagrams. Identify whether each glacier is advancing or retreating.

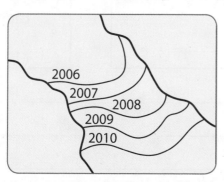

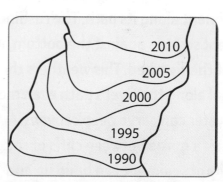

Can Waves Cut Caves?

Water carries dirt down the drain when you wash your hands. It also carries rocks and sediment down a river or along a shoreline.

Active Reading As you read the text, circle one effect of water erosion.

Moving water causes weathering and erosion. A flowing river picks up sediment along its path. The rushing sediment scrapes against the bottom and sides of the riverbed. This weathers the material along the river's path even more. River water can carve deep *canyons*. A canyon is a gorge between cliffs of rock. Deposits of sediment can build up and force river water to change directions. Curves in a river's path change over time and produce different landforms.

▶ Write how water caused these landforms. Explain how the two causes differ.

	→ sea arch
	→ canyon

_____

_____

_____

_____

Arizona, United States

The Colorado River slowly carved the Grand Canyon. This process occurred over millions of years.

As a river gets older, its course may change. The banks become less steep, and the distance across gets wider.

A sea arch forms when waves erode a cave all the way through a narrow cliff.

Ocean waves crash forcefully into rocks along the shore. The waves weather cliffs, erode away pieces of broken rock, and deposit the sediment in new places. Waves can cut caves into shoreline cliffs. The sediment from eroding shorelines becomes fine particles of sand. Beaches form where the sand is deposited at the water's edge.

▶ What do you think will eventually happen to this sea arch? Explain.

_____

_____

_____

WASHED AWAY BY WATER!

Do Plants Protect Soil?

The Great Plains of the United States can be a very dry, windy area. Grasses that naturally grow there keep moisture in the soil. Their roots hold the soil in place.

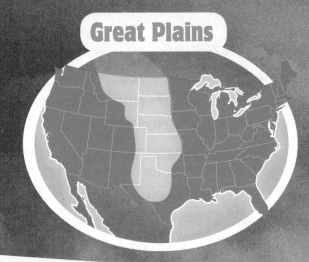

Great Plains

In the early 1900s, many families made their living in the central plains by farming. They deeply plowed hundreds of thousands of square kilometers of land where natural grasses had grown before. In between crop seasons, fields of loose soil were left exposed to the wind.

During the 1930s, the plains experienced severe drought. The bare soil turned to fine, dry dust. Then, the high winds blew the soil away in gigantic dust storms. Clouds of dust traveled as far as New England and even out over the Atlantic Ocean! Dust fell like snow.

A dust storm can travel up to 120 km/h (75 mph)!

These dust storms occurred regularly for years. Wind erosion stripped away much of the soil that had made the region good for farming. Families had to move away and find other ways to survive. Many starved and suffered terribly hard times. That region of the country became known as the Dust Bowl. It taught a valuable lesson about erosion problems caused by removing all the plants from an area.

Now, farmers plant different crops at different times to keep soil covered year-round. In yards and small fields, fencerows and lines of trees break the wind. Adding plants to hillsides protects soil from water erosion as well as from wind.

▶ Add to the drawing to show what you could do to prevent erosion. Explain what you drew.

Sum It Up!

When you're done, use the answer key to check and revise your work.

Use the information in the summary to complete the cause-and-effect graphic organizers.

Summarize

Over time, wind, water, ice, gravity, plants, and animals cause rocks to break down into smaller pieces. Bits of broken-down rock, or sediment, are eroded by such agents as wind and flowing water. Eventually, the sediment is deposited. Deposited sediment forms landforms, such as deltas and sand dunes.

1

| Water enters the cracks in a rock and freezes into ice. | → | _____ _____ _____ |

2

| _____ _____ _____ | → | Sediment is deposited at the mouth of the river and forms a delta. |

© Houghton Mifflin Harcourt Publishing Company   (tr) ©Lindsey Stock/Alamy; (br) ©NPA/Getty Images

Answer Key: 1. The ice causes the rock to crack and break apart. **2.** A river erodes sediment and carries it downstream.

Name _____

Word Play

1 Use the words in the box to complete the puzzle.

Across

1. What process causes rocks to break down into smaller pieces?

4. What process causes eroded sediments to be dropped off in another place?

6. What is a land feature such as a sea arch or a canyon called?

7. What landform moves in the direction of the wind?

Down

2. What process carries away weathered rock?

3. What is a large sheet of flowing ice called?

5. What landform is caused by sediment deposited at the mouth of a river?

7. What are broken-down pieces of rock called?

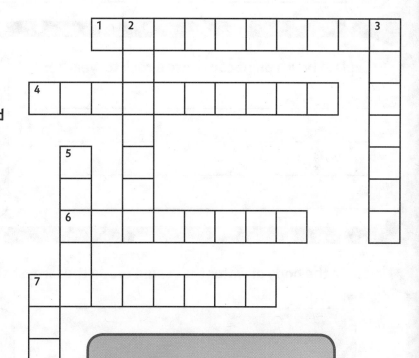

delta   deposition*   erosion*   glacier

landform   sand dune   sediment*   weathering*

*Key Lesson Vocabulary

Apply Concepts

2 Make a list of things that can weather rock.

_____   _____

_____   _____

_____   _____

_____   _____

3 Explain how a plant can cause a rock to weather.

_____

_____

_____

_____

4 Circle the body of water that could erode the largest sediments.

Name _____

5 For each landform shown, write the word that tells what caused the landform to form. Choose from the list of words below.

wind ice water

_____

_____

_____

6 For each landform below, write whether the landform was formed by erosion or by deposition. Describe how you know your answer is correct.

_____
_____
_____
_____

_____
_____
_____
_____

_____
_____
_____
_____

_____
_____
_____

Take It Home!

With your family, walk through your neighborhood or local park. Find objects that have been left outside for a long time. Describe how you think weathering has changed these objects.

Extreme Weather Gear

To survive in extreme cold, people need special clothing. Layers that serve different purposes provide the protection. But the layers can't be too bulky, or the wearer won't be able to move around easily.

Headwear

Down coat

Mittens/gloves

Boots need to be waterproof, warm, and lightweight. Your feet are far from your heart, so it is harder for warm blood to keep them warm. So gear for hands and feet must be very effective.

Down pants

Insulated boots

This fabric's outer layer keeps out water and wind. Inner layers provide insulation and help keep the body dry.

Think About It

Keeping warm is important, but so is keeping dry! Clothing that causes a person to sweat can be dangerous. Wet skin can chill quickly. How could extreme-weather clothing be designed to prevent that?

_____

_____

Dressing to deal with extreme weather conditions applies not only to the cold. The body needs protection in extreme heat as well.

What gear would you wear to protect yourself in the environment below? Draw the gear, and explain what protection it provides.

_____

_____

_____

You are going on a hike. The weather forecast predicts rain. What would you wear? From what materials should your clothing be made?

_____

_____

Build On It!

Rise to the engineering design challenge—complete **Design It: Build a Seismograph** in the Inquiry Flipchart.

Name _____

Essential Question

How Does Water Change Earth's Surface?

Set a Purpose
What will you learn from this activity?

_____

_____

_____

Think About the Procedure
1. What do the materials in the activity represent?

_____

_____

_____

2. Why do you position the tray to produce a slope?

_____

_____

_____

Record Your Data
Use the table below to record your observations. Draw or describe your model's appearance before and after you pour the water.

	Top view	Front view	Side view
Before water			
After water			

Draw Conclusions

What happened to the sugar under the clay?

_____

_____

_____

Describe how your model demonstrates a process that shapes landforms.

_____

_____

_____

_____

Analyze and Extend

1. What would you expect to happen in places with steeper slopes where water moves downhill faster?

_____

_____

_____

2. What would you expect to happen in places where it rains daily compared to places that receive very little rain?

_____

_____

_____

3. What is the role of the clay in this model? What does it represent?

_____

_____

_____

4. What additional factors could affect the rate of cave formation?

_____

_____

_____

5. Explain how you could test the effect of one of the factors you listed in question 4.

_____

_____

_____

_____

6. What other questions do you have about how water weathers rock?

_____

_____

_____

Essential Question

How Do Movements of the Crust Change Earth?

Engage Your Brain!

Find the answer to the following question in the lesson and record it here.

How does Earth's interior shape its surface?

_____

_____

_____

Active Reading

Lesson Vocabulary
List the terms. As you learn about each one, make notes in the Interactive Glossary.

crust	fault
mantle	earthquack
core	egicenter
Plate tectonics	volcano

Signal Words: Sequence
Many ideas in this lesson are connected by a sequence, or order, that describes the steps in a process. Active readers look for a sequence when they read about one step in a process and move on to another.

INSIDE THE EARTH

Have you ever dug a hole in the ground? What do you think you would find if you could dig a hole all the way to Earth's center?

Active Reading As you read these two pages, put brackets [ ] around four words for the layers of Earth's interior.

It's not really possible to dig a hole to the center of Earth. But scientists have done research with technology to learn what is beneath Earth's surface. Earth is a sphere made up of very different layers.

▶ Identify each Earth layer by its description. Then draw a line from your answer to that layer on the diagram.

Largest portion of Earth's interior

mantle

Made of molten metal

outer core

Made of solid iron and nickel

inner core

Thin, rigid rock layer

core

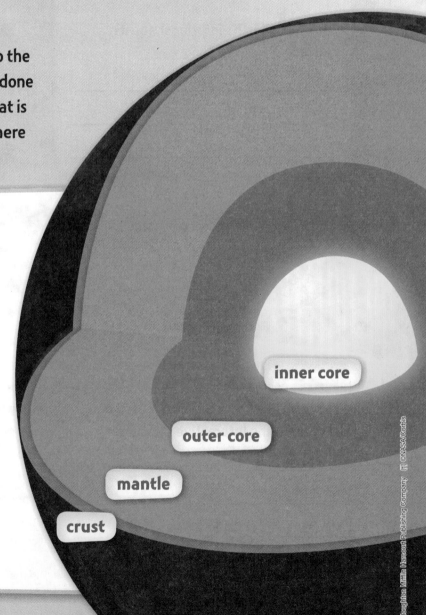

inner core

outer core

mantle

crust

If you look closely at a slice of bread, you'll see that the crust is very thin compared to the inside of the bread. The same is true of Earth. Earth's **crust** is its rocky outer layer. The crust is hard and made of many minerals. Earth's crust is thinnest under the oceans and thickest under mountains. The crust makes up only about one percent of Earth's mass.

The layer below Earth's crust is the **mantle**. The mantle is the thickest layer, making up about two-thirds of Earth's mass. The mantle contains some liquid rock but is mostly solid. High heat and pressure in the mantle cause it to flow slowly like warm plastic.

At the center of Earth is a **core** made of metal. The *inner core* is solid iron and nickel. The *outer core* is molten, liquid metal. The metal core makes up about one-third of Earth's mass and is extremely hot.

5–70 km (3–43 mi)

2,885 km (1,790 mi)

2,270 km (1,410 mi)

1,210 km (750 mi)

diagram not to scale

▶ You can learn different things from these two diagrams of Earth's layers. Explain the difference.

I can learn the km and the mi. And the names

PLATE TECTONICS

You can see objects in motion all around you. Did you know the surface of Earth beneath your feet is in motion, too?

Active Reading As you read these two pages, draw boxes around the names of two things that are being compared.

Earth's crust is a hard shell of rock, but it is not one solid piece. Many pieces of crust, called *plates*, fit together like a jigsaw puzzle. The plates rest on Earth's mantle. If Earth's mantle flows like warm plastic, do the plates move, too? Yes, they do! The motion of Earth's plates is very slow, however. It happens too slowly to see.

The theory that Earth's crust is divided into plates that are always moving is called **plate tectonics**. Some plates contain mostly continental crust. Others contain mostly oceanic crust. Many plates are made of a combination of the two. In some places, plates are moving toward each other. In other places, the plates are spreading apart.

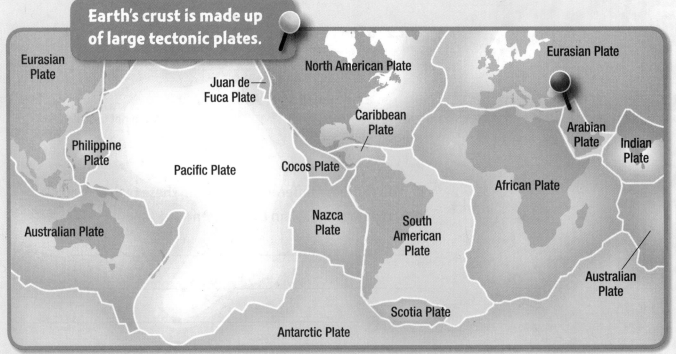

Earth's crust is made up of large tectonic plates.

Eurasian Plate

North American Plate

Juan de Fuca Plate

Caribbean Plate

Philippine Plate

Pacific Plate

Cocos Plate

Eurasian Plate

Arabian Plate

Indian Plate

African Plate

Nazca Plate

South American Plate

Australian Plate

Australian Plate

Scotia Plate

Antarctic Plate

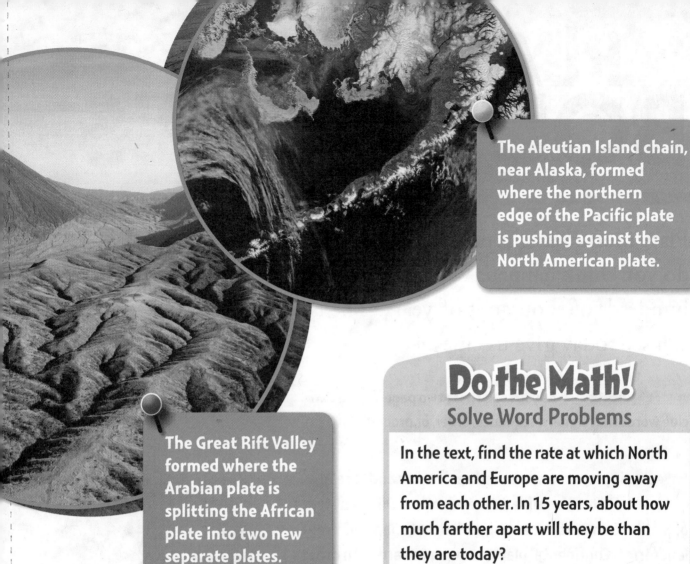

The Aleutian Island chain, near Alaska, formed where the northern edge of the Pacific plate is pushing against the North American plate.

The Great Rift Valley formed where the Arabian plate is splitting the African plate into two new separate plates.

Do the Math!
Solve Word Problems

In the text, find the rate at which North America and Europe are moving away from each other. In 15 years, about how much farther apart will they be than they are today?

_____

_____

▶ What can you tell by comparing the shapes of the continents with the shapes of Earth's plates?

the plate are
pushing the continents

_____

_____

_____

Look on the map at the plates that contain North America and Europe. Each year, North America and Europe are about 19 mm farther apart!

Certain land features form where plates collide. Other features form where plates separate. Mountain ranges, island chains, and enormous valleys are some likely signs of a plate boundary.

PLATE BOUNDARIES

Plate motion might be too slow to see, but what do you think happens where two plates meet over hundreds of thousands of years? The landforms we can see today give us clues.

Active Reading As you read these two pages, circle two clue words that signal a sequence, order, or process.

Tectonic plates move toward each other and spread apart. Plates also slide past each other. Different types of plate motion produce boundaries that shape different landforms. Continental plates moving toward each other push up mountains. When an oceanic plate moves toward another oceanic plate, one of them is pushed down under the other. This collision can cause a deep-ocean trench and an arc of volcanic islands to form. When an oceanic plate collides with a continental plate, the denser oceanic plate sinks under the continental plate, causing mountains and volcanoes to form along the boundary between the plates. When plates pull apart, new crust forms a ridge on both sides of the boundary.

The Himalayas

Two plates can slide sideways past each other. Earthquakes occur often at these boundaries. At the San Andreas Fault in California, the North American plate is moving southward, and the Pacific plate is moving northward.

Two plates can pull away from each other. On land this forms a rift, or separation. Iceland sits across the separating boundary between the North American plate and the Eurasian plate. It will eventually become two separate landmasses.

As two continental plates move together, their edges fold and bend, pushing up mountain ranges. The Himalaya Range in Asia includes the world's highest mountain peaks. The Himalayas are still growing today as the Indo-Australian plate pushes against the Eurasian plate.

▶ Draw arrows on the diagram to show a kind of plate boundary. Then draw a landform that could occur at that kind of boundary.

EARTHQUAKES

Movement of whole tectonic plates is very slow, but once in a while a small piece of Earth can shake enough to crumble buildings to the ground!

Seismographs are used to record and predict earthquakes.

A **fault** is a break in Earth's crust where rock on one side can move in relation to rock on the other side. As plates move, pressure builds up along the fault. When the pressure becomes too great, the rock on one side of the fault suddenly snaps free and slides past the rock on the other side. This release of energy and shaking of the ground is called an **earthquake**.

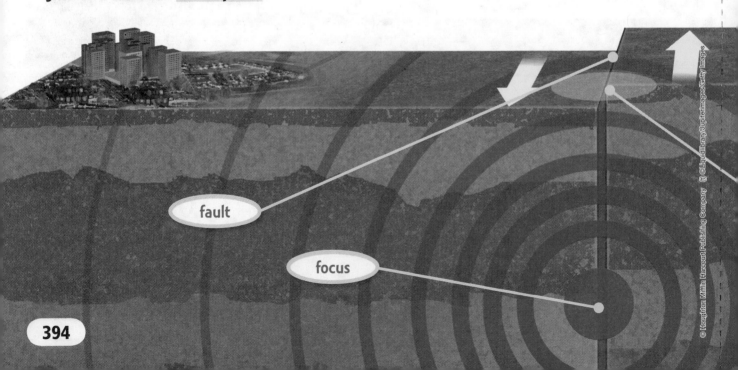

fault

focus

© Houghton Mifflin Harcourt Publishing Company (t) ©Liquidlibrary/Jupiterimages/Getty Images

The point inside Earth where an earthquake begins is called the *focus*. The energy from an earthquake travels away from the focus in waves. When the energy waves reach the surface, the ground shakes. The point on Earth's surface directly above the focus is called the **epicenter**. Earthquake motion is most severe at the epicenter.

Smaller waves of energy occur near the focus before an earthquake. The tremors may not be felt at the surface, but a device called a seismograph can graph them. Scientists can use a seismograph to predict if an earthquake is likely to occur. There is no way to prevent earthquakes, though. To avoid injuries during an earthquake, avoid buildings, bridges, or other structures that are likely to fall down. Earthquakes can be dramatic and can cause great damage to built structures.

When the ground at a fault shifts, it moves structures built on it.

▶ Compare what the motion of the ground was probably like during these two earthquakes as shown from a seismograph.

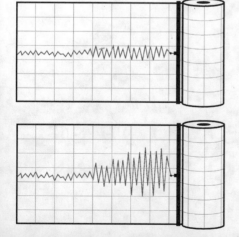

the first one is a small earth-quack, and the second one is a big earthquack

epicenter

energy waves

MEASURING EARTHQUAKES

How do scientists describe the strength of an earthquake? Do they measure the size of its energy waves? Do they figure out the total amount of energy it produces? They do both.

Active Reading As you read these two pages, draw boxes around the names of two things that are being compared.

An earthquake's *magnitude* is the amount of energy it releases. The *Richter scale* measures the magnitude of earthquakes on a scale from 1 to 10. The scale uses the size of waves on a seismograph to determine an earthquake's strength. An earthquake that measures 2.0 on the Richter scale is too mild to feel. About 8,000 earthquakes measuring below 2.0 on the Richter scale occur every day!

An earthquake in Italy in 2009 caused extensive damage.

Presidential Palace, Haiti

Before

After

Moment magnitude	Earthquake location and year
9.5	Chile, 1960
8.3	Kuril Islands, Russia, 2006
7.9	Sichuan Province, China, 2008
7.0	Haiti, 2010
8.8	Chile, 2010

Each one-point increase on the Richter scale means an increase in strength of about 31 times. An earthquake measuring 6.0 or higher on the Richter scale can cause heavy damage in populated areas. Earthquakes measuring 6.0 or stronger occur about 120 times per year.

The Richter scale was developed in 1935. Scientists have since developed a more accurate way to measure the magnitudes of larger earthquakes. The moment magnitude scale uses a mathematical formula to calculate the total energy that an earthquake releases. The moment magnitude scale also assigns numbers between 1 and 10. In January of 2010, an earthquake measuring 7.0 on the moment magnitude scale caused catastrophic damage to a densely populated area in Haiti.

▶ Explain which of these locations would experience greater earthquake damage.

9.5 chile 1960

city

country

VOLCANOES

The heat and pressure in Earth's interior are intense enough to melt rock. Does that liquid rock ever make it to the surface? Yes, it does!

Active Reading As you read these two pages, draw boxes around the names of two processes that are being compared.

Over 450 active volcanoes line the rim of the Pacific plate. The belt is called the Ring of Fire.

The liquid rock below Earth's crust is called *magma*. At boundaries where plates are either moving toward each other, pulling away from each other, or at hotspots in the middle of plates, openings in the crust can occur. A **volcano** is an opening that allows magma to reach Earth's surface. *Lava* is the molten rock that erupts from the volcano along with ash and hot gases.

The shape of a volcano depends on how that volcano erupts. Some volcanoes erupt explosively, spewing lava, ash, and gases high into the air. Other volcanoes erupt with a slower, steadier flow of lava.

Nonexplosive lava flows form shield volcanoes. Broad sheets of lava steadily build up to form the wide, low shape of a warrior's shield. The island of Hawai`i is made up of five shield volcanoes.

Explosive eruptions form cinder cone volcanoes. Lava explodes into the air and quickly hardens. The fragments fall and collect to form the volcano's steep slope. Paricutín is a cinder cone volcano in Mexico.

Alternating types of eruptions form composite volcanoes. Explosive eruptions produce the steeper slope, and liquid lava flows cement the fragments in place. Mount St. Helens, in Washington State, is a composite volcano.

▶ Which type of volcano does the photo show? Describe the formation process.

Nonexplosive is lava form shield.
Explosive is a cinder cone volcano in
mexico. Alternating is a typ of eruption form.

Sum It Up!

When you're done, use the answer key to check and revise your work.

I. Write the vocabulary term that matches each definition.

A. _outer core_   Earth's liquid metal layer

B. _crust_   The rigid, rocky layer of Earth

C. _mantle_   The thickest layer of Earth

D. _inner core_   Earth's solid metal layer

E. _volcano_   An opening in Earth's crust where magma can reach the surface

II. Summarize

Pieces of Earth's crust move in a process called _Plates tectonics_. Motion of the _Plate fault_ causes pressure to build up. Eventually, the pressure causes rock on one side of a _fault track_ to snap free and slide past the rock on the other side. This shakes the ground, producing an _earthquake_. The point inside Earth where an earthquake begins is called the _foucs_. The _epicenter_ is the point on Earth's surface directly above the focus.

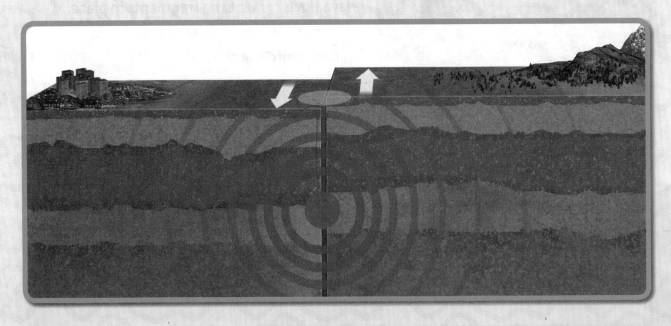

Name _____

Word Play

1 Unscramble the words in the word box, and then write the correct word on each line.

scouf ~~fouse~~   uftal ~~faut~~ _fault_   cusrt _crust_   reco _core_
telnam _mantle_   reeahaqukt   reeptinec
                    earthquake   _epicenter_

fouse _____ The strongest surface point of an earthquake

mantle _____ Contains most of Earth's mass

fault _____ A break in the crust where rock can slide past other rock

earthquake _____ Shaking ground at a moving fault

crust _____ Earth's outermost layer

epicenter _____ The point where an earthquake begins

core _____ Earth's innermost section, made of two layers

True or False:

The temperature of Earth gets colder the closer you move toward the core. _false_

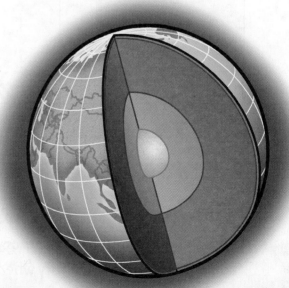

Apply Concepts

2 Identify each type of volcano.

explosive   Nonexplosive   Alternating

3 Describe the process that is causing the Himalayas to continue to grow.

Himalays keep grow because of the plates.

4 Compare and contrast the Richter scale and the moment magnitude scale.

the richter scale is increase and moment magnitude use Mathematical

5 Explain the difference between the two seismograph readings.

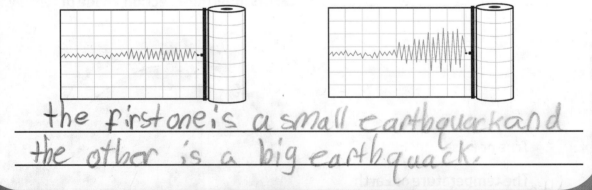

the firstone is a small earthquark and the other is a big earthquack.

Take It Home!

Research the locations of faults on the Internet with the help of an adult. Make a map to identify where faults are located in the United States.

Ask a Seismologist

Q. What do seismologists do?

A. They use advanced tools to detect the tiniest movements in Earth's crust. They can learn a lot about earthquakes this way.

Q. Why is seismology important?

A. Seismologists warn people about where some earthquakes might happen in the future. They can also warn people when earthquakes happen under the ocean.

Q. How do seismologists know where natural disasters will happen?

A. Seismologists watch places where Earth's plates rub and move. They also watch hot spots around the world. These are places where magma from under Earth's crust comes to the surface. Hot spots are among the places where volcanoes form.

Be a Seismologist!

Look at the world map. Numbers are placed where earthquakes are most likely. Write each number below the description that correctly explains why earthquakes happen there.

Pacific Ring of Fire: A place where many volcanoes are found because of ocean trenches and plate movements

_____

hot spot: A place far from tectonic plate boundaries where a plate moves slowly over a hole below it that lets out magma

_____

plate boundaries: A place where tectonic plates push against each other and shift positions

_____

mountain-building area: A place where plates move under or over each other to raise the surrounding land

_____

Name _____

Essential Question

How Do Plates Move?

Set a Purpose
What will you model during this activity?

_____

_____

_____

Think About the Procedure
What do the materials in this activity represent?

_____

_____

_____

_____

Record Your Data
Describe what happens as you push the strips of paper up through the slit in the box.

_____

_____

Draw your model from two angles and label the parts in each.

Draw Conclusions

What does the rising paper in the model represent?

_____

_____

_____

Infer what happens to the continental crust as plates move apart.

_____

_____

_____

Analyze and Extend

1. Plates can move toward or slide past each other. Use your model to demonstrate these other plate movements. Draw and describe what happens to the continents.

_____

_____

_____

2. By observing and using models, scientists infer how the continents move. Based on your model, what can you infer about the positions of these four continents millions of years ago?

_____

_____

_____

What do you predict will happen to these four continents over the next five million years?

_____

_____

3. If the clay represents the crust and the paper strips represent the mantle, how might this explain how the continents move?

_____

_____

_____

_____

4. What other questions would you like to ask about plate movement?

_____

_____

_____

_____

Unit 8 Review

Vocabulary Review

Use the terms in the box to complete the sentences.

> core
> crust
> deposition
> epicenter
> mantle
> sediment
> volcano
> weathering

1. Motion of the ground is most severe at an earthquake's

   _____.

2. Tectonic plates move over the partly melted layer of Earth called

   the _____.

3. Deltas, canyons, and caves are all parts of Earth's

   _____.

4. An opening from which lava erupts is

   a(n) _____.

5. Weathering by wind, water, and ice produces

   _____.

6. Earth is made of many layers. The densest layer of Earth is the

   _____.

7. The process of wearing away rock is known as

   _____.

8. A landslide quickly erodes sediment on a steep hill. When the
   landslide reaches the bottom of the hill, it slows down and finally
   comes to rest. The sediments it leaves are called

   _____.

Science Concepts

Fill in the letter of the choice that best answers the question.

9. Wind, water, and ice can change rocks. So can living things.

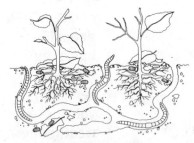

Look at the drawing. Which of these statements is **true**?

(A) The worms are eroding sediment.

(B) The plant roots are depositing sediment.

(C) The pill bugs are causing chemical weathering.

(D) All of the living things are dropping sediment to form deltas.

10. Alexa observed this landform on a trip to Alaska.

What is this landform and how did it form?

(A) It is a valley that was carved by a glacier.

(B) It is a dune that formed as wind eroded sand.

(C) It is an arch that was carved by a slow-moving river.

(D) It is a delta that formed when a river deposited sediment.

11. Look at the drawing. It is a cut-away view that shows Earth's structure.

To which layer of Earth is the arrow pointing?

(A) crust   (C) outer core

(B) mantle   (D) inner core

12. Volcanoes and earthquakes are two effects of plate tectonics. What does the theory of plate tectonics state?

(A) Earth's mantle is solid.

(B) Earth's crust is divided into parts that move.

(C) Earth's inner core causes changes in the crust.

(D) Earth's outer core is liquid, and its inner core is solid.

13. Why do earthquakes occur along faults?

(A) Rocks along a fault are stable.

(B) Rocks along a fault are easily eroded.

(C) Rocks along a fault are under pressure.

(D) Rocks along a fault are easily weathered.

14. Places where tectonic plates meet are called boundaries. Different landforms form along different boundaries.

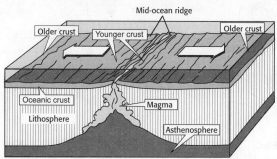

If this boundary is on the ocean floor, what type of landform will form as the plates move?

(A) an ocean trench

(B) a shield volcano

(C) a mountain chain

(D) an arc of volcanoes

15. Natural processes change Earth's surface. Some of these processes affect humans and human-made structures.

Which Earth process **most likely** caused the damage in this picture?

(A) an earthquake

(B) a volcanic eruption

(C) erosion by strong winds

(D) water freezing in a crack in the road

16. The shape of a volcano depends on how the volcano erupts. Examine the drawing.

Based on the information given and the drawing, which is a valid conclusion?

(A) The eruption is explosive.

(B) The eruption is nonexplosive.

(C) The volcano is a shield volcano.

(D) The volcano is in the Ring of Fire.

17. A scientist is studying a volcano that is made of alternating layers of liquid lava and explosive materials such as ash. What type of volcano is it?

(A) cinder cone

(B) shield volcano

(C) lava flow cone

(D) composite cone

Apply Inquiry and Review the Big Idea

Write the answer to these questions.

18. Anish is doing a science activity. Her setup is shown here.

Identify two Earth processes being modeled. Describe what will happen when Anish pours the water over the sand. Predict what would happen if Anish propped up one end of the pan before she poured the water over the sand.

_____

_____

_____

19. In the activity *How Do Plates Move?*, you used a shoebox, strips of paper, and clay to model what happens when plates move apart. Explain how you could add to the model to show what happens at places where plates come together.

_____

_____

_____

20. Jenna is modeling the movement of plates. She is using a beaker of water, a hot plate, and some pieces of foam. Explain what each part of the model represents and how it would work.

_____

_____

_____

_____

The Rock Cycle

Big Idea

Rocks and minerals are formed and changed through different Earth processes.

I Wonder Why

The Bingham Canyon Mine is about 0.75 mi deep and 2.5 mi across. Why would people dig a hole that big? *Turn the page to find out.*

Here's why Bingham Canyon Mine in Utah has produced many tons of copper ore, from which the metal copper is made. Copper is used in many products from electric wires to teapots.

In this unit, you will explore this Big Idea, Essential Questions, and investigations on the Inquiry Flipchart.

Levels of Inquiry Key ■ DIRECTED ■ GUIDED ■ INDEPENDENT

Track Your Progress

Big Idea Rocks and minerals are formed and changed through different Earth processes.

Essential Questions

Now I Get the Big Idea!

Science Notebook

Before you begin each lesson, be sure to write your thoughts about the Essential Question.

Essential Question

What Are Minerals?

Engage Your Brain!

Find the answer to the following question in this lesson and record it here.

You find a clear mineral that can't be scratched by any other minerals. It has a glassy luster. What mineral did you probably find?

_____

_____

_____

_____

Active Reading

Lesson Vocabulary

List the terms. As you learn about each one, make notes in the Interactive Glossary.

_____

_____

_____

_____

Visual Aids

Charts, diagrams, and photos add information to the text that appears on the page with them. Active readers pause their reading to review each visual aid and decide how the information in the visual aid adds to what is provided in the running text.

What Are Minerals?

What do copper, table salt, and diamonds have in common? They are all minerals!

A **mineral** [MIN•er•uhl] is any nonliving solid that has a crystal form. All minerals form in nature—under the ground, in caves, and even in the air. Plastic and bricks are not minerals; they are made by people. There are over 4,700 different minerals found on Earth.

When you think of crystals, you may think of ones like those in caves. Yet not all crystals look like those. Mineral crystals come in different shapes, but there is something that is the same. The particles in a crystal combine to form a shape that is repeated over and over again. It is this repeated structure that defines a crystal.

Minerals are the same in another way. Each mineral is made up of the same set of nonliving things called elements. For example, the mineral calcite is always made of the elements calcium, carbon, and oxygen. Rubies are always made of aluminum and oxygen. Diamonds are always made of carbon.

Do the Math!
Identify Shapes

One characteristic that can help you identify minerals is crystal shape. Draw a line from the name of each shape to the crystal that best matches that shape.

Square Pyramid	Square Prism	Hexagonal Prism

Pyrite

Fluorite

Beryl

Which Mineral Is Which?

With more that 4,700 minerals in the world, how can you tell one mineral from another?

Active Reading On this page, underline two mineral properties.

Hardness is one property used to identify minerals. *Hardness* is a mineral's ability to scratch another mineral. In 1812, a scientist named Friedrich Mohs [mohz] developed a scale to compare the hardnesses of different minerals.

On the Mohs scale, a mineral with a higher number can scratch another mineral with a lower or equal number. The softest minerals score a 1. Every other mineral can scratch minerals with a hardness of 1. The hardest mineral—a diamond—scores a 10 on the Mohs scale. A diamond can't be scratched by any mineral except another diamond.

Another property used to tell one mineral from another is luster. *Luster* describes how minerals reflect light. The minerals copper, gold, and silver each have a metallic luster. Talc and gypsum [JIP•suhm] each have an earthy luster.

The Mohs Scale

talc	gypsum	calcite	flourite	apatite
1	2	3	4	5

▶ Suppose you found this bright purple mineral. How would you describe its luster?

_____

_____

The mineral can be scratched by diamond but not by feldspar. What could the mineral's hardness be?

_____

earthy luster

metallic luster

Luster can be described using words such as *metallic, earthy,* and *glassy.*

glassy luster

You can scratch minerals with a hardness of 2 or less with a fingernail. You can scratch minerals with a hardness of 6 or less with a steel nail.

feldspar	quartz	topaz	corundum	diamond

6   **7**   **8**   **9**   **10**

Magnetite attracts things that have iron in them.

Unique Properties of Minerals

You can use all sorts of properties to identify minerals. Some are more useful, some less. But use all of them, and you'll probably identify the mineral.

Active Reading Underline the name of the mineral that has a greenish-black streak.

The color of a mineral may vary, but its streak is always the same.

You've learned that mineral crystals come in different shapes. Mineral crystals also break in a certain way. The way a mineral breaks can be used to identify it. When some minerals break, the broken sides are smooth and straight. Minerals that break this way have *cleavage*. Minerals that do not break along smooth lines have *fracture*.

To identify a mineral, you can rub the mineral against a white tile called a streak plate. The color left behind is called the mineral's *streak*. Sometimes a streak is the same color as the mineral itself. But this is not true for many minerals. Pyrite has a gold color, but its streak is greenish-black.

A mineral can come in different colors. Corundum [kuh•RUHN•duhm] crystals can be red, blue, green, yellow, purple, or brown. Yet no matter what color the corundum crystal is, its streak is always white. Because of this, streak color is useful when identifying a mineral.

Some minerals have other properties. Calcite and fluorite glow under a black light. Calcite also fizzes when you put a drop of vinegar on it. Quartz can conduct electricity.

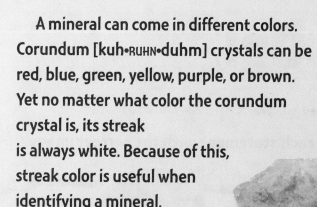

This piece of mica [MY•kuh] has cleavage. It breaks into thin, flat sheets.

Confused by Color?

Look at the minerals shown here. They are all quartz. How could you show that they are all quartz? What tests could you use?

_____

_____

_____

_____

Sum It Up!

When you're done, use the answer key to check and revise your work.

Read the summary statements. Then match each statement with the correct image.

1 Minerals are nonliving solids that have crystal shapes. Garnet crystals are shaped almost like soccer balls. _____

A

2 A mineral's hardness can help to identify it. Fluorite has a hardness of 4. It can be scratched with a steel nail. _____

B

3 Different minerals reflect light in different ways. This property is called luster. Gold has a metallic luster. _____

C

4 Minerals that break in straight lines have cleavage. The mineral mica breaks into thin, flat sheets. _____

D

5 You can see a mineral's streak color using a streak plate. Each mineral has a characteristic streak color. Graphite has a black to gray streak. _____

E

Answer Key: 1. C 2. A 3. E 4. B 5. E

Word Play

Name _____

1 Use the words in the box to complete each sentence. Then use the circled letters to answer the question below.

cleavage	crystal	hardness	luster	minerals*	streak

* Key Lesson Vocabulary

1. You can find out a mineral's ◯_ _ _ _ _ _ _ by seeing what other minerals it can scratch.

2. A nonliving solid that has a _ _ _ _ _◯_ form is called a mineral.

3. Gold, silver, copper, and pyrite each have a metallic ◯_ _ _ _ _ .

4. Fluorite, talc, diamond, gold, and quartz are all examples of _ _◯_ _ _ _ _ _ .

5. The color left behind when a mineral is rubbed across a white tile is its _ _◯_ _ _ _ .

6. A mineral that breaks along straight, smooth lines is said to have _ _ _◯_ _ _ _ _ .

I "ROCK" AT WORD PLAY!

Question:

Which mineral is also known as table salt?

◯ ◯ ◯ ◯ ◯ ◯

Apply Concepts

2 Make a list of the different properties that can be used to identify a mineral.

_____   _____

_____   _____

_____   _____

3 Magnetite has a metallic or earthy luster, a gray-black streak, and a hardness of 5–7. Circle the mineral that is most likely magnetite.

Mohs Hardness Scale	
1	Talc
2	Gypsum
3	Calcite
4	Fluorite
5	Apatite
6	Feldspar
7	Quartz
8	Topaz
9	Corundum
10	Diamond

This mineral can scratch talc but not calcite.

This mineral can scratch apatite but not quartz.

This mineral can scratch apatite but not quartz.

4 Which part of the description helped you identify the mineral?

_____

_____

5 Which mineral did you rule out first? How?

_____

_____

Take It Home!

Using building blocks, chenille sticks, or other items, build a model of a crystal. Your crystal can be any shape, but remember that crystals have a repeating shape.

Bernard Hubbard

As a child, Bernard Hubbard collected rocks from Prospect Park and Central Park in New York City. During high school, he entered his collection in a rock and fossil contest. He won third place. He went on to become a geologist. Today, Dr. Hubbard helps find places around the world that may have volcanic activity. Hubbard's work with the U.S. Geological Survey helps people know where to avoid building structures.

Meet the Geniuses of Geology

Florence Bascom

In 1896, the U.S. Geological Survey hired its first woman—Florence Bascom. She became interested in geology as a child while on a driving tour with her father and his friend, a geology professor. Bascom spent much of her career studying an area called the Piedmont. It is a plateau region in the eastern United States. She also taught geology at a women's college in Pennsylvania. Bascom collected crystals, minerals, and rocks for the college. Several of her students followed in her footsteps and became geologists, too.

Identify Mystery Minerals

Geologists have identified thousands of minerals based on their properties. Read the description of each mineral below. Match the mineral to the correct picture based on its description. Then write the name of the mineral next to its picture.

Apatite is usually green or gray. It has a hardness of 5 and can be scratched with a knife. It has a glassy or greasy luster.

Talc is usually white to almost silver in color. It has a hardness rating of 1 and can leave a mark when rubbed on paper. It has a dull luster.

Diamond is usually colorless. It has a hardness rating of 10 and can be scratched only by another diamond. A diamond has a shiny or waxy luster.

Gypsum is usually white or gray. It has a hardness rating of 2 and can be scratched with a fingernail. It has a glassy or pearly luster.

Dull luster, 1 on the Mohs scale

_____

Glassy luster, 2 on the Mohs scale

_____

Glassy luster, 5 on the Mohs scale

_____

Name _____

What Are Properties of Minerals?

Set a Purpose

Why is it important to know how to classify things?

_____

_____

_____

Think About the Procedure

Name three mineral properties you will be using in this activity.

_____

_____

_____

Record Your Data

In the table below, record your observations. Beneath the table, describe how you would classify the minerals into groups using one of the properties in the table.

Mineral Sample	Luster	Streak	Hardness

_____

_____

Draw Conclusions

Which mineral that you tested is the hardest? Which is the softest? Explain how you know.

_____

_____

_____

_____

How did you classify the mineral samples?

_____

_____

_____

_____

_____

_____

Did you classify your minerals in the same way as other students? Why or why not?

_____

_____

_____

_____

Analyze and Extend

1. What are some other ways minerals can be classified?

_____

_____

_____

_____

_____

2. Based on your observations, which property or properties do you think are most helpful in identifying a mineral? Explain.

_____

_____

_____

_____

_____

_____

3. What other questions would you like to ask about the properties of minerals?

_____

_____

_____

_____

Essential Question

How Can Rocks Be Classified?

Engage Your Brain!

Find the answer to the following question in this lesson and record it here.

Mount Rushmore National Memorial in South Dakota was carved out of granite that formed from cooled magma. What type of rock matches this description?

_____

_____

_____

_____

Active Reading

Lesson Vocabulary

List the terms. As you learn about each one, make notes in the Interactive Glossary.

Rhyolite rock cool
down from lava quickly

_____

_____

Sequence

Many ideas in this lesson are connected by a sequence, or order, that describes the steps in a process. Active readers stay focused on the sequence when they mark the transition from one step in a process to another. Focus on the sequence of formation as you read about different classifications of rocks.

Gabbro forms below Earth's surface as magma cools slowly. It contains large crystals of the mineral quartz.

Like gabbro, granite forms below Earth's surface and has large mineral crystals.

Igneous Rock

A volcano erupts. Hot lava sprays into the air and flows over the ground. As lava cools, it hardens. It's a rock factory in production mode. What type of rock forms this way?

Active Reading As you read these two pages, **underline** the sentences that describe how igneous rocks form.

Just what is a rock? A **rock** is a natural solid that is made of one or more minerals. Rocks are classified by how they form. The three types of rocks are igneous, sedimentary, and metamorphic.

One way that rock forms is when melted rock, called magma or lava, cools and hardens. Rock that forms when magma or lava harden is called **igneous rock** [IG•nee•uhs]. Igneous rock can form deep inside Earth as magma slowly cools. It can also form on Earth's surface when a volcano erupts and the lava cools.

Basalt has very small mineral crystals. It forms at Earth's surface and is the most common igneous rock on Earth.

Basalt columns in Ireland

Rhyolite forms as lava cools quickly at Earth's surface. It has small mineral crystals.

An igneous rock's appearance gives clues about where it formed. When magma cools slowly beneath Earth's surface, large mineral crystals form. The rock that forms from these minerals has crystals that you can see with the unaided eye. Gabbro and granite are examples of rocks that form this way. When lava at Earth's surface cools quickly, mineral grains do not have time to grow. As a result, igneous rocks that form at Earth's surface, such as rhyolite and basalt, contain small mineral crystals. To study the small crystals in basalt, you need a magnifying glass or, sometimes, a microscope.

Clues from Crystals

Look at the two igneous rocks shown here. Which rock cooled more quickly? How do you know? Infer how each rock formed.

Porphyry   Obsidian

Porphry cools down quickly. Obidian cools down not that fast

Lava cools very quickly at Earth's surface. Mineral crystals have little time to form and remain small.

The temperature of magma can range from 700 °C (1,292 °F) to 1,200 °C (2,192 °F). Below Earth's surface, magma cools more slowly than it does at or near the surface. Because it cools more slowly, mineral crystals have time to form and become large.

sedimentary Rock

Rocks are broken by ice, wind, and water. The pieces are moved from place to place and fall like a gentle rain out of the water and wind that carry them. How can those pieces form another kind of rock?

Active Reading As you read the next page, write 1, 2, and 3 in the margin next to the sentences that give the sequence in which sedimentary rock forms.

What would happen if you placed a flower under a stack of books? Eventually, the weight of the books would flatten the flower. The same thing happens to deposited sediment. *Sediment* is particles of weathered rock. **Sedimentary rock** [sed•uh•MEN•tuh•ree] forms from sediment that gets cemented together under pressure.

Sediment from weathered and eroded rock collects in loose layers.

More layers of sediment are deposited on top. The additional weight presses on the layers underneath.

Over time, the sediment at the bottom becomes cemented, or glued, together.

Rock salt forms from salt left behind when salt water evaporates. The main mineral in rock salt is halite. It is one source of the salt you sprinkle on your food.

Houghton Mifflin Harcourt Publishing Company (bg) ©Kerrick James/Alamy; (t) ©D. Meissner/Ace Images GmbH/Alamy

The sandstone walls of Antelope Canyon in Arizona have been carved and smoothed by flowing water. You can see layers of sediment in the rock.

Conglomerate forms from pebble-sized particles with smooth, round edges.

As layers of sediment are deposited, bottom layers get pressed together by the weight of the layers above. Air and water in the spaces between the sediment layers are squeezed out. Over time, sediment becomes cemented together and forms sedimentary rock.

Sandstone, shale, and conglomerate are distinguished by the size of the sediment they contain. Shale is made of very fine sediment. Sandstones have larger sediment than shale does. Conglomerates contain even larger sediment. Sometimes sedimentary rock contains fossils, too. A *fossil* is the remains or the signs or trace of a living thing, such as a bone, a shell, a leaf imprint, or a fossil footprint.

Some sedimentary rock forms through chemical processes. Rock salt and limestone are two types of sedimentary rock that form when minerals dissolved in water come out of solution.

Limestone is often formed from the shells of animals that live in the sea. These shells are made up of the mineral calcite. When the animals die, the shells are left behind. They are crushed into sand-sized particles, which become cemented together. Sometimes within the limestone, you can find whole shell fossils.

Where Are Fossils Found?

Why aren't fossils found in igneous rock?

it has basalt and has very small mineral crystal.

431

Metamorphic Rock

Squeeze and squeeze and squeeze and squeeze—then add a little, or a lot, of heat—and you get a different kind of rock. How do pressure and temperature change the rock?

Active Reading As you read these two pages, write a *P* next to the paragraph that explains how metamorphic rocks form.

Rock that forms when earth processes change the texture and the mineral content of rock is called **metamorphic rock**. Metamorphic rock can form as a result of high pressure, high temperature, a combination of high temperature and high pressure, or when super-hot fluids such as water come into contact with rock. The word *metamorphic* [met•uh•MAWR•fik] comes from the Greek word that means "to change form." The temperature at which metamorphic rock forms is never high enough to melt the rock. P

Marble and quartzite are examples of metamorphic rocks. Marble forms when increased temperature and pressure act on the sedimentary rock limestone. Marble is used in buildings and carved sculptures. Quartzite can form when sandstone is exposed to heat and pressure. Quartzite is used in construction of roof tiles or floors.

Most of the changes that cause rock to become metamorphic rock happen deep inside Earth. That is why most rocks you find are igneous or sedimentary, not metamorphic.

Shale is a type of sedimentary rock that forms from very fine sediment.

With high pressure and somewhat increased temperature, the layers of shale are flattened and the structures and minerals within the rock change. Shale becomes the metamorphic rock slate.

With even greater temperatures and pressure, minerals in slate can become other minerals. The way they are arranged in the rock can change. The rock can break easily along the planes where the minerals have lined up. In this way, slate can become schist, another type of metamorphic rock.

Mountains can form when two large pieces of Earth's crust push against each other. The force that pushes the mountains up also causes rocks in the growing mountains to change. Pressure builds up. Rock layers may bend, twist, and break under the pressure. Over time, many of the rocks become metamorphic rocks. You can see such metamorphic rock exposed in some mountain ranges and in areas like the Piedmont in the eastern United States.

Under intense pressure, the minerals in schist separate into bands. New minerals may form, too. This new metamorphic rock is called gneiss [NYS].

Do the Math!
Use Fractions and Percentages

This circle graph shows the relative amounts of different kinds of rock on Earth's surface.

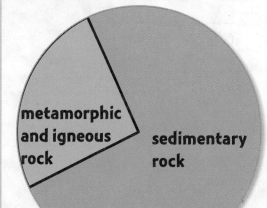

metamorphic and igneous rock

sedimentary rock

1. What fraction of Earth's surface is sedimentary rock?

_____

_____

2. Ninety-five percent of igneous rocks and metamorphic rocks are below Earth's surface. Why is this true?

_____

_____

_____

_____

The twisted rock in this landform was formed by heat and pressure.

The Rock Cycle

Once a rock, always a rock? Well, not exactly. After rock forms, it does not stay the same forever. The rock may be broken down by water and wind. It may be heated and squeezed or melted by pressure inside Earth.

Active Reading On the diagram, draw a star next to the arrow that shows the sequence of how an igneous rock becomes a sedimentary rock.

Any type of rock can become any other type of rock. Let's take sedimentary rock as the example. After molten rock has cooled to form igneous rock, weathering and erosion can break down the rock to form sediment. The sediment is deposited and layers build up and become cemented over time to form rock.

Metamorphic rock can be broken down in the same way and become sediment, which in turn becomes rock. Not even sedimentary rock is safe! It too can be broken down, transported, and deposited to become new sedimentary rock.

In the same way, temperature and pressure can act on any type of rock to transform it into metamorphic rock. Any type of rock can be melted and then cooled to become igneous rock. The continuous process of rock changing from one type to another is known as the *rock cycle.*

The rock cycle diagram summarizes the processes that work to transform Earth's rock.

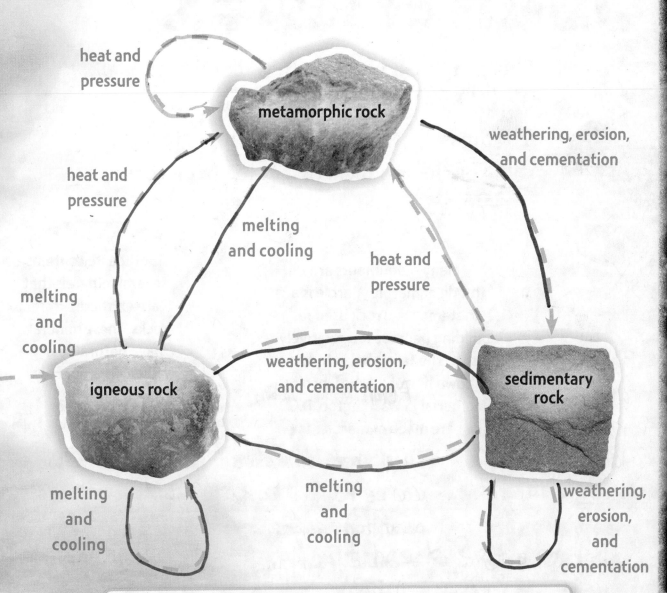

heat and pressure

metamorphic rock

weathering, erosion, and cementation

heat and pressure

melting and cooling

heat and pressure

melting and cooling

weathering, erosion, and cementation

igneous rock

sedimentary rock

melting and cooling

melting and cooling

weathering, erosion, and cementation

Changing Rocks

In the rock cycle diagram, trace all the arrows that show melting in red. Trace the arrows that show heat and pressure in green. Trace the arrows that show weathering, erosion, and cementation in brown.

Polished stones are used in jewelry and decorations.

Uses of Rock

Did you brush your teeth, walk on a sidewalk, or pass by a stone-faced building today? Toothpaste, cement, and buildings are just some of the products that come from rocks.

Many monuments are made of marble. Marble is a metamorphic rock used for building because it is relatively soft. The Taj Mahal in India, shown here, and the Lincoln Memorial in Washington, D.C., are made of marble.

Toothpaste contains several minerals that are extracted from rocks. These minerals have natural cavity-fighting properties.

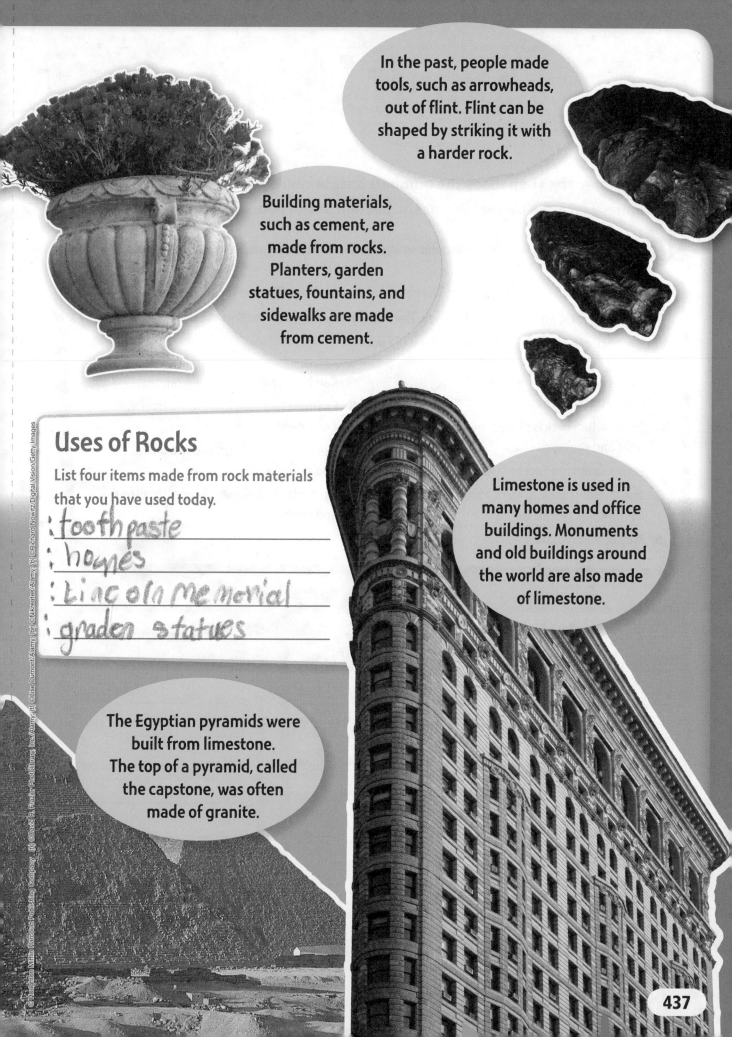

In the past, people made tools, such as arrowheads, out of flint. Flint can be shaped by striking it with a harder rock.

Building materials, such as cement, are made from rocks. Planters, garden statues, fountains, and sidewalks are made from cement.

Uses of Rocks

List four items made from rock materials that you have used today.

- tooth paste
- homes
- Lincoln memorial
- graden statues

Limestone is used in many homes and office buildings. Monuments and old buildings around the world are also made of limestone.

The Egyptian pyramids were built from limestone. The top of a pyramid, called the capstone, was often made of granite.

Sum It Up!

When you're done, use the answer key to check and revise your work.

Read the summary. Then place the numbered statements below the summary into the correct box at the bottom of the page.

Summarize

Rocks are classified by how they form. The three kinds of rock are igneous rock, sedimentary rock, and metamorphic rock. The rock cycle shows that each of these kinds of rock can change into any other kind of rock.

1. Forms when sediments are cemented together
2. Forms when rock is placed under great heat and pressure
3. Forms when magma or lava cools
4. The longer it took to form, the larger its mineral crystals will be
5. May contain fossils
6. Can be found in mountain ranges
7. Examples include marble, quartzite, and gneiss
8. Examples include granite, obsidian, and rhyolite
9. Examples include sandstone, limestone, and shale

Igneous

Forms when magma or lava cools. The longer it took to form larger it's mineral crystal. granite, obsidian rhyolite.
3, 4, 8

Sedimentary

May contain fossils. Form when sediments are cemented together sandstone, limestone and shale
1, 5, 9

Metamorphic

Form when rock is placed under great heat and pressure
2, 6, 7

Answer Key: Igneous: statements 3, 4, and 8 Sedimentary: statements 1, 5, and 9 Metamorphic: statements 2, 6, and 7

Word Play

1 Draw a line from each term to its definition.

1. Rock

2. Igneous rock

3. Sedimentary rock

4. Metamorphic rock

5. Sediment

6. Rock cycle

7. Magma

8. Fossil

A. A rock that forms from bits of weathered rock

B. A rock that forms by great heat and pressure deep within Earth

C. A rock that forms from magma or lava

D. The natural processes that cause one kind of rock to change into another kind

E. Remains or traces of a once-living thing sometimes found in sedimentary rock

F. Bits of weathered rock

G. Melted rock below the ground

H. Made up of one or more minerals

Riddle

Why did the rock collector like his collection of metamorphic rocks so much?

Metamorphic Black

_____

Apply Concepts

2 What is the relationship between minerals and rocks?

_____

_____

_____

3 Draw a picture of a place on Earth where you think igneous rock would form.

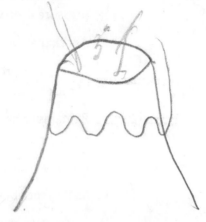

4 Circle the rock below that is most likely a sedimentary rock. How do you know?

_____

5 In the three boxes below, draw and label diagrams showing how sedimentary rock forms.

Diagram 1   Diagram 2   Diagram 3

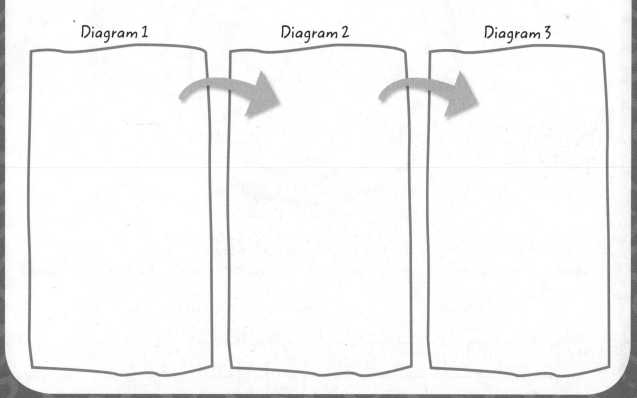

6 Circle the rock below that is most likely a metamorphic rock. How do you know?

_____

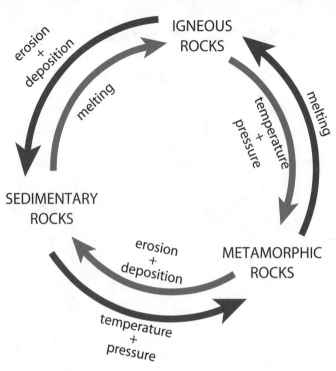

7 Look at the rock cycle diagram. How does igneous rock become metamorphic rock?

<u>temperature + pressure</u>

8 How does sedimentary rock become igneous rock?

<u>melting</u>

Take It Home!

Go on a hike or take a "walk" on the Internet with your family. Observe rocks you find. Try to identify the rocks as being igneous, sedimentary, or metamorphic.

Tools That Rock

Geologists study Earth materials and often work outdoors. They use some tools you are probably familiar with, but they might use them in unexpected ways.

Hand-held GPS device

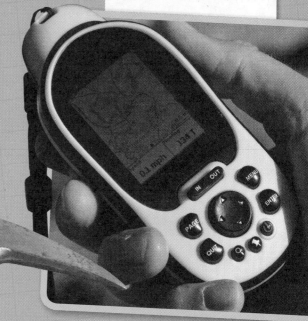

Geologists use physical tools such as this rock hammer to collect rock samples. They also use electronic technology, such as GPS for mapping and computers for recording and processing data.

Critical Thinking

Name three tools a geologist uses that are not shown here. Describe what each tool is used for.

_____

_____

_____

After collecting rocks, a geologist uses different tools to identify the samples.

How can a geologist use each of these tools below to identify a rock sample?
Do research to find out, and write your explanations below.

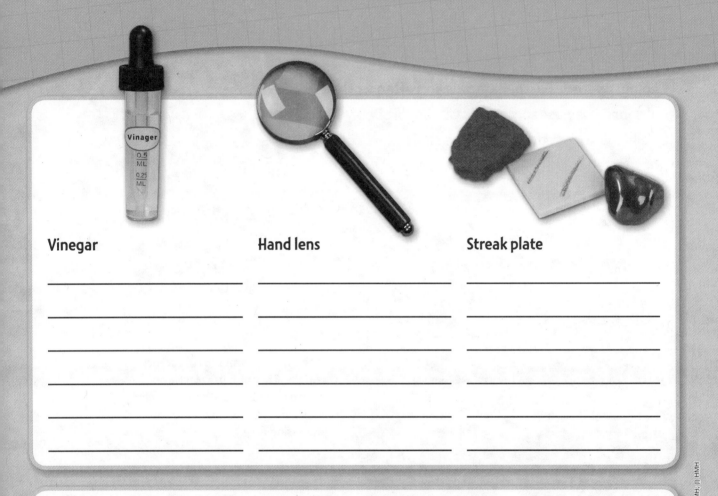

Vinegar

_____

_____

_____

_____

_____

_____

Hand lens

_____

_____

_____

_____

_____

_____

Streak plate

_____

_____

_____

_____

_____

_____

One new technology geologists use is GPS. Research how they use GPS, and write about why it is useful for geologists.

_____

_____

Build On It!

Rise to the engineering design challenge—complete **Improvise It: Separating By Size** in the Inquiry Flipchart.

Name _____

How Can You Model Changes in Rock?

Set a Purpose
What will you learn from this activity?

_____

_____

_____

_____

Think About the Procedure
How is a model useful to a student?

_____

_____

_____

Why is it important to think about what each step in this procedure models in real life?

_____

_____

_____

Record Your Observations
Draw the side view of what you made in Steps 1–4. Identify the type of rock you modeled and describe your observations.

_____

_____

_____

Draw the type of rock you modeled in Step 5. Identify the type of rock you modeled and describe your observations.

[blank drawing box]

_____

_____

_____

Draw Conclusions

What force are you modeling when you use the books?

_____

_____

In order for your model to show how metamorphic rock changes into igneous rock, what could you do?

_____

_____

_____

Analyze and Extend

1. How might using models help scientists understand the ways rocks form?

_____

_____

_____

_____

2. Explain how you could represent weathering and erosion as part of your model.

_____

_____

_____

3. How does your model represent the rock cycle?

_____

_____

_____

_____

4. What other questions do you have about how rock forms?

_____

_____

_____

_____

446

Unit 9 Review

Vocabulary Review

Use the terms in the box to complete the sentences.

> fossil
> igneous rock
> luster
> metamorphic rock
> mineral
> rock
> sedimentary rock
> streak

1. Any nonliving solid with a crystal form is called

   a(n) _____.

2. A rock that forms from lava or magma is classified as

   a(n) _____.

3. A mineral that reflects light like a piece of foil has a

   metallic _____.

4. A rock that forms when heat or pressure changes an existing rock

   is classified as a(n) _____.

5. The color a mineral leaves on a white tile is called

   its _____.

6. A rock that forms from sediment that gets cemented together

   under pressure is classified as a(n) _____.

7. A naturally formed solid made of one or more minerals is

   a(n) _____.

8. The impression of a leaf in a sedimentary rock is an example of

   a(n) _____.

Science Concepts

Fill in the letter of the choice that best answers the question.

9. The Mohs hardness scale is shown below.

Mineral	Hardness
Talc	1
Gypsum	2
Calcite	3
Fluorite	4
Apatite	5
Feldspar	6
Quartz	7
Topaz	8
Corundum	9
Diamond	10

The hardness of a steel nail is about 5.5. A certain mineral scratches a steel nail but does not scratch quartz. What could the hardness of the mineral be?

Ⓐ 4

Ⓑ 5

Ⓒ 6

Ⓓ 7

10. Scientists can manufacture diamonds from carbon by using heat and pressure. These diamonds, however, are not classified as minerals. Which statement explains why?

Ⓐ They are made from glass.

Ⓑ They are not made in nature.

Ⓒ They do not have an orderly crystal structure.

Ⓓ They do not have the same color as other diamonds.

11. Jamal is testing some minerals to try to identify them. Look at the drawing.

What property is Jamal testing?

Ⓐ cleavage   Ⓒ luster

Ⓑ hardness   Ⓓ streak

12. Erika is using a hand lens to examine a piece of granite. She observes large black and white pieces that glitter as she moves the sample under a light. What is Erika seeing?

Ⓐ fossils   Ⓒ sediment

Ⓑ minerals   Ⓓ glass shards

13. What is the main difference between igneous rocks and metamorphic rocks?

Ⓐ Metamorphic rocks are always banded.

Ⓑ Metamorphism does not involve melting.

Ⓒ Igneous rocks cannot be metamorphosed.

Ⓓ Igneous rocks are smaller than metamorphic rocks.

14. Tamika made a visual display for her science project on metamorphic rocks. This is her drawing.

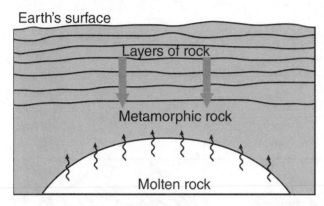

Earth's surface
Layers of rock
Metamorphic rock
Molten rock

According to her drawing, what produced the metamorphic rock?

Ⓐ pressure from the magma

Ⓑ pressure from above and heat from the magma below

Ⓒ water in the rock layers above the metamorphic rock

Ⓓ weathering of the rocks above the metamorphic rock

15. The rock cycle includes all of the processes that change rocks. This drawing shows one version of this cycle.

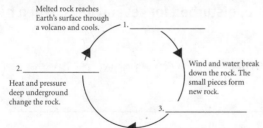

Melted rock reaches Earth's surface through a volcano and cools.
1. _____
Wind and water break down the rock. The small pieces form new rock.
2. _____
Heat and pressure deep underground change the rock.
3. _____

Suppose this drawing were on your science test. Which of these terms would you write on the line labeled 1 to make the drawing correct?

Ⓐ sediment   Ⓒ sedimentary rock

Ⓑ igneous rock   Ⓓ metamorphic rock

16. Which of these processes would change limestone into marble?

Ⓐ heat and pressure

Ⓑ melting and cooling

Ⓒ volcanism and erosion

Ⓓ weathering and cementation

17. Jada was classifying minerals by their properties. Which property would be **least** useful in classifying minerals?

Ⓐ luster   Ⓒ color

Ⓑ hardness   Ⓓ streak

18. Tyrone was given samples of four minerals. To test the hardness of each mineral, he tried to scratch each one with his fingernail, a copper penny, and a steel nail. The results of his tests are shown in the table below.

Mineral	Fingernail	Copper penny	Steel nail
Calcite	no	yes	yes
Quartz	no	no	no
Gypsum	yes	yes	yes
Fluorite	no	no	yes

Which mineral tested is the hardest?

Ⓐ calcite   Ⓒ gypsum

Ⓑ fluorite   Ⓓ quartz

Apply Inquiry and Review the Big Idea

Write the answer to these questions.

19. Val has three different minerals. All are white. Her brother Josh, who is a geologist, tells her that the minerals are quartz, calcite, and fluorite. Josh also tells Val that she can perform only two tests on each mineral to tell which is which. What should Val do?

_____

_____

_____

_____

20. Alé made a model of a rock in science class. A drawing of her rock is shown.

a. Based on her drawing, what type of rock could this be?

_____

_____

b. Alé's rock is made of very thin sheets of wax. Describe how she could do an activity to change her rock into another type of rock. Include the names of rock cycle processes.

_____

_____

21. Aldo made a model of a rock. He half-filled a paper cup with a sugar-water solution. Then he carefully added gravel and sand. He let the cup sit undisturbed for several days. When he removed the paper cup, he had a model rock.

a. Use rock cycle terms to explain how Aldo's rock formed.

_____

_____

b. Explain how Aldo could improve his model rock to make it more like an actual sedimentary rock.

_____

Fossils

©Houghton Mifflin Harcourt Publishing Company (bg) ©Sinclair Stammers/Science Photo Library/Photo Researchers, Inc.; (inset) ©Francois Gohier/Photo Researchers, Inc.; (border) ©NDisAge Fotostock

Big Idea

Fossils help us understand Earth's history.

I Wonder Why

These are shellfish fossils. Animals like these live in the ocean. Why were these fossils found on mountaintops? *Turn the page to find out.*

Here's why Fossils can tell scientists about past environments. Ocean, or marine, fossils found on mountaintops in Texas indicate that the area was once covered by an ocean. Over time the land changed, and the layers that contained the fossils rose above sea level.

In this unit, you will explore the Big Idea, the Essential Questions, and the Investigations on the Inquiry Flipchart.

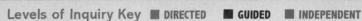

Levels of Inquiry Key ■ DIRECTED ■ GUIDED ■ INDEPENDENT

Track Your Progress

Big Idea Fossils help us understand Earth's history.

Essential Questions

○ **Now I Get the Big Idea!**

Science Notebook

Before you begin each lesson, be sure to write your thoughts about the Essential Question.

Essential Question

What Are Fossils?

Engage Your Brain!

Find the answer to the following question in this lesson and record it here.

These animals no longer live on Earth. What can scientists learn about Earth's history by studying these animals?

_____

_____

_____

Active Reading

Lesson Vocabulary

List the terms. As you learn about each one, make notes in the Interactive Glossary.

_____

_____

_____

_____

Main Ideas

The main idea of a paragraph is the most important idea. The main idea may be stated in the first sentence, or it may be stated elsewhere. Active readers look for main ideas by asking themselves, What is this section mostly about?

453

Insects can get trapped in tree sap. Hardened sap is called amber. Insect parts and even whole insects are often preserved in amber.

Sometimes, whole organisms can be preserved as fossils. This baby mammoth was frozen in ice. Its soft tissues were preserved along with its bones and teeth.

Traces of the Past

You can find seashells on many ocean beaches. These shells are from animals that are living today. Suppose you found a rock that had something in it that looks like a seashell. This is a trace of an animal that lived long ago. What other traces of past life might you find?

Active Reading As you read, underline each type of fossil discussed.

All living things contain the element carbon. Some plant tissues get preserved as *carbon films* in rock.

Footprints are examples of trace fossils. These features show that an animal was there, even though none of its parts were preserved.

The preserved remains or traces of a living thing is called a **fossil**. Fossils can be made of an organism's hard parts or its soft parts. Hard parts include bones, teeth, and shells. Soft parts are tissues such as skin and organs. Because bacteria quickly break down soft tissue, soft parts are rare as fossils. Soft-part fossils can be original tissue if it has been frozen or dried out as in a mummy. They can also be preserved as an impression in a rock.

Most fossils are found in sedimentary rock. One common way that fossils form is shown at right. Another way fossils form occurs as minerals, such as quartz, replace the shell or plant material that made up the organism. This is how *petrified* wood forms. Sometimes, the replacement is so perfect that even the bark and wood grain are visible.

These mold and cast fossils were made when a leaf was pressed into soft mud, leaving a hollow space called a **mold**. A **cast** can form if the mold is later filled with mud that hardens.

What Might You Leave Behind?

Draw a set of footprints or other trace that you might leave. Explain what part of your body would make the trace and what your trace fossil would tell future scientists.

_____

_____

The plants and animals shown on these pages are fossils. Scientists study many types of fossils to help them learn about ancient life on Earth.

Fossil Formation

1. An animal dies and settles on the bottom of a body of water.

2. Sediment buries the animal. Over time, the soft parts of the animal decay.

3. Hard parts are preserved in sediment as a fossil.

How Coal Forms

1. Plants die and settle to the bottom of a body of water. They are buried by sediment.

2. The temperature and pressure rise. Much of the water in the remains is squeezed out. The remains change into peat. Peat doesn't give off a lot of heat. It produces a lot of smoke when it burns.

3. Peat continues to be compressed and heated. Over time, all of the water is gone. Coal forms. It is hard and made of pure carbon. Coal produces a lot of heat and little smoke.

Fossils That Burn

Not all organisms are fossilized in rock. What else may happen to organisms when they die? The fossilized remains of the plant shown in this photo may give you a clue.

Active Reading As you read these pages, draw two lines under the main idea of each paragraph.

Coal forms from dead plants. When plants die, they sometimes end up at the bottom of a lake or pond. Sediment buries the plants. Over many years, the heavy layers of sediment cause the temperature and pressure underground to rise. This causes the plant material to change into coal. The higher the temperature and pressure, the better the type of coal that forms. Because the coal we use today comes from ancient plants, it is a fossil fuel. A **fossil fuel** is an energy-rich resource formed from the buried remains of once-living organisms. Coal formation is continuing in peat bogs found around the world.

How Oil and Natural Gas Form

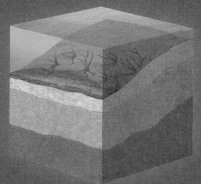 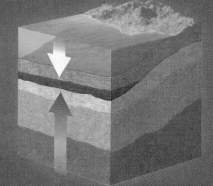 

1. Many tiny sea organisms die and settle to the bottom of the ocean where they are buried by sediment.

2. Over time, the weight of both the sediment and the water above it cause the temperature and pressure to rise.

3. Eventually, all that's left of the organisms is hydrogen and carbon. Oil and natural gas form from these elements.

Tiny diatoms are organisms that help form oil and natural gas. Imagine how many millions of them were needed to produce the fossil fuels we use today!

Oil and natural gas take millions of years to form. So the organisms that made the fuels we are using today are very old. Just like coal, oil and natural gas are fossil fuels. Today, large amounts of oil and natural gas are trapped beneath layers of rock deep below Earth's surface. Pumps remove the oil and natural gas from the ground.

Do the Math!
Use a Data Table

Products Made from a Barrel of Crude Oil (Liters)	
Diesel Fuel	35 L
Jet Fuel	15 L
Other Products	40 L
Gasoline	70 L

Oil that is pumped from the ground is called crude. Crude oil is refined to make many different products, such as gasoline for cars and fuel for jets.

About how many total liters are refined from a barrel of crude oil?

_____

How much crude oil remains after gasoline is refined from the oil?

_____

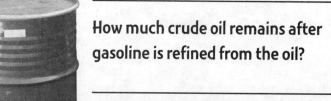

What Fossils Tell Us

Jawless fish

Armored fish

Fossils can tell us a lot about what life on Earth was like in the past.

Scientists who study fossils are called *paleontologists*. They study fossils to learn what life on Earth was like long ago. Fossils show that some types of plants and animals have changed a lot. Other plants and animals have hardly changed at all.

The woolly mammoth is related to modern elephants. It lived during the Ice Age when the climate was very cold. Today's elephants live mostly in warm climates.

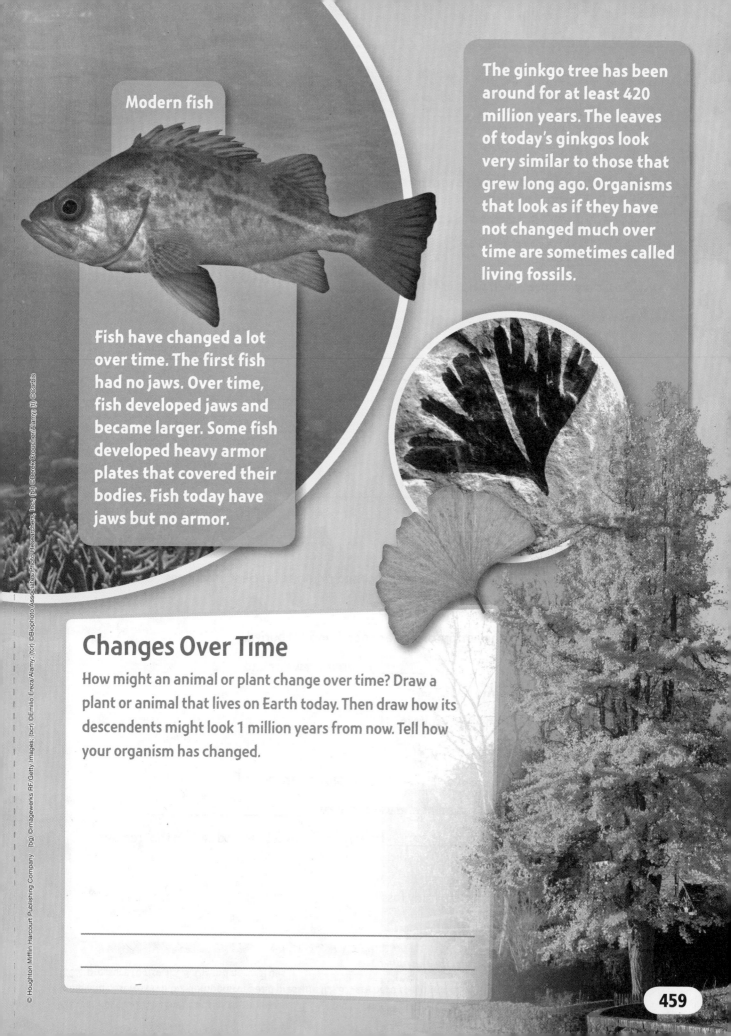

Modern fish

The ginkgo tree has been around for at least 420 million years. The leaves of today's ginkgos look very similar to those that grew long ago. Organisms that look as if they have not changed much over time are sometimes called living fossils.

Fish have changed a lot over time. The first fish had no jaws. Over time, fish developed jaws and became larger. Some fish developed heavy armor plates that covered their bodies. Fish today have jaws but no armor.

Changes Over Time

How might an animal or plant change over time? Draw a plant or animal that lives on Earth today. Then draw how its descendents might look 1 million years from now. Tell how your organism has changed.

_____

_____

When you're done, use the answer key to check and revise your work.

Complete the outline below to summarize the lesson.

Summarize

I. Traces of the Past

    A. Fossils are the preserved parts or traces of past life.

    B. How Fossils Form

        1. Organisms die and settle on the bottom of a lake or ocean.

        2. _____.

        3. _____.

    C. Kinds of Fossils

        1. preserved in amber or ice

        2. _____

        3. carbon film or trace fossil

II. Fossils That Burn

    A. Fossil fuels are fuels that come from the decay and change of ancient organisms.

    B. How Coal Forms

        1. Plants die, settle to the bottom of a lake or pond, and are buried.

        2. _____ drive off water and

          change the remains into peat.

        3. More compression and heat results in _____.

    C. How Oil and Natural Gas Form

        1. Tiny ocean organisms die and settle to the bottom and are buried.

        2. The weight of overlying sediment and water causes _____.

        3. _____ form from the hydrogen and carbon that remain.

III. What Fossils Tell Us

    A. Scientists called paleontologists study fossils.

    B. How life has changed on Earth

Answer Key: I.B.2. Sediment buries the animal. I.B.3. Soft parts decay; hard parts are preserved. I.C.2. mold and cast fossils II.B.2. Temperature and pressure II.B.3. very hard coal made of pure carbon. II.C.2. pressure to rise. II.C.3. Oil and natural gas

Name _____

Word Play

1 Read the summary statements below. Each statement is incorrect. Change the part of the statement in blue to make it correct. Use the word bank if you need help.

carbon film	fossil*	fossil fuels*	mold*
mud	paleontologist	petrified wood	trace fossil

* Key Lesson Vocabulary

1. A carbon film can be footprints preserved in rock. _____

2. A cast forms when a shell leaves its shape in the mud. _____

3. A mummy is a scientist who studies fossils. _____

4. Coal, oil, and gas are trace fossils. _____

5. The preserved remains or traces of a once-living organism is a mold.

   _____

6. A fossil leaf that is made only of carbon preserved between two rock layers is called a fossil fuel. _____

7. A cast forms when minerals fills a mold and hardens. _____

8. A paleontologist forms when minerals replace the plant material in a piece of wood.

   _____

Apply Concepts

2 Number the diagrams in the correct order to show how fossils can form.

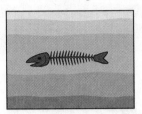      

_____   _____   _____

3 Which would have a better chance of becoming a fossil: a fish that dies and settles to the ocean floor or a mouse that dies on the ground in a forest? Explain your answer.

_____

_____

4 What is a living fossil?

_____

_____

5 Choose one type of fossil. Draw a three-panel comic strip to show how the fossil forms. Write a description and labels for each picture to show how the fossil forms.

Take It Home!

Make one kind of fossil using a grape. Set up an area where you can leave the grape sitting undisturbed for several days. Examine the grape each day and note any changes. When would you consider the grape a fossil?

How It Works:

Walk This Way

Measuring the distance between fossil footprints gives scientists clues about how dinosaurs walked. Studying fossilized bones tells scientists how dinosaur joints moved. Scientists use these data with the aid of computers to see what a walking dinosaur would have looked like.

A computer model starts with a skeleton. Then virtual muscles are added. Finally scientists are able to animate *Triceratops* in motion.

Troubleshooting

Study the pictures of the walking *Triceratops* below. Describe how it moves.

_____

_____

_____

S.T.E.M.

continued

Before moving-picture cameras and computer technology, people began to study animal motion by finding ways to take rapid series of still photographs. They could look at the pictures in order to understand the animal's motion.

This famous set of images shows how a horse gallops. At one point in its stride, a horse has all four feet in the air. Write another detail that you observe about how the horse moves.

_____

_____

Research how a hummingbird flies. Draw separate images of a hummingbird in flight. How is high-speed video of hummingbirds shot?

_____

_____

_____

Build On It!

Rise to the engineering design challenge—complete **Make a Process: Design a Fossil Exhibit Hall** in the Inquiry Flipchart.

Essential Question

What Was Ancient Earth Like?

Find the answer to the following question in this lesson and write it here.

This scene shows an environment on Earth millions of years ago. How are scientists able to hypothesize about what Earth looked like long ago?

_____

_____

_____

_____

_____

Active Reading

Lesson Vocabulary

List each term. As you learn about each one, make notes in the Interactive Glossary.

_____

_____

_____

Main Ideas and Details

In this lesson, you will read about Earth's ancient environments. Detail sentences throughout the lesson will provide information about this topic. The information may be examples, features, characteristics, or facts. Active readers stay focused on the topic when they ask, What fact or information does this sentence add to the topic?

How *Rocks* and *Fossils* Tell a Story

Sedimentary rock forms in layers. Many sedimentary rocks contain fossils. How can you tell the age of these layers and of the fossils within them?

Active Reading Underline the sentences on this page that provide details about relative age.

You can learn about an area's history by studying its rocks and fossils. For example, you can tell how old the rock is compared to other rocks. You can also tell how living things and environments changed in that area over time. If you study rocks in different places, you can tell about large changes to Earth's surface and to life on Earth.

Imagine making a stack of newspapers in the order they were printed. When you look at the stack, you'll find the oldest paper on the bottom and the newest on the top. Rock layers work the same way. The oldest rock layers are at the bottom and the youngest rock layers are at the top. The *relative age* of a layer of rock is the age of that layer when you compare it to other layers—older, younger, or the same.

Each rock layer of the Grand Canyon formed at a different time in Earth's history and in a different environment.

Rock Layers of the Grand Canyon

Fossils form when sediment buries dead organisms. As a result, fossils are often found in sedimentary rocks. Scientists use fossils they find in rocks to help figure out the relative age of rock layers.

The *fossil record* is made up of all the fossils in Earth's rock layers. Fossils show how life on Earth has changed over time. So the *fossil record* contains information about Earth's history and the history of life on Earth.

Over time, movement of Earth's crust can cause layers of rock to become tilted. These movements can also lift rocks that were formed in the ocean to new positions high above sea level. The rock layers of the Grand Canyon were tilted and lifted millions of years ago.

The fossils in this layer of rock show that they were formed in an ocean.

This layer of rock is older than the layers above it. It contains a fossil imprint, or mold, of a plant.

Fossils like these are found in another layer of rock also formed in the ocean.

This layer of rock is one of the lower layers of the canyon, and is older than all of the rocks above. It contains fossils of trilobites, small animals like horseshoe crabs, that lived in ancient seas.

Relative Age

Suppose you find a fossil that looks like the second one from the top on this page. What can you say about its relative age?

_____

_____

_____

Divisions in Time

When you talk about your past, do you say how old you were when events happened? Scientists use similar references to describe Earth's history. Scientists who study Earth's history divide time into large groups.

Flowering plants, such as grasses, appeared before the first Ice Age. Saber-toothed cats lived during the ice ages.

Active Reading As you read the captions on this page, circle the first Ice Age, the Age of Dinosaurs, and the Age of Trilobites.

Trees that produce seeds in cones appeared at the beginning of the Mesozoic Era. The middle and end of the Mesozoic Era is known as the Age of Dinosaurs. Large animals such as Stegosaurus lived during this time.

Large tree ferns were common during the late Paleozoic Era. The large coal deposits in the eastern United States formed from plants like these. Trilobites were so common that the earliest part of the Paleozoic was called the Age of Trilobites.

All the rocks on Earth are a record of Earth's long history. Scientists developed the *geologic time scale* to divide Earth's history into manageable units. The fossils each unit contains define it.

Some fossils are more help than others. **Index fossils** help to identify a very short period of Earth's history. Index fossils must meet four requirements.

1. The organisms from which they formed lived during a short period of Earth's history.
2. The organisms must have had large populations so that many fossils formed.
3. The fossils must be widespread.
4. The fossils must be easily recognized.

Pterosaurs lived during the Mesozoic. These animals were not dinosaurs. They were flying reptiles. The largest pterosaur had a wingspan of at least 12 m (39 ft)!

Do the Math!
Read the Geologic Time Scale

Geologic Time Scale			
Cenozoic Era **65 mya–present**			Age of Mammals
146	Mesozoic Era	Cretaceous	Age of Dinosaurs
200		Jurassic	
251		Triassic	
299	Paleozoic Era	Permian	Age of Fishes
359		Carboniferous	
416		Devonian	
444		Silurian	
488		Ordovician	
542		Cambrian	
Precambrian time **4,600–542 mya**			1st life on Earth [stromatolites]

million years ago (mya)

Use the geologic time scale to answer the questions.

Which time interval was the longest?

_____

Which era was the shortest?

_____

How many years did each of the three eras last?

_____

_____

_____

How long did Precambrian time last?

_____

BIG
Changes on Earth

Fossils tell about how life on Earth has changed over time. They also can give clues to how Earth's continents and landforms have changed.

Mesosaurus fossils are found in South America, Africa, Antarctica, Australia, and India.

Active Reading   As you read these pages, underline details that provide evidence for continental drift.

Fossils can tell us about the relative ages of rocks. From fossils we can learn about changes in life through the divisions of geologic time. Fossils can also provide evidence about other larger changes to Earth's surface. Using fossils, you can identify areas of Earth that are now in different places than they once were.

Scientists have found the same type of fossil on both sides of the Atlantic Ocean. They are fossils of a small lizard-like reptile called *Mesosaurus* that lived in fresh water. At first, scientists thought that *Mesosaurus* swam from one side of the ocean to the other. But *Mesosaurus* was too small to have been able to swim across the salty Atlantic!

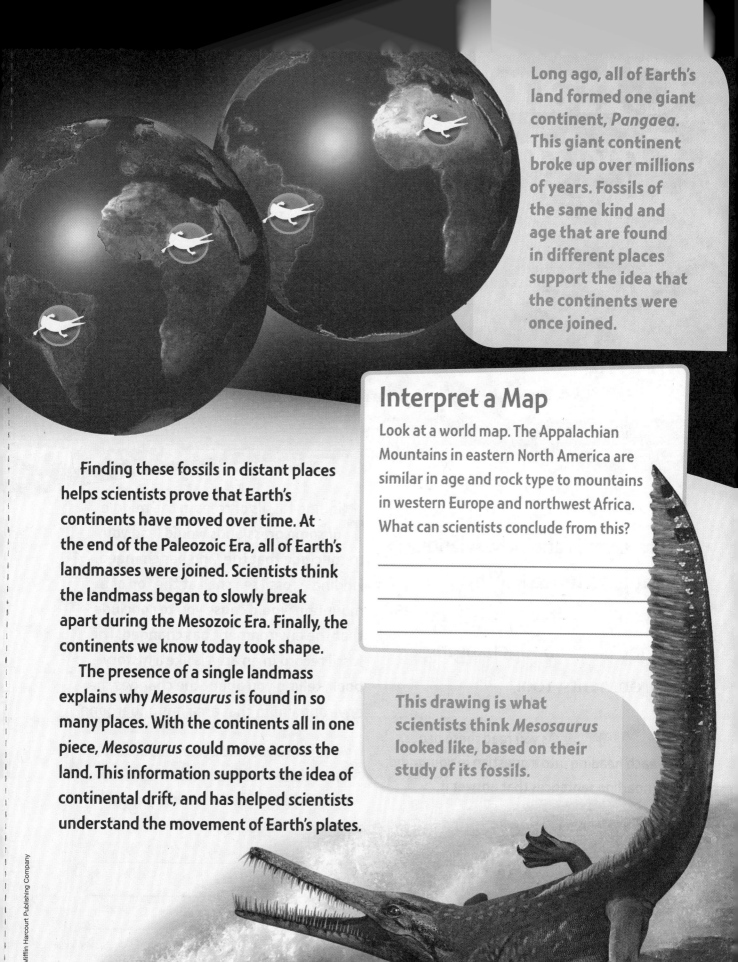

Long ago, all of Earth's land formed one giant continent, *Pangaea*. This giant continent broke up over millions of years. Fossils of the same kind and age that are found in different places support the idea that the continents were once joined.

Finding these fossils in distant places helps scientists prove that Earth's continents have moved over time. At the end of the Paleozoic Era, all of Earth's landmasses were joined. Scientists think the landmass began to slowly break apart during the Mesozoic Era. Finally, the continents we know today took shape.

The presence of a single landmass explains why *Mesosaurus* is found in so many places. With the continents all in one piece, *Mesosaurus* could move across the land. This information supports the idea of continental drift, and has helped scientists understand the movement of Earth's plates.

Interpret a Map

Look at a world map. The Appalachian Mountains in eastern North America are similar in age and rock type to mountains in western Europe and northwest Africa. What can scientists conclude from this?

_____

_____

_____

This drawing is what scientists think *Mesosaurus* looked like, based on their study of its fossils.

Changing Environments

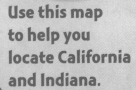

© Houghton Mifflin Harcourt Publishing Company   (b) ©Pat Morris/Ardea London Limited

Use this map to help you locate California and Indiana.

The La Brea Tar Pits
40,000 years ago

You can use fossils to tell how old a rock layer is and how a landmass might have moved. What else can you learn from fossils? Fossils provide clues about changing environments, too.

Active Reading As you read these pages, turn each heading into a question in your mind, and underline sentences that answer it.

Rancho La Brea today

Finding fossils of trees in the middle of some grasslands would lead you to conclude that the land has changed. Finding a fossil sea snail at the top of a mountain would cause you to conclude that the environment has changed. The fossil record in an area is like a history book, telling you about the changes the environment in that area has undergone.

▶ Suppose you find a fossil seashell in the rocks in your local park. What does this tell you about the environment that was once there?

_____

_____

_____

The Devonian Sea
380 million years ago

Falls of the
Ohio State Park today

The La Brea Tar Pits

The La Brea Tar Pits are located in Los Angeles, California, where tar still seeps from the ground. About 40,000 years ago, the area looked like the picture shown on the facing page. Scientists have collected fossils of thousands of plants and animals from the pits. Scientists know that those plants lived in a climate only a little wetter and cooler than it is today. In other words, the climate has not changed much in this area over the last 40,000 years.

Falls of the Ohio

Today the Falls of the Ohio is a state park in Indiana, tucked into a bend of the Ohio River where the land is flat and often dry. The summers are hot, and the winters are cold and snowy. But the rocks at the Falls of the Ohio State Park tell a different story. The rocks are filled with fossils of coral, clams, and other organisms that lived in shallow, warm, tropical seas. You can see on the map that Indiana is far from the ocean today. These fossils show that the climate in this area has changed a lot over the last 380 million years.

The Great Die Offs

When scientists look at the fossil record, they compare fossils to organisms living today. Scientists have discovered that many organisms have become extinct. There are times in Earth's history when a great many organisms became extinct all at once. How did this happen?

Active Reading As you read these pages, circle the possible causes of mass extinctions.

Sometimes only one species becomes extinct at a time. The passenger pigeon became extinct in 1914. Hunting and loss of habitat are likely causes. At several times during Earth's history, many species became extinct at the same time. These large events, caused by climate change, are called **mass extinctions**.

Worldwide volcanic eruptions can cause mass extinctions. These eruptions blow large amounts of ash and dust into the air. Sunlight is blocked, so plants can't grow. Other plants die when the ash settles on

Changing climate affects rainfall. Too much rain can cause flooding, which can destroy habitats. Too little rainfall means no plant growth and no water to drink. The result is death for many living things.

The last large meteor to hit Earth is thought to have been at least 16 km (10 mi) across. Craters such as this one in Arizona show the result of meteor impacts.

them and smothers them. If plants die, the animals that eat them also die.

Objects from outer space can cause mass extinctions. At the end of the Mesozoic, an asteroid crashed into what is now Mexico. The impact sent huge amounts of dust into the air. The dust blocked out sunlight. Changes in climate occurred that were similar to those caused by large volcanic eruptions. These changes may have caused the extinction of many animals, including the last of the dinosaurs.

Summarizing Mass Extinctions

Fill in the chart to explain some causes of mass extinctions.

Cause	Effect	Result
volcanic eruption		
	flooding	
no rain		
	dust and ash in the air	

Volcanic ash can change climate.

Sum It Up!

When you're done, use the answer key to check and revise your work.

The statements below are incorrect. Replace the words in blue to correct each statement.

1. The units of the geologic time scale are defined the by the thickness of the rock layers. _____

2. The relative age of a fossil tells whether it is 1,000 years old or 1 million years old. _____
_____

3. Rocks that contain fossils of brachiopods, crinoids, and jawless fish formed in a desert environment. _____

4. The Age of Dinosaurs is known for the large number of animals, such as the saber-toothed cat, that were able to live in a cold environment.
_____

5. Index fossils must be found over a large area, be easily recognized, have lived during the Paleozoic, and have large populations.
_____

6. Support for continental drift includes different fossils found on the same continents. _____

7. Fossils of the reptile *Mesosaurus* are used to explain the movement of continents because this reptile lived in the desert.
_____

8. When volcanic eruptions send dust and ash into the air, increases in animal and plant populations can occur. _____
_____

Name _____

Word Play

1 Use the clues to complete the puzzle.

Clues

Across

2. can be used to help identify the relative age of a rock layer

4. unit of time that contains the Age of Dinosaurs

6. occurs when many species die out at the same time

7. a geologic chart that divides Earth's history into units

8. common fossil animal from the Paleozoic

Down

1. used to describe if a fossil is older or younger than another fossil

3. all of the fossils in Earth's rock layers

5. giant continent that existed in Earth's past

fossil record	Mesozoic Era
geologic time scale	Pangaea
index fossil*	relative age
mass extinction*	trilobite

* Key Lesson Vocabulary

Apply Concepts

2 What does this fossil tell you about Antarctica's past environment?

_____

_____

_____

_____

3 The county is building a new road near your school. Bulldozers have dug up fossils of trees, leaves, and horses. Draw a picture of what the environment might have looked like when these plants and animals were living.

4 Place the following geologic time units in their correct order from oldest to most recent.

Cenozoic Era   Precambrian Time   Mesozoic Era   Paleozoic Era

_____

_____

5 What information in the picture supports the idea that Earth's continents have moved over time?

_____

_____

6 Read each description. Circle the fossil that is an index fossil.

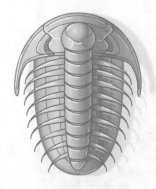 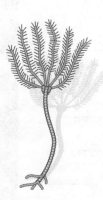 

This animal lived for a short time during the late Paleozoic. Many of its fossils are found all over the United States.

This animal lived during the early and middle Paleozoic. Its fossils have only been found in a few parts of Indiana.

This tooth is from a shark that is living today. Many similar teeth have been found on the shores of Virginia.

7 Draw a three-panel comic strip that shows one way that a mass extinction might occur.

Cause	Effect	End Result

8 Which rock layer is the oldest? Which is the youngest? Explain how you know.

_____

_____

_____

_____

_____

_____

_____

Take It Home!

Take a walk with an adult around your neighborhood. Think about how the area might change over the next 5, 10, 50, 100, or 1,000 years. What clues would tell future paleontologists about how your area looks today?

Meet Some Paleontology Pioneers

Luis and Walter Alvarez

In 1980, a father-and-son geology team had an idea. They knew that dinosaurs may have become extinct around 65 million years ago when a huge asteroid hit Earth. To look for evidence of this, they looked at the layer of rock from that time period. The rock had a lot of the same chemical elements as asteroids. The Alvarezes hypothesized that an asteroid impact sent enough smoke and dust into the atmosphere to block out sunlight. Now many scientists agree with their idea.

Karen Chin

Karen Chin knows that we learn about animals by studying what they eat. That is why she studies the fossils of dinosaur dung! She learns a lot about dinosaurs this way. She can tell how they interacted with the plants and animals in their ecosystems. Dr. Chin was the first person to identify and study *Tyrannosaurus rex* poop! From her research, she could show that *Tyrannosaurus rex* ate *Triceratops*. And it didn't just eat meat from its prey. It ate bones and all.

Describe Dinosaurs

Look at each skeleton below. Answer the questions to compare and contrast the dinosaurs.

Stegosaurus

What do you think the plates on *Stegosaurus's* **back were for?**

_____

_____

_____

Why do you think *Stegosaurus's* **tail was so long?**

_____

_____

What do you think *Tyrannosaurus rex* **ate? Why do you think so?**

_____

_____

_____

Tyrannosaurus rex

Why do you think *Tyrannosaurus rex's* **legs were longer than its arms?**

_____

_____

_____

How do scientists find data to answer these questions?

_____

_____

_____

What do scientists learn from locations of dinosaur fossils?

_____

_____

_____

Name _____

Essential Question

How Can Scientists Use Fossils?

Set a Purpose
What will you learn from this activity?

_____

_____

_____

_____

State Your Hypothesis
Write your hypothesis or testable statement.

_____

_____

_____

_____

Think About the Procedure
Why is it important to examine the fossil symbols carefully?

_____

_____

How would the results change if only one fossil symbol was drawn on each card?

_____

_____

_____

_____

Record Your Data
Record your results in the space below.

Sequence of Rock Layers (Oldest to Youngest)	Fossil Symbols
Youngest	
Oldest	▲ ☆

Draw Conclusions

Use your card stack to order the fossils from oldest to youngest, according to when they last appeared in the rock record. Record your sequence on the lines below and in the chart.

_____

_____

_____

Oldest to Youngest	Fossil Symbols
Youngest	
Oldest	

Is the fossil $ older or younger than the fossil ♥?

_____

_____

Analyze and Extend

1. Scientists use time-space relationships to compare rock layers around the world. What can you tell about the age of the fossil ✚ using this information?

    Fossil ◯ is 25 to 50 million years old.
    Fossil ● is 75 to 110 million years old.

    _____

    _____

    _____

2. What has most likely occurred if a fossil that appeared in an older rock layer does not appear in a younger rock layer?

    _____

    _____

    _____

3. Suppose fossil # appeared in each rock layer. Would fossil # make a good index fossil? Explain.

    _____

    _____

    _____

4. What other questions do you have about how scientists use fossils?

    _____

    _____

Unit 10 Review

Vocabulary Review

Use the terms in the box to complete the sentences.

> cast
> fossil
> fossil fuel
> index fossil
> mass extinction
> mold

1. A fuel formed from the remains of once living things is

   a(n) _____.

2. The remains or traces of a plant or animal that lived long ago is

   a(n) _____.

3. An event that results in the dying off of many species is called

   a(n) _____.

4. An impression of an organism, formed when sediment hardens

   around the organism, is called a(n) _____.

5. A model of an organism, formed when sediment fills a mold and

   hardens, is a(n) _____.

6. A fossil of a type of organism that lived in many
   places during a relatively short time span is called

   a(n) _____.

Science Concepts

Fill in the letter of the choice that best answers the question.

7. Not every animal or plant becomes a fossil when it dies. Which event **best** helps a fossil form?

   (A) Water washes away dirt.

   (B) Animals eat the soft tissues.

   (C) Wind blows the dead organism away.

   (D) Sediment quickly buries the dead organism.

8. Josh read about a land animal whose fossils were found in similar rock layers in Africa and South America. What can he conclude from this discovery?

   (A) Animal fossils all look alike.

   (B) The landmasses were once joined.

   (C) The animals swam across the ocean.

   (D) The fossils formed in an ocean and washed ashore.

Science Concepts

Fill in the letter of the choice that best answers the question.

9. Nkomo found a piece of amber. Which object shown below would the amber most likely contain?

(A)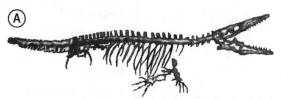

(B)

(C)

(D)

10. Malaya was collecting fossils. She found one whose original material had been replaced by quartz. What type of fossil did she find?

(A) trace fossil
(B) carbon film
(C) petrified wood
(D) mummified body

11. Suppose you found fossils of sharks and other fish in a nearby forest. What could you infer about the area from these discoveries?

(A) The area was once a desert.
(B) The area was once an ocean.
(C) The area was once a forest.
(D) The area was once an ice field.

12. Over time, the materials that form coal change. What was once a product that burns with a lot of smoke and little heat changes to a product that produces a lot of heat with little smoke.

Which graph correctly shows what happens underground as the coal improves in quality?

(A)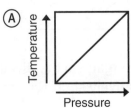

(C)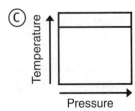

(B)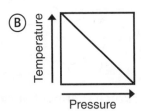

(D)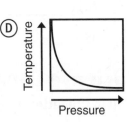

13. Dana researched the uses of crude oil. She made the following list. What can she conclude about the uses of crude oil?

Products Made from Crude Oil	
diesel motor fuel	crayons
heating oil	dishwashing soap
jet fuel	deodorant
gasoline	eyeglasses
CDs and DVDs	tires

- (A) Crude oil is used to heat homes.
- (B) Crude oil is used to make products other than fuel.
- (C) The fuel made from crude oil causes pollution.
- (D) Crude oil is used to produce only fuel for motor vehicles.

14. Oil and natural gas start out as tiny sea organisms. Over time, their remains change so that eventually only two elements are left. Which two elements make up oil and natural gas?

- (A) carbon and oxygen
- (G) carbon and hydrogen
- (C) oxygen and hydrogen
- (D) hydrogen and nitrogen

15. What is a "living fossil"?

- (A) a fossil that is easily identified
- (B) an organism that is at least 100 years old
- (C) a fossil that is well known in the scientific community
- (D) a living organism that looks similar to its ancient ancestors

16. Study the rock layers in the diagram below.

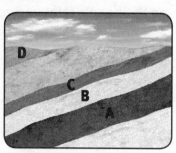

Which rock layer is probably the oldest?

- (A) Layer A
- (C) Layer C
- (B) Layer B
- (D) Layer D

17. Which life forms were common during the Mesozoic Era?

- (A) dinosaurs
- (C) tree ferns
- (B) mammoths
- (D) trilobites

18. Paul visited several western state capitals on his vacation. The map below shows the stops on his trip.

Paul said that he had found index fossils. Which one requirement for an index fossil had Paul **completely** satisfied?

- (A) The fossil is from an organism that lived during a short period of Earth's history.
- (B) The fossil is from an organism that had a large population.
- (C) The fossil is widespread.
- (D) The fossil is easily recognized.

Apply Inquiry and Review the Big Idea

Write the answer to these questions.

19. Leeza wanted to know the relative age of a fossilized bone she found. How can she use the rock layers shown below to help determine the bone's relative age?

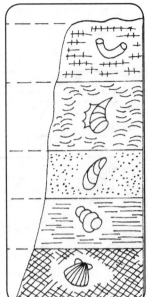

_____

_____

_____

_____

_____

20. Two fifth graders are planning to give a presentation about fossils to the class.

a. Ronda must explain how scientists use the fossil record to learn about ancient environments. Write at least two things that she should include in her presentation.

_____

_____

_____

b. Gabe must explain how scientists use fossils found in areas such as the Grand Canyon to demonstrate how life forms have changed over time. Write three things that Gabe should include in his presentation.

_____

_____

_____

_____

UNIT 11
Earth's Oceans

Big Idea

Oceans are complex systems that interact with Earth's land, air, and organisms.

I Wonder Why

Surf's up! Is the water really carrying him toward the beach? Nope. So, why is he moving forward? *Turn the page to find out.*

Here's why Waves of energy moving through the ocean do not actually move any water forward. They leave water in the same place. A passing wave pushes the surface of the water up, though, and when the wave passes, the surface drops back. The surfer glides down the front of the wave as if he were sliding down a snowy hill on a sled!

In this unit, you will explore the Big Idea, the Essential Questions, and the Investigations on the Inquiry Flipchart.

Levels of Inquiry Key ■ DIRECTED ■ GUIDED ■ INDEPENDENT

Track Your Progress

Big Idea Oceans are complex systems that interact with Earth's land, air, and organisms.

Essential Questions

Now I Get the Big Idea!

Science Notebook

Before you begin each lesson, be sure to write your thoughts about the Essential Question.

Essential Question

What Are the Oceans Like?

Engage Your Brain!

Find the answer to the following question in this lesson and record it here.

Oceans cover most of Earth's surface. How do oceans affect life on land?

_____

_____

_____

_____

_____

Active Reading

Lesson Vocabulary

List the terms. As you learn about each one, make notes in the Interactive Glossary.

_____

_____

_____

_____

_____

Main Idea and Details

Detail sentences give information about a topic. The information may be examples, features, characteristics, or facts. Active readers stay focused on the topic when they ask, What fact or information does this sentence add to the topic?

That's a Lot of Water!

On their way to the moon, astronauts looked back and took pictures of Earth. Those photos inspired Earth's nickname—the "blue marble." The view from space dramatically shows how much of our planet is covered with water.

Active Reading As you read these two pages, put brackets [ ] around four details. Underline the main idea the details help explain.

People who live toward the middle of a continent might go their entire lives without ever seeing an ocean, but oceans are truly all around us! Five oceans separate and surround Earth's landmasses. They are, from largest to smallest, the Pacific, Atlantic, Indian, Southern, and Arctic Oceans. You can also think of the world's oceans as one giant body of water. Most of Earth's water is contained in the world ocean. If there were 100 jugs of water on Earth, 97 of them would be salty ocean water. Only three would be fresh water!

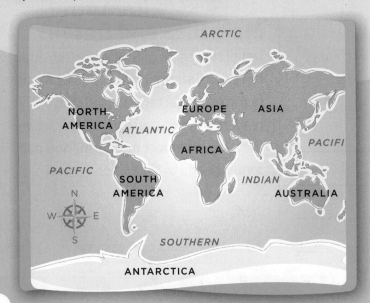

People use geographic lines on maps to describe ocean locations, but ocean water knows no boundaries. Water flows freely throughout the world ocean.

If we could fit all of Earth's oceans into gallon jugs, we could fill trillions of jugs!

343,000,000,000,000,000,000,000! (343 billion billion)

Oceans cover about 71% of Earth's surface, almost three times the area that land covers.

Do the Math!
Interpret Data with a Graph

The Pacific Ocean covers 155,557,000 square kilometers (km^2). The Arctic Ocean covers 14,056,000 km^2. The surface areas of the Atlantic, Indian, and Southern Oceans are 76,762,000 km^2, 68,566,000 km^2, and 20,327,000 km^2, in that order. Label the graph with the ocean names to show their part of the world ocean surface area.

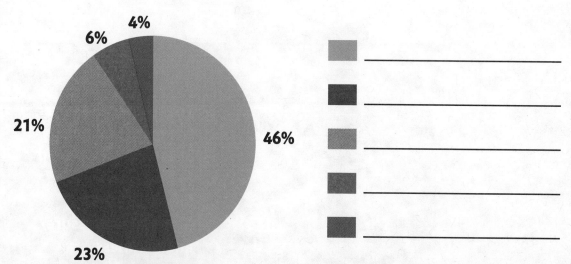

4%

6%

21%

46%

23%

Same Ocean, Different Water

You might think people have traveled everywhere there is to go on Earth. The oceans are largely unexplored, though. Some places are simply too deep, dark, and cold to visit!

Active Reading As you read these two pages, circle phrases that describe the problems of ocean exploration.

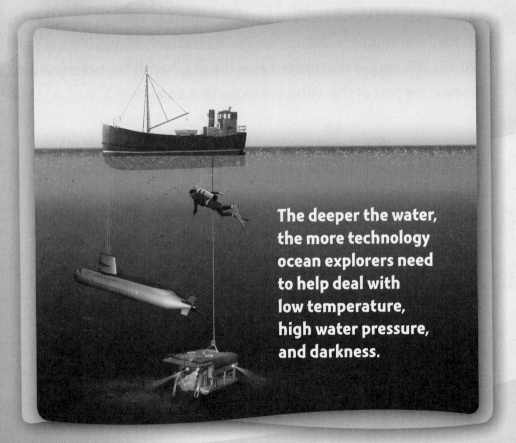

The deeper the water, the more technology ocean explorers need to help deal with low temperature, high water pressure, and darkness.

You can travel across the ocean by boat, but you'll need to pack your drinking water. Ocean water is salty, so you can't drink it. The saltiness of water is its **salinity**. Salinity makes water denser, so boats float a bit more easily in the ocean than they do in fresh water.

To explore beneath the ocean's surface, you'll have to pack your air, of course. You'll also need protection from the cold. The deeper the water, the less sunlight reaches to warm it. Divers breathe air from SCUBA tanks and also wear suits to keep warm.

At a certain depth, water pressure becomes too great for divers to withstand. **Water pressure** is the force of water pressing against whatever it surrounds. To visit those ocean depths, explorers must travel in an underwater vehicle called a *submersible*. Some places are too deep even for human-driven submersibles to visit. People can only explore these deepest ocean spots using robotic submersibles.

Submersibles provide passengers with air, light, and protection from water pressure and the cold.

▶ Write solutions to two of the problems you circled in the text.

_____

_____

Is the Ocean Floor Flat?

If you hiked across the continent, you would walk across hills and valleys, mountains, and plains. Would a walk across the ocean floor be much different?

Active Reading As you read these two pages, underline the names of two things that are being compared.

The continental slope is the steep area where the ocean rapidly gets deeper. It can reach 3,000 m (10,000 ft) below the surface. The *continental rise* is the lower portion of the continental slope. It reaches 4,000 m (13,000 ft) below the surface.

The coastal plain is the flat, low-lying land area at the seacoast.

An oceanic trench is a deep valley in the ocean floor. The deepest one is 11,000 m (36,000 ft). An *oceanic ridge* is a system of underwater mountains and valleys, usually parallel to an oceanic trench.

The continental shelf is the underwater border of each continent. The average depth is 140 m (460 ft).

The floors of all the world's oceans share roughly these same features.

Imagine a walk across the ocean floor. You begin on a coastal plain and enter the water onto the continental shelf. Along some coastlines, the continental shelf is more than 1,000 km wide, but a few coastlines have little shelf at all.

At the edge of the shelf, the continental slope drops sharply. The drop levels out gradually where sediment has collected at the bottom of the slope. This is the continental rise.

In the deep, open ocean you reach a vast, flat region of abyssal plain. Abyssal plains cover more than 50% of Earth's surface. After a long trek across the abyssal plain, you find another steep drop. This oceanic trench is a deep valley in the abyssal plain.

You also cross a mid-ocean ridge, an underwater range of mountains and valleys. Some volcanic mountains rise so high, they break through the surface of the water. The exposed mountaintops are islands.

Volcanic mountains on the ocean floor become islands where they are tall enough to break through the water's surface.

▶ If you traveled from west to east across the ocean floor pictured on these pages, what features would you find, from first to last?

1. _____

2. _____

3. **continental slope**

4. _____

5. _____

6. _____

7. **volcanic mountain**

8. _____

An abyssal plain is a vast, flat area on the deep ocean floor. The average depth is 4,500 m (15,000 ft).

Islands Come and Go

The processes that shape landforms usually take a very long time. Tomorrow there might be a new island in the middle of the ocean, though, where there isn't one today!

Active Reading As you read these two pages, draw one line under a cause. Circle the effect.

Earth's crust is made up of plates that move. Oceanic trenches form where two plates meet. One plate sinks beneath the other, and magma comes out at the boundary. New crust forms, building a ridge of volcanic mountains.

The volcanoes can grow in height until they poke through into the open air. When this happens, volcanic islands are born! These islands stop growing when their volcanoes become inactive. The islands weather and erode over time. Eventually, they disappear beneath the water again.

Volcanic island chains form at plate boundaries all over the world.

In tropical regions, coral reefs form in the shallow water around volcanic islands. A reef can grow until it completely encircles an island. The reef itself can come out from the water, forming land that surrounds a lagoon of shallow water.

When a volcanic island sinks far enough to disappear, the ring of coral is left encircling the lagoon. The ring-shaped coral island is called an *atoll*. Atolls form only in tropical waters because the corals that build reefs live only in warm water.

The movements of plates cause islands to shift and sink. Eventually, due to plate movement, even the atoll will sink and no land will be visible above the water. Waves erode the land under the water. This submerged feature is called a *guyot* [GEE•yo].

> The volcanic island of Bora Bora is weathering and eroding. Eventually, the central island will disappear, leaving just an atoll surrounding the lagoon.

▶ Draw what this island might look like at two points in the future. Explain the process that your drawings show.

Now   **1,000 years**   **10,000 years**

_____

_____

_____

When you're done, use the answer key to check and revise your work.

1

Identify each feature on the ocean floor.

a. _____

e. _____

c. _____

b. _____

d. _____

Summarize

2 Fill in the missing words to describe oceans.

The world ocean is made up of the _____, _____,

_____, _____, and _____ Oceans.

All ocean water is _____, the measure of which is the

water's _____. At a certain depth, _____ becomes too

great for divers to withstand. Explorers must visit greater depths in _____.

As the plates that make up Earth's crust move, _____ islands may form.

Over time, coral reefs grow and surround the island. An _____ forms when

the island sinks and the coral is left behind.

1. a. continental shelf b. continental slope c. oceanic trench d. abyssal plain e. volcanic island 2. Arctic, Atlantic, Indian, Pacific, Southern, salty, salinity, water pressure, submersibles, volcanic, atoll

 **Brain Check**

Lesson **1**

Name _____

Word Play

1 Unscramble the words in the box. Use the words to complete the sentences.

The flat, low-lying land area at the seacoast is the

— — — — — — — — — — — —.

The underwater border of each continent is the

— — — — — — — — — — — — — — — —.

The steep area where the ocean rapidly gets deeper is the

— — — — — — — — — — — — — — — —.

The lower portion of the continental slope is the

— — — — — — — — — — — — — — — —.

A vast, flat area on the deep ocean floor is an

— — — — — — — — — — — — —.

A deep valley in the ocean floor is an

— — — — — — — — — — — — — —.

A range of underwater mountains and valleys is an

— — — — — — — — — — — — — —.

cloaats ailnp _____   lctoanntine efslh _____

ntinloentac psleo _____   ontaiclnent iser _____

basasly pinal _____   coicena threcn _____

anoccei gried _____

© Houghton Mifflin Harcourt Publishing Company

501

Apply Concepts

2 Draw a region of the ocean floor. Label at least three features.

3 Describe three problems of exploring the deep ocean that are solved by submersibles.

_____

_____

4 What protection can a diver's suit and gear provide? What deep ocean problem can the suit not solve?

_____

_____

_____

5 Why is the deep ocean cold and dark?

_____

_____

_____

_____

_____

_____

_____

_____

Take It Home!

Ask an adult at home to do some research on the Internet with you. Determine the nearest ocean to where you live. Find out how far this ocean is from your hometown.

How It Works:
Seeing the Sea Floor

Scientists use GPS and sonar to map an ocean floor too big and too deep and dark to see. GPS is a tool that tells the exact point of a location on Earth. Sonar uses sound to measure underwater distances.

Ocean floor map

Sonar sends sound toward the ocean floor and detects the sound's echo. The device uses the speed of sound to calculate the distance the sound traveled. That shows the depth of the ocean at the place the echo bounced back from. GPS pinpoints the place. Repeating the process over and over adds up to making a picture of many points on the ocean floor.

Critical Thinking

Draw arrows on the picture to show how sound travels from the ship to the ocean floor and back. Why does detailed ocean floor mapping require both sonar and GPS?

_____

_____

GPS uses *trilateration* to determine a point on Earth. Trilateration is a way of finding a point in space by using at least four other points as a reference. *Triangulation* is the technique for a flat surface. It uses three reference points.

Draw a circle with a 1.5-inch radius around the baseball diamond. Then, draw a 1-inch radius circle around the pond. Finally, draw a circle with a 1.5-inch radius around the playground.

A picnic will be at the place where all three circles intersect. Where is it located? _____

Build On It!

Rise to the engineering design challenge—complete **Design It: Build a Working Submarine Model** in the Inquiry Flipchart.

Essential Question

How Does Ocean Water Move?

Engage Your Brain!

Find the answer to the following question in this lesson and record it here.

The movement of ocean water affects a lot of things outside the ocean. What are some things that happen because of the ways ocean water moves?

_____

_____

_____

_____

Active Reading

Lesson Vocabulary

List the terms. As you learn about each one, make notes in the Interactive Glossary.

_____   _____

_____   _____

_____   _____

Compare and Contrast

Many ideas in this lesson are connected because they explain comparisons and contrasts—how things are alike and different. Active readers stay focused on comparisons and contrasts when they ask themselves, How are these things alike? How are these things different?

Catch a Wave

From gentle ripples to crashing giants, the surface of the ocean is in constant motion. Waves carry energy from place to place.

Active Reading As you read these two pages, draw a box around an effect. Circle the cause of each effect.

Based on this photo, you might think that waves push huge amounts of water on shore. Actually, the water in waves doesn't move forward, it moves up and down. A **wave** is the up-and-down movement of surface water. A wave carries energy, not water, forward. Inside the wave, the water itself moves in small ovals. As waves approach shore, where water is shallow, the waves slow down. The bottom of a wave slows most, and the top gets ahead. Eventually, the top falls over, or breaks. Breaking waves are what you see crashing onto the shore.

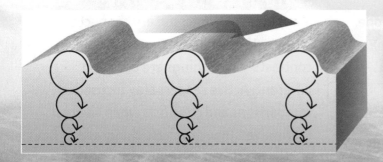

Surface waves are caused by wind pushing against the surface of the water. Because the open ocean is large and there is nothing in the way to stop the wind, the surface keeps collecting energy from the wind. With enough wind, what starts as a small ripple can build into a wave the height of a building!

Waves constantly affect the shoreline. Even gentle waves weather and erode rock and transport sand. Powerful hurricane winds produce much larger waves. The winds of a hurricane can cause a *storm surge*, or an unusually high water level. Then water can flood far inland into areas that are usually dry.

The energy in waves is not only destructive. People have built devices that float in the ocean and convert the energy of waves into electrical energy. As the technology for these devices improves, they will provide a steady source of electricity, because wave motion never stops!

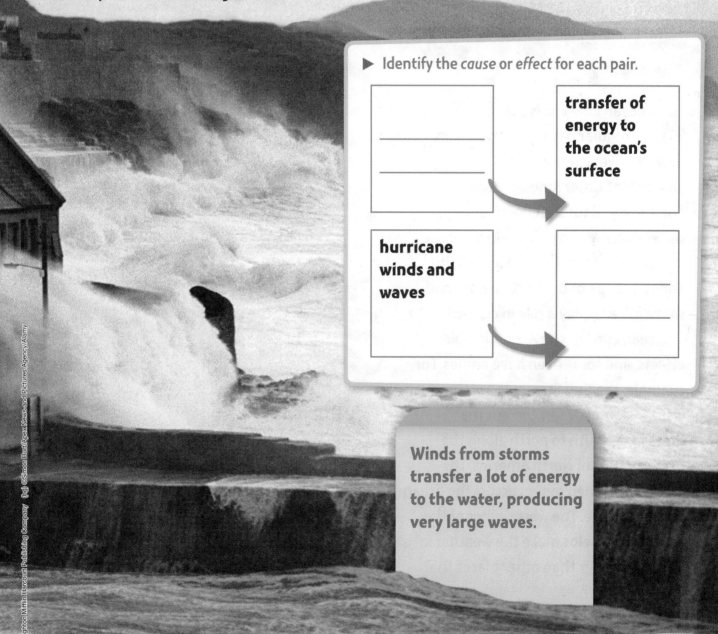

▶ Identify the *cause* or *effect* for each pair.

| _____ _____ | → | **transfer of energy to the ocean's surface** |

| **hurricane winds and waves** | → | _____ _____ |

Winds from storms transfer a lot of energy to the water, producing very large waves.

Go With the Flow

Is there a river near where you live? You might have watched the water flow steadily by. There are areas in the ocean where the water flows steadily in a direction, too.

Active Reading As you read these two pages, underline the ocean feature that is similar to a river.

An ocean **current** is a steady flow of water in a regular pattern in the ocean. Currents flow like rivers in the ocean, moving large amounts of water long distances. The steady winds that flow from the equator to the poles help drive currents. Temperature, water salinity, and the shape of both ocean floor and shoreline also play a role in currents.

Ocean currents have predictable effects, and some even have names. For example, the Gulf Stream is a warm-water Atlantic Ocean current that flows from south to north along the eastern coast of North America. The Gulf Stream then moves across the ocean toward Europe. The warm water of the Gulf Stream helps make the weather in Europe warmer than other places that are as far north.

Water that steadily flows outward from the shore against the direction of incoming waves is called a rip current. You can spot a rip current as a smooth gap, or rip, in a regular pattern of waves.

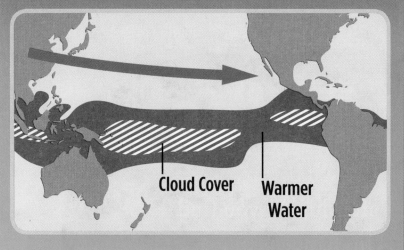

Cloud Cover

Warmer Water

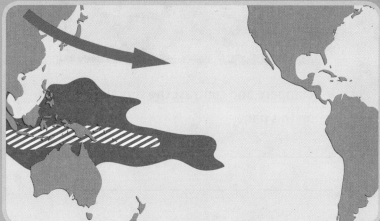

Sometimes, the water in the South Pacific Ocean gets unusually warm. This produces a climate pattern called El Niño. An El Niño season disrupts normal weather patterns. It causes extreme weather, such as droughts and flooding, in different regions of the world.

North Pacific Ocean

North Atlantic

Equator

South Pacific

▶ Draw arrows that show the direction water is flowing in this rip current.

The Turning Tides

Suppose you take a walk on a beach before breakfast. When you return after lunch, you find the same area under water. This happens twice every day along ocean beaches!

Active Reading As you read the next page, underline two things that are being contrasted.

▶ Compare and contrast the shoreline images on this page.

_____

_____

_____

_____

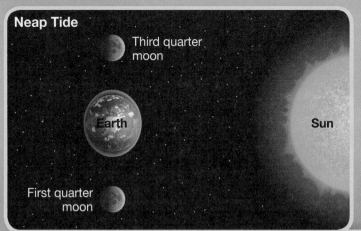

Neap Tide

Third quarter moon

Earth

Sun

First quarter moon

Spring Tide

Full moon

Earth

New moon

Sun

Spring tides are the highest high tides and the lowest low tides. Neap tides are the high and low tides that are closest to the same level.

The level of the ocean rises and falls in a cycle. This rise and fall in the water level of the ocean is called a **tide**. Tides are caused by the "pull" of the sun and moon on Earth's oceans.

The moon's gravity pulls on Earth. As a result, two bulges form in Earth's oceans. One bulge is on the side of Earth facing the moon. The other is on the side facing away from the moon. The higher water level in the bulges produces a *high tide.* Between the bulges, the water level is lower. There, a *low tide* occurs.

When Earth, the sun, and the moon are in a straight line, their combined gravity causes the most dramatic differences in the levels of the tides. The high tides are highest, and the low tides are lowest. When the sun, Earth, and the moon are positioned in an L shape, the difference between the levels of high tide and low tide is the smallest.

Do the Math!
Tide Times

Low	High
12:25 a.m.	6:42 a.m.
12:55 p.m.	7:07 p.m.

What is the amount of time from one high tide to the next?

_____

What is the time difference between two low tides?

_____

What is the time span between the first high tide and the low tide that follows?

_____

Changing Shorelines

What do you imagine when you think of a trip to the seashore? A long, sandy beach? Not all beaches are sandy. Some are rocky and some have towering cliffs.

Active Reading As you read these two pages, circle two problems. Underline their solutions.

Waves and ocean currents carry sand to and away from this beach. The same wind that drives the waves also weathers the cliffs.

Land at the edge of the ocean is called **shore**. The action of wind and ocean waves constantly changes the shore. Rocks and cliffs weather slowly, but the ocean can carry sand away from beaches in a short time. In fact, a big storm can erode a beach almost entirely in a day! People can restore the beach by replacing and stabilizing the sand.

People also build structures to prevent a steady current from moving sand. A **jetty** is a structure, often made of piles of rock, that the current cannot move. It stands against the flow of water. Jetties can both preserve beaches and keep sand from accumulating and making waterways too shallow for boats.

To restore this beach, sand was pumped from beneath the water back up onto the beach.

▶ Describe how this shoreline might be different without the jetty.

_____

_____

_____

513

Sum It Up!

When you're done, use the answer key to check and revise your work.

1

Write the vocabulary word that matches each description.

_____ 1. A built structure that the current cannot move

_____ 2. The land at the edge of the ocean

_____ 3. The periodic change of the ocean water level

_____ 4. Continuous flow of ocean water in a regular pattern

_____ 5. The transfer of energy through the water

Summarize

Fill in the missing words to describe how ocean water moves.

If you look at the surface of the ocean, you see the constant motion of 6. _____

caused by 7. _____. Waves do not actually 8. _____

much water. They move 9. _____ the water. Ocean water does flow like a

10. _____ in various 11. _____. The water level at the

shore also rises and falls in a cycle called the 12. _____.

Name _____

Word Play

1 Unscramble the words in the targets. Use the letter in the center as the first letter of the first word. Each answer contains more than one word.

R T E
U **S** G
O R
S M

_____

Abnormally high water level during a hurricane

O
I **E** Ñ
N L

_____

A severe weather season caused by an unusually warm South Pacific current

H
I **H** D
G E
I T

_____

The point at which the water reaches its highest regular place on the shore

E
D **L** O
T W
I

_____

The point at which the water reaches its lowest regular place on the shore

N A D
N **S** O
U N
M O

_____

Two objects that affect the tides

Write a single sentence that uses three of the answers above.

_____

Apply Concepts

2 Draw the positions of Earth, the sun, and the moon during a spring tide.

3 Circle the diagram that shows an El Niño season.

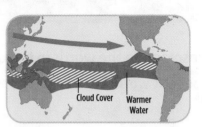

4 Describe how a particle of water moves as energy passes through in a wave.

_____

_____

_____

_____

_____

5 Draw a diagram of the Gulf Stream.

Take It Home!

Build a model of a shoreline in a shoebox with a family member. Make labels that tell about different ways that water moves at the shore.

Name _____

Essential Question

How Can You Model Ocean Water?

Set a Purpose
What will you learn from this experiment?

_____

_____

_____

Think About the Procedure
What are the conditions that you will control and try to make the same for each trial?

_____

_____

Why is it important to repeat the procedure with the bottles in different positions?

_____

_____

_____

_____

_____

Record Your Data
Use the chart below to record your observations. Describe what you see during each observation.

_____

_____

_____

	Starting position of the bottles	Behavior of the water
Trial 1		
Trial 2		
Trial 3		
Trial 4		
Trial 5		
Trial 6		

517

Draw Conclusions

Which trial produced the fastest results?
Draw what you observed.

_____
_____
_____

Which is more dense: salt water or fresh
water? How do you know?

_____
_____
_____
_____

How did changing the temperature of
the water affect the outcome of the last
three trials?

_____
_____

Analyze and Extend

1. How does this activity relate to
   currents in the ocean?

   _____
   _____
   _____
   _____

2. Overall, how does colder, saltier water
   behave in the ocean?

   _____
   _____
   _____

3. How does the behavior of colder,
   saltier water affect warmer, less
   salty water?

   _____
   _____
   _____

4. What other questions would you like
   to ask about ocean water?

   _____
   _____
   _____

Essential Question

What Are Some Ocean Ecosystems?

Engage Your Brain!

Find the answer to the following question in this lesson and record it here.

Which part of the ocean is home to the most organisms?

_____

_____

_____

_____

Active Reading

Lesson Vocabulary

List the terms. As you learn about each one, make notes in the Interactive Glossary.

_____

_____

_____

_____

Using Headings

Active readers preview headings and use them to ask questions to answer during the reading. Reading with this purpose helps active readers focus on understanding and recalling what they read in order to answer their questions.

Where the Ocean Meets the Land

The ocean is full of life, right up to the high-tide line. What happens at the high-tide line when the water level drops at low tide? Do plants and animals move down the beach to stay in the water?

Active Reading What can you tell about the location of this ecosystem from the headings on this page? Circle the heading that describes the location of the intertidal zone.

Looking into a tide pool, you can observe ocean life without actually going into the ocean!

The intertidal ecosystem provides a habitat for more than underwater organisms. At low tide, sea birds feed on many organisms they couldn't reach at high tide.

The Intertidal Zone

The **intertidal zone** is the area between the high- and low-tide lines. At high tide, the area is completely under water. At low tide, the area is exposed to air. Intertidal habitats depend on land features at the shore. Low parts of rocky cliffs might be covered with barnacles and plants that can survive out of water when the tide is low. Sandy beaches hide crabs and clams that burrow beneath the sand to await the rising tide. River inlets branch into marshes and mud flats full of grasses with mollusks at their roots.

In many places, rocky bowls hold pools of water while the tide is low. Animals in a tide pool remain in their own natural aquarium. Tide pools commonly include crabs, small shrimp, sea anemones, sea stars, sea cucumbers, snails, and a variety of small plants.

Tide pool organisms are sheltered from large fish at high tide because of the crashing waves. Organisms in tide pools are in danger of being eaten by birds at low tide. Small fish may swim into the area when the tide is high, remain in the pool through low tide, and swim away when the area is fully underwater again. Or, they might become a meal for an anemone!

Two Worlds in One

Choose two organisms in the intertidal zone. Write what the animal does during low tide.

Organism	How it behaves at low tide

The Richness of the Reef

The ocean is shallowest near the shore. Sunlight warms the water and supports plant life. Animals feed on the plants. This area is rich with life. The area between the intertidal zone and the open ocean is the near-shore zone.

Active Reading What can you tell about the location of this ecosystem from the headings on these pages? Underline the term in the heading that tells where coral reefs are found.

The Near-Shore Zone

The near-shore zone is home to many species of fish, jellyfish, and seaweed. Plants and small fish attract hungry larger animals such as dolphins and sharks. Corals also live in the near-shore zone. Coral individuals, called polyps, live in colonies. Polyps produce hard exoskeletons attached to those of their neighbors. **Coral reefs** are the branch-like structures built by colonies of coral polyps. The branched reefs provide habitats for many organisms. The organisms form a complex community and food web.

If the coral in an area are healthy, the rest of the organisms that live near them tend to thrive. If the coral in an area die, the whole ecosystem is affected. Why is this important? If the ocean were divided into 1,000 parts, coral reefs would take up the space of only one part. But as many as 25% of all the oceans' species would live in that one part!

Individual coral polyps are tiny. The reefs they build are massive enough to spot from airplanes and even from orbiting spacecraft!

Underwater Buffet

Small fish find shelter amongst the branching coral.
How does this make the reef a hearty food web?

_____

_____

_____

The Wide and the Deep

If you looked across the open ocean, you would see a huge span of blue that seemed the same throughout. The open ocean is not a single kind of ecosystem. Conditions change the deeper the water gets.

Active Reading What can you tell about the location of this ecosystem from the headings on this page? Circle the ways in which the open ocean differs from the ecosystems you read about on these two pages.

The Open-Ocean Zone

Animals at the surface in the open ocean are much like those that live near shore. Many fish, sea turtles, and whales move back and forth between the near-shore zone and the open ocean at different times during the year. As you move deeper in the ocean, light decreases, pressure increases, and the temperature drops. Organisms that live in those extreme conditions are very different from those organisms that live near the surface.

Too little sunlight reaches below 200 m to allow photosynthetic organisms to survive. Squid are one kind of animal that live in the region from 200 to 1,000 m deep. Pilot whales can dive into those depths to feed on squid, but they must return to the surface to breathe. Many animals that live below 200 m move toward the surface at night to feed.

Most squid are shorter than your arm. However, giant squid can grow to over 40 m long!

Some whales filter krill and tiny plankton from the water. Others hunt squid and larger prey.

Almost no light reaches below 1,000 m. The water is extremely cold and contains little oxygen. Still, organisms do live on the ocean floor. Communities of shrimp, crabs, tubeworms, slugs, and even fish form around hydrothermal vents. A *hydrothermal vent* is a volcanic spot on the ocean floor. Bacteria there eat dissolved chemicals in the heated water. The bacteria start the food chain for larger organisms.

Some varieties of angler fish live in total darkness near the sea floor. They lure prey with a body part that gives off its own light.

Do the Math!
Interpret Data

Open ocean zones are nicknamed by their depths. In a 1 m^2-wide column of ocean water, how much water would each of these zones contain?

Zone	Depth	Amount of water
sunlit	200 m	
twilight	1,000 m	
midnight	4,000 m	
lower midnight	11,000 m	

How much water in the column gets enough light to support plant life?

_____

How much water in the column does not get enough light to support plant life?

_____

The Most Important Organism You Never See

If you dove into the open ocean, you might look as far as you could see in every direction and not see a plant, fish, or mammal. However, you would still be surrounded by life!

Plankton are drifting organisms that inhabit the wide open ocean. Most plankton are microscopic. Plankton aren't a single species. They are a group that includes plantlike organisms, animal-like organisms, and bacteria. Plantlike plankton make their own food through photosynthesis. Animal-like plankton feed on other plankton. Animals large and small filter plankton from the water as their food. Smaller fish, in turn, become food for bigger predators.

Plantlike plankton are important. Not only are they food for many other organisms, they also take carbon dioxide out of the atmosphere and release oxygen back into it during photosynthesis, enabling us to breathe!

Plankton blooms can last for a few days or several weeks. Plankton reproduce in such massive numbers that they form clouds in the water visible from space!

Fishing for Plankton?

Describe two ways that this fisher relies on plankton.

_____

_____

_____

_____

_____

_____

_____

When you're done, use the answer key to check and revise your work.

Write the words from the word box in the category for the appropriate environment. You may use words more than one time.

> anemones, barnacles, beach, birds, coral reef, crabs, dark, dolphins, high tide, hydrothermal vents, jellyfish, low tide, marshes, mollusks, mud flats, plants, sharks, shore, shrimp, squid, sunlight, tide pool, tubeworms, whales

1. Intertidal zone

_____

_____

_____

2. Near-shore zone

_____

_____

_____

3. Open ocean

_____

_____

_____

4. Write three things you learned about ocean ecosystems.

_____

Brain Check

Name _____

Word Play

1 Use the words from the lesson to complete each sentence.

The intertidal zone is under water during __ __ __ __ __   __ __ __ __ __.

Coral polyps live together in __ __ __ __ __ __ __ __ __ __ __.

The area between the intertidal zone and the open ocean is the

__ __ __ __ __   __ __ __ __ __ __ zone.

The widest and deepest ecosystems are in the __ __ __ __ __   __ __ __ __ __ __ __.

Compared to the open ocean, the near-shore zone is warm and

__ __ __ __ __ __ __ __ __.

Many intertidal organisms are exposed to air during __ __ __ __   __ __ __ __ __.

Birds can feed on animals exposed in a __ __ __ __ __   __ __ __ __ __.

A group of microscopic organisms of different types drifting in the ocean are

__ __ __ __ __ __ __ __ __ __.

Figure out how to place the answers in the boxes below so that the letters in the red boxes answer the riddle.

Riddle: Where do fish meet new friends? _____

Apply Concepts

2 Draw a tide pool, and write the names of three organisms that live there.

_____

_____

_____

3 Draw a hydrothermal vent, and write the names of three organisms that live there.

_____

_____

_____

4 Explain why photosynthetic organisms are more plentiful in the near-shore zone than in the open ocean.

_____

_____

5 Identify what has happened in these before-and-after pictures.

_____

 **Take It Home!** Ask an adult at home to do some research online with you. How are ocean food webs similar to land food webs? How are they different? Make a three-dimensional model of an ocean food web.

Meet the Ocean Explorers

Evan B. Forde

Since graduating from college in 1974, Evan B. Forde has been an oceanographer. He has explored many underwater canyons. He also studies how hurricanes start over ocean water. To educate students and teachers about oceanography, Forde often speaks at schools. He explains that a big part of a scientist's job is solving mysteries.

Eugenie Clark

Eugenie Clark's love for fish started on a trip to an aquarium at the age of nine. Being one of the world's leading experts on sharks and their behavior has earned her the nickname the Shark Lady. Dr. Clark learned how to scuba dive so she could study fish up close. She has written many books and traveled all over the world talking to people about what she has learned.

Classifying Ocean Life

One important job of oceanographers is classifying ocean life. Look at the dichotomous key. Then answer the questions.

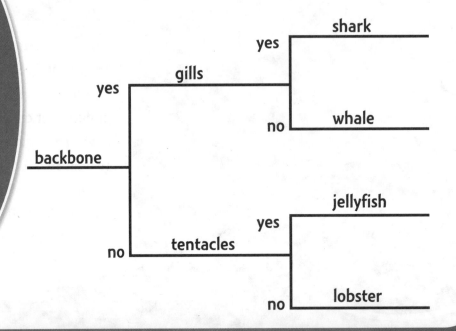

backbone

— yes — gills — yes — shark
— no — whale

— no — tentacles — yes — jellyfish
— no — lobster

Which animal does not have gills?

_____

Which animal has tentacles?

_____

How does a shark breathe?

_____

Unit 11 Review

Vocabulary Review

Use the terms in the box to complete the sentences.

> abyssal plain
> continental shelf
> continental slope
> current
> shore
> storm surge
> tide
> wave

1. The regular rise and fall of the ocean's surface, caused by the gravitational pull of the moon and sun on Earth, is

   a(n) _____.

2. When surface water is disturbed by energy moving through the water, it moves up and down in a pattern called

   a(n) _____.

3. A continuous, regular pattern of water flow is called

   a(n) _____.

4. The abnormal rise of ocean water level due to high winds, large waves, and other causes is called

   a(n) _____.

5. The land along the edge of the ocean is called the

   _____.

6. The vast floor of the deep ocean is called the

   _____.

7. The gradually sloping portion of the ocean floor that forms the underwater border of a continent is the

   _____.

8. The steeply sloping part of the ocean floor where the ocean

   rapidly gets deeper is called the _____.

Science Concepts

Fill in the letter of the choice that best answers the question.

9. Soon-Yi studied a cross-section diagram of ocean floor features. Then she predicted that one of the features would someday become an island. Which feature was she **most likely** referring to?

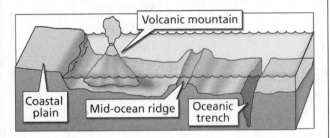

(A) coastal plain

(B) mid-ocean range

(C) oceanic trench

(D) volcanic mountain

10. A hurricane was expected to make landfall. Tuan heard a weather report that advised people to leave coastal areas and go inland. What hazardous effect was expected that could be caused by hurricane-force winds?

(A) tides

(B) rip currents

(C) very large waves

(D) beach restoration

11. At a beach near where Tara lives, the mouth of an inlet keeps filling with sand. The ocean current flows south to north past the inlet.

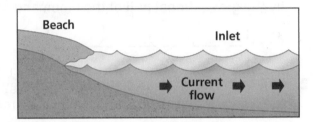

What could be expected to happen if a jetty were built to the **south** of the entrance to the inlet?

(A) Less sand would block the inlet.

(B) Sand would completely fill the inlet.

(C) Less sand would remain on the beach to the left of the jetty.

(D) More sand would build up on the beach to the right of the inlet.

12. On a field trip to the coast, Rani observes sea anemones, crabs, small shrimp, sea stars, snails, and small fish in rocky pools. What ocean ecosystem is she observing?

(A) hydrothermal vent

(B) intertidal zone

(C) near-shore zone

(D) open-ocean zone

13. The picture shows how the shore looked when Yuri arrived at the beach in the morning. He saw many seabirds landing on the beach. When he left in the afternoon, the area was covered with water. Most of the birds were gone.

Which sentence **best** explains why the seabirds left the shore?

Ⓐ It was high tide in the morning and low tide in the afternoon.

Ⓑ The organisms in the tide pool were more exposed at high tide.

Ⓒ The organisms in the tide pool were more exposed at low tide.

Ⓓ The organisms in the tide pool were washed away by the rising water.

14. The living community surrounding a hydrothermal vent is different from other ocean ecosystems. What is the **main** reason for the difference?

Ⓐ It has fewer types of organisms.

Ⓑ Whales, sea turtles, and squid swim in and out of this ecosystem.

Ⓒ Its food chains do not depend upon solar energy or plant life.

Ⓓ It is faster to build a living community because of volcanic activity.

15. Look at the map.

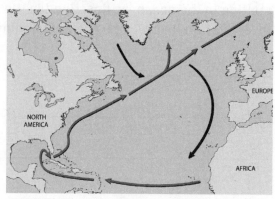

What does the dark arrow represent?

Ⓐ winds caused by El Niño

Ⓑ the movement of all water in the Atlantic Ocean

Ⓒ the movement of water in the Gulf Stream

Ⓓ movement and deposition of sand along a coast

16. Scientists in a submersible travel deep into the ocean. Which of the following factors of the environment will **increase** the deeper the scientists go?

Ⓐ light   Ⓒ temperature

Ⓑ oxygen   Ⓓ water pressure

17. An iceberg made mostly of fresh water is melting. Which sentence describes the **most likely** effects of this process?

Ⓐ The surrounding water will decrease in salinity and increase in temperature.

Ⓑ The surrounding water will increase in salinity and temperature.

Ⓒ The surrounding water will develop a warm current like the Gulf Stream.

Ⓓ The surrounding water will decrease in salinity and temperature.

Apply Inquiry and Review the Big Idea

Write the answers to these questions.

18. Erik wants to model the effect on the surrounding water of an iceberg melting in the ocean, as described in the previous question. Describe an investigation he could carry out, including ways to measure the results.

_____

_____

_____

_____

19. Explain the importance of a submersible in helping scientists study the ocean.

_____

_____

_____

_____

20. The chart gives information about the different zones of the open ocean. What can you infer about the physical environment of each zone? What differences would you expect to observe in the ecosystems of these zones?

Zone	Depth
sunlit	0–200 meters
twilight	200–1,000 meters
midnight	1,000–4,000 meters
lower midnight	4,000–11,000 meters

_____

_____

_____

UNIT 12

The Solar System and the Universe

Big Idea

Earth is part of a solar system, which is made up of many different objects orbiting a sun.

I Wonder Why

Why are most observatories built far from large cities? *Turn the page to find out.*

Here's why Most observatories are built far from cities to avoid the brightening of the night sky caused by artificial outdoor lighting, which can make it impossible to see dim lights from stars.

In this unit, you will explore the Big Idea, the Essential Questions, and the Investigations on the Inquiry Flipchart.

Levels of Inquiry Key ■ DIRECTED ■ GUIDED ■ INDEPENDENT

Track Your Progress

Big Idea Earth is part of a solar system, which is made up of many different objects orbiting a sun.

Essential Questions

Now I Get the Big Idea!

Science Notebook

Before you begin each lesson, be sure to write your thoughts about the Essential Question.

ential Question

What Objects Are Part of the Solar System?

Engage Your Brain!

Find the answer to the following question in this lesson and record it here.

Which planets have rings, and what are the rings made of?

_____

_____

_____

Active Reading

esson Vocabulary

t the terms. As you learn about each one, ke notes in the Interactive Glossary.

_____ _____

_____ _____

_____

Compare and Contrast

Many ideas in this lesson are connected because they explain comparisons and contrasts—how things are alike and different. Active readers stay focused on comparisons and contrasts when they ask themselves, How are these things alike? How are they different?

The Solar System

The sun, Earth, and its moon form a system in space. Earth revolves around the sun. That means Earth travels around the sun in a path called an orbit. The moon revolves around Earth. Read on to learn about other objects in space.

Active Reading As you read this page, underline two details that tell how all planets are alike.

Earth and its moon are part of a larger system in space called a solar system. A **solar system** is made up of a star and the planets and other space objects that revolve around it. A **planet** is a large, round body that revolves around a star. In our solar system, the planets and other objects revolve around a star we call the sun.

There are eight planets in our solar system. All of them rotate, or spin, about an axis. This is an imaginary line that goes through the center of a planet. Earth rotates on its axis once every 24 hours. This is the length of one day on Earth.

Unlike planets, some objects don't revolve directly around the sun. *Moons* are small natural objects that revolve around other objects. Many planets have moons. Earth has only one. It revolves once around Earth about every 27 days.

Earth is about 150 million kilometers from the sun!

Diagrams not to scale.

The planets in our solar system are very far from each other.

The orbits of the planets in our solar system are not perfect circles. They are oval-shaped, or elliptical [eh•LIP•tuh•kuhl].

Some planets have many moons. Earth has only one. Venus and Mercury have none!

Around and Around

Draw an orbit for the planet. Then draw a moon and its orbit.

sun

planet

The Inner Planets

At times, the brightest object in the night sky is not the moon or a star. It is Venus, one of Earth's closest neighbors in space.

Active Reading As you read this page, underline ways in which the inner planets are alike.

Mercury

Mercury, the smallest planet in our solar system, is less than half the size of Earth. Its surface is filled with craters, much like Earth's moon. Mercury is the closest planet to the sun. On Mercury, the sun would look three times as large as it does on Earth.

Planets in our solar system can be classified based on their distance from the sun. The four inner planets are the closest to the sun. In order from closest to farthest, the inner planets are Mercury, Venus, Earth, and Mars.

The inner planets are very dense and rocky. They have thin atmospheres and small diameters. A planet's diameter is the distance from one side of the planet, through its center, to the other side. The inner planets have large solid cores at their centers. They have few moons, and their revolution times are short compared to the other planets in the solar system.

Venus

Venus is so hot that lead would melt at its surface! Thick clouds surround Venus, and its atmosphere is made up mostly of carbon dioxide. Lava flows from more than 1,000 volcanoes on Venus's surface.

Planets not to scale.

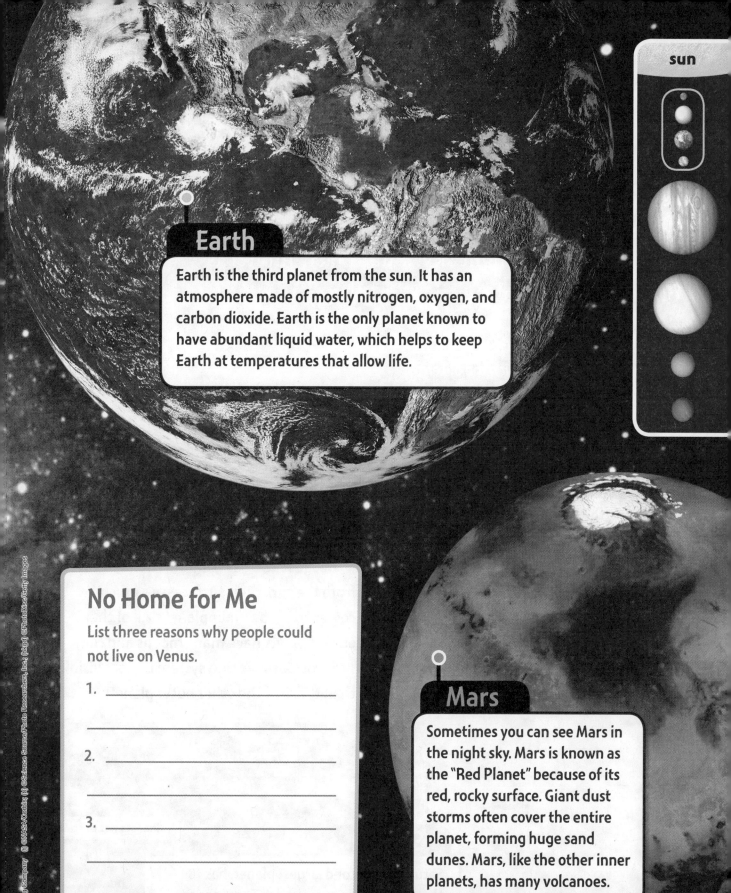

sun

Earth

Earth is the third planet from the sun. It has an atmosphere made of mostly nitrogen, oxygen, and carbon dioxide. Earth is the only planet known to have abundant liquid water, which helps to keep Earth at temperatures that allow life.

No Home for Me

List three reasons why people could not live on Venus.

1. _____

   _____

2. _____

   _____

3. _____

   _____

Mars

Sometimes you can see Mars in the night sky. Mars is known as the "Red Planet" because of its red, rocky surface. Giant dust storms often cover the entire planet, forming huge sand dunes. Mars, like the other inner planets, has many volcanoes.

The Outer Planets

On a clear night, Jupiter might appear to be a large, bright star in the night sky. But in fact, Jupiter is one of the outer planets in our solar system.

Great Red Spot

Jupiter

Jupiter is the largest planet in the solar system. In fact, all of the other planets would fit inside Jupiter! Its Great Red Spot is about as wide as three Earths. The red spots are massive, spinning storms. Jupiter's faint rings were discovered by the *Voyager 1* space probe in 1979.

Jupiter, Saturn, Uranus, and Neptune are the outer planets. In that order, they are the farthest planets from the sun. The outer planets are also called the gas giants, because they are huge and made up mostly of gases. They don't have a solid surface, and their cores are very small.

Because the gas giants are so far away from the sun, their surfaces are much colder than the inner planets. All of the outer planets have many moons and ring systems. Saturn's ring system is more visible than those of the other outer planets.

Planets not to scale.

Saturn

Saturn, the second largest planet, has thousands of rings around it. The rings are made up of ice and chunks of rock. Some of Saturn's moons are found inside these rings. Like Jupiter, Saturn has large storms.

Houghton Mifflin Harcourt Publishing Company   (t) ©NASA/JPL/University of Arizona; (b) ©NASA/JPL ©Getty Images/PhotoDisc; (bkgd) ©PhotoDisc/Getty Images

What Makes Them Unique?

Write one thing that is unique about each of the outer planets.

Jupiter

_____

_____

Saturn

_____

_____

Uranus

_____

_____

Neptune

_____

_____

Uranus

The axis of Uranus is tilted so far that, compared to other planets, it rotates on its side. This makes seasons on Uranus last more than 20 years! Deep inside Uranus, heated gases bubble and burst onto the surface, causing bright clouds to form. Uranus has a system of at least 13 faint rings.

Neptune

Neptune is the windiest planet in our solar system. Its winds move at speeds of about 2,000 km/hr (1,243 mi/hr). These winds blow Neptune's Great Dark Spot around the planet. This spot is a storm, about the size of Earth, known to vanish and reform! Neptune has nine rings around it.

Compare Inner and Outer Planets

Size, surface features, and distance from the sun are just some differences between the inner and outer planets. Look at this chart to learn about other differences.

Planet	Period of Revolution (in Earth days and years)	Period of Rotation (in Earth hours and days)	Temperature (°C) (inner planets: surface range; outer planets: top of the clouds)	Number of Moons	Density (g/cm³)	Diameter
INNER PLANETS						
Mercury	88 days	59 days	−173 to 427	0	5.43	4,878 km (3,031mi)
Venus	225 days	243 days	462	0	5.24	12,104 km (7,521 mi)
Earth	365 days	1 day	−88 to 58	1	5.52	12,756 km (7,926 mi)
Mars	687 days	about 1 day	−87 to −5	2	3.94	6,794 km (4,222 mi)
OUTER PLANETS						
Jupiter	12 years	about 10 hours	−148	63	1.33	142,984 km (88,846 mi)
Saturn	29 years	about 10 hours	−178	61	0.70	120,536 km (74,898 mi)
Uranus	84 years	about 17 hours	−216	27	1.30	51,118 km (31,763 mi)
Neptune	165 years	about 16 hours	−214	13	1.76	49,528 km (30,775 mi)

Do the Math!

Find an Average

In the space below, find the average density of the four inner planets. Repeat for the four outer planets.

Inner planets:

Outer planets:

How do the average densities compare?

_____

_____

_____

The density of water is 1 gram per cubic centimeter (g/cm³). Saturn would float because its density is less than the density of water. Earth would sink.

Patterns in Data

Look at the data table on the previous page. Describe two trends in the data between the inner and outer planets.

_____

_____

_____

_____

The Flying Objects

Besides planets, there are many other bodies that orbit the sun. Let's find out more about some of them.

Active Reading As you read these two pages, find and underline two facts about asteroids.

Moons

Other moons are very different from Earth's moon. Europa, one of Jupiter's moons, may have a liquid ocean under a layer of ice. Another of Jupiter's moons, Io [EYE•oh], has the most active volcanoes of any body in the solar system.

Io

Dwarf Planets

Pluto was once called a planet. But in 2006, it was reclassified as a dwarf planet. **Dwarf planets** are nearly round bodies whose orbits cross the orbits of other bodies. Most are found in a region of the solar system beyond Neptune's orbit called the Kuiper belt. These objects are far away and hard to study. Quaoar, shown above, was discovered in 2002.

Asteroids

Asteroids are rock and iron objects that orbit the sun. Millions of them are found in the wide region between Mars and Jupiter known as the *asteroid belt*. Some asteroids are as small as a city block. Others could fill up an ocean. Some asteroids even have their own moons!

Meteoroids, Meteors, and Meteorites

Each day, tons of meteoroids hit Earth's atmosphere. *Meteoroids* are pieces of rock that break off of asteroids and travel through space. Most meteoroids burn up in Earth's atmosphere, causing a streak of light called a *meteor*. Meteoroids that reach Earth's surface are called *meteorites*.

Where's the Sun?

In the drawing of a comet, put an *S* to indicate the direction toward the sun. Put a *T* over each tail.

Comets

A **comet** is a chunk of frozen gases, rock, ice, and dust. Comets have long orbits around the sun. As comets pass close to the sun, part of their frozen surface begins to break away and turn into gases and dust. These particles reflect the sun's light and become visible as long tails. A comet's tails always point away from the sun.

Space Watch

Some objects in space cross each others' orbits. Often, nothing happpens. But sometimes the objects hit each other. Scientists look out for objects that may cross Earth's orbit.

Pictures of the surface of the moon tell a story. Over millions of years, space objects such as comets, meteoroids, and asteroids have impacted, or hit, the moon. Impact craters of all sizes can be found on the moon's surface.

Space objects have also hit other bodies in the solar system. A comet named Shoemaker-Levy 9 impacted Jupiter in 1994. Pictures of the impact were taken by the *Galileo* space probe.

Scientists know that large objects have also hit Earth. In fact, a huge one impacted Earth about 65 million years ago. Many scientists think it caused changes in the environment that killed all the dinosaurs. Luckily, impacts like that one do not happen often.

Scientists use telescopes to scan space for near-Earth asteroids. These are objects that may cross Earth's orbit. Scientists keep track of their size, position, and motion. They analyze this data to determine if the objects could impact Earth.

The impact of Shoemaker-Levy 9 caused bubbles of hot gas to rise into Jupiter's atmosphere, as well as dark spots to form on its surface.

The Barringer Meteor Crater, in Arizona, was formed by a meteorite that struck Earth about 50,000 years ago.

Impacts can happen anywhere on Earth! This map shows some impact crater sites from around the world.

Impact Crater Diameter

- 10–25 km
- 25–50 km
- greater than 50 km

▶ On these pages, underline effects of impacts. Then circle a picture that shows evidence of an impact on Earth.

Observatories have powerful telescopes that enable scientists to track the movement of objects in space.

Sum It Up!

When you're done, use the answer key to check and revise your work.

Read the summary, and then place the information in the list into the correct box below.

The sun is at the center of the solar system. Planets, dwarf planets, moons, and other smaller objects make up the solar system. The eight planets in the solar system can be divided into inner planets and outer planets. Each group has different characteristics.

small and dense	longer revolutions	many moons	few moons
giant size	closest to sun	gaseous surface	low density
rings	rocky surface		

1 **Inner Planets**

2 **Outer Planets**

Fill in the missing information to describe the object shown below.

3

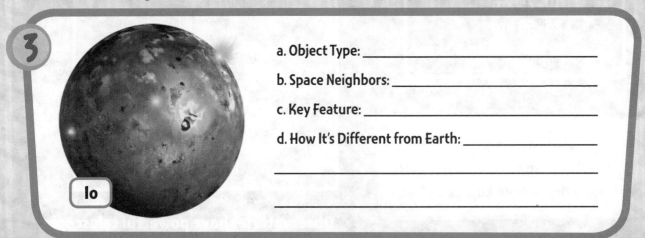

Io

a. Object Type: _____

b. Space Neighbors: _____

c. Key Feature: _____

d. How It's Different from Earth: _____

_____

_____

© Houghton Mifflin Harcourt Publishing Company

Brain Check

Lesson 1

Name ______________________________

Word Play

1 Use each of the terms in the box to label the objects in the diagram below.

planet	comet	asteroid	solar system	dwarf planet
moon	orbit	gas giant	sun	* Key Lesson Vocabulary

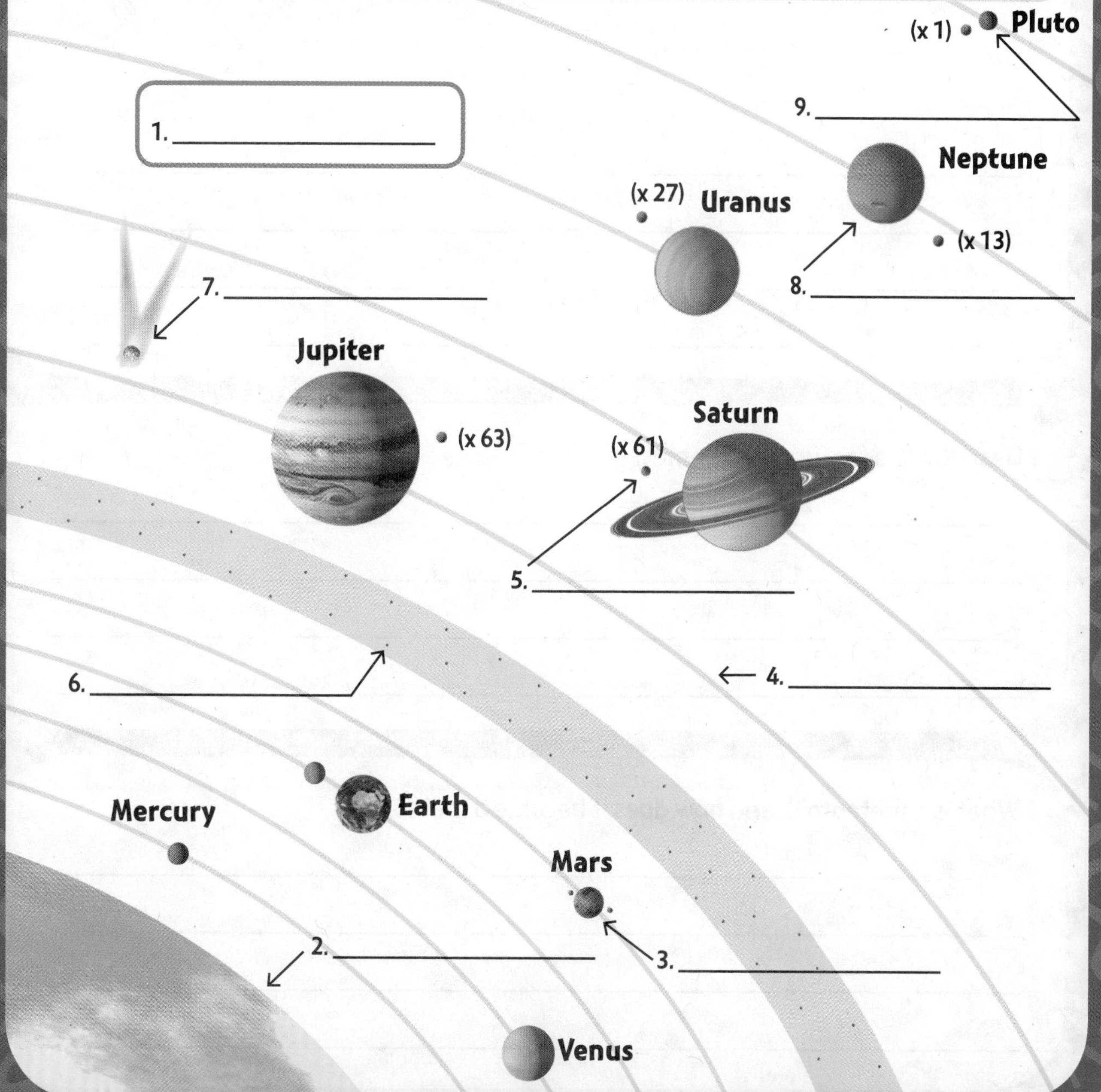

(x 1)
Pluto
9. ______________
1. ______________
Neptune
(x 27)
Uranus
(x 13)
8. ______________
7. ______________
Jupiter
(x 63)
Saturn
(x 61)
5. ______________
6. ______________
4. ______________
Earth
Mercury
Mars
2. ______________
3. ______________
Venus

Apply Concepts

2 In the space below, draw pictures to show the key physical characteristics of an inner planet and an outer planet. Then describe your drawings.

_____   _____

_____   _____

_____   _____

_____   _____

3 Describe the features of a comet.

_____

_____

_____

_____

4 What is a meteoroid, and how does it become a meteorite?

_____

_____

_____

_____

5 Identify each of the following large objects in the solar system. Write how you are able to identify each one.

_____
_____

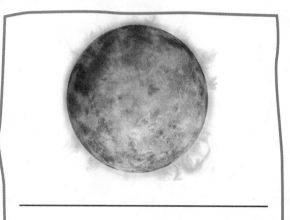

_____
_____

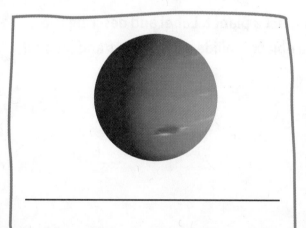

_____
_____

_____
_____

6 A scientist discovers an object in the solar system. She describes it as bigger than an asteroid, smaller than Mercury, and farther from the sun than Neptune. What kind of object could it be? Explain.

_____
_____

7 Complete the Venn diagram in order to compare and contrast an asteroid and a comet.

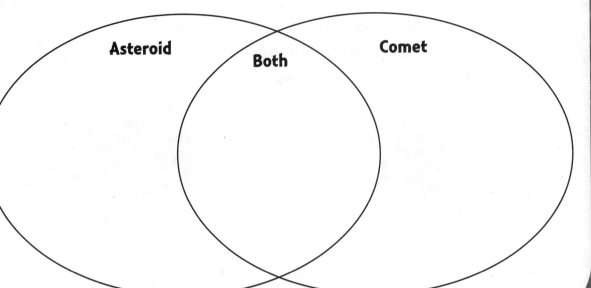

Asteroid   Both   Comet

8 Draw a picture of an object that might impact a planet. Label and describe the object. What evidence is there that these objects collide with planets and moons?

_____

_____

_____

Take It Home!

Many newspapers give the location of Venus, Mars, and Jupiter in the sky. Find out where in the sky these planets may appear. See if you can find them. They are among the brightest objects in the night sky.

Meet Two Space Explorers

On her first mission, Kalpana Chawla traveled more than six million miles in 15 days!

Kalpana Chawla

As a little girl in India, Kalpana Chawla dreamed about flying airplanes. She came to the United States and studied hard. She soon earned her degree as an aerospace engineer. Kalpana Chawla could fly many kinds of airplanes. Her dreams had come true! But she kept dreaming. She wanted to fly in space. She went to work for NASA and became an astronaut. Soon, Kalpana Chawla became the first Indian-born woman in space!

Claudia Alexander

Claudia Alexander explores outer space, too. But she never leaves Earth! She studies the moons of the planet Jupiter. She was in charge of NASA's *Galileo* mission. The mission sent an unmanned spacecraft to Jupiter. The spacecraft left Earth in 1989. It took six long years to reach Jupiter. Claudia Alexander directed it over 385 million miles! Under her command, *Galileo* was the first spacecraft to take detailed photos of Jupiter and its moons.

Galileo space probe

Two Ways to Study Space

Kalpana Chawla and Claudia Alexander study space in different ways. Write the statements that apply to each scientist in the correct circle.

Kalpana Chawla

_____

_____

_____

_____

_____

The Hubble Space Telescope sends scientists pictures of space from its orbit high above Earth.

- I lead space missions without leaving Earth.
- I traveled on the space shuttle.
- I study the moons of Jupiter.
- I grew up in India and learned to fly many types of airplanes.
- I study objects in space.

Claudia Alexander

_____

_____

_____

_____

Many scientists study space from Earth by using a telescope, such as this one, in an observatory.

Name _____

Essential Question

How Do We Observe Objects in the Solar System?

Set a Purpose
What do you think you will learn from this investigation?

_____

_____

_____

Think About the Procedure
Why do you think you will observe the object in different ways?

_____

_____

_____

_____

Why is it important that you work together as a team in this investigation?

_____

_____

Record Your Data
In the space below, record the observations you made using all three methods.

_____

_____

_____

Draw Conclusions

Think about how scientists view objects in space. What did observing the object from far away represent?

_____

_____

_____

What did using binoculars represent?

_____

_____

_____

What did viewing the object up close represent?

_____

_____

_____

Analyze and Extend

1. How did your observations from far away differ from those made using binoculars? Give an example.

_____

_____

_____

2. How did your observations made using binoculars differ from the observations made when a student walked to the poster? Give an example.

_____

_____

_____

_____

3. How do space probes help scientists learn about objects in space?

_____

_____

_____

_____

4. Think about objects in the solar system. How do scientists use time and space relationships to observe them?

_____

_____

_____

_____

5. Think of other questions you would like to ask about how scientists study objects in space. Write your questions.

_____

_____

_____

sential Question

What Are Stars and Galaxies?

Engage Your Brain!

Find the answer to the following question in this lesson and record it here.

Space is not completely empty. There are small particles in space. What happens when these particles come together?

_____

_____

_____

A nebula, such as the Pelican Nebula shown here, is a giant cloud of gas and dust.

Active Reading

esson Vocabulary

st the terms. As you learn about each one, ake notes in the Interactive Glossary.

_____

_____

_____

_____

Signal Words: Details

Signal words show connections between ideas. _For example, for instance,_ and _such as_ signal examples of an idea. _Also_ and _in fact_ signal added facts. Active readers remember what they read because they are alert to signal words that identify examples and facts about a topic.

TWINKLING STARS

You see stars as tiny points of white light in the night sky. Stars are not tiny, and they are not all white. Find out how scientists study stars.

Active Reading As you read these two pages, draw boxes around words or phrases that signal a detail or an added fact.

People have always looked at objects in the sky. **Astronomy** is the study of objects in space and their characteristics. *Astronomers* are scientists who study space and everything in it. They use many types of telescopes to observe objects in space, such as stars and planets.

Stars are huge balls of hot, glowing gases that produce their own heat and light. The sun is the star you know the most about. It seems much larger than other stars only because it is much closer to Earth.

Do the Math!
Dividing by 3-digit Numbers

A small telescope magnifies objects 150 times. A large observatory telescope magnifies an object 3,300 times. How many times as great is the magnification of the observatory telescope than the small telescope?

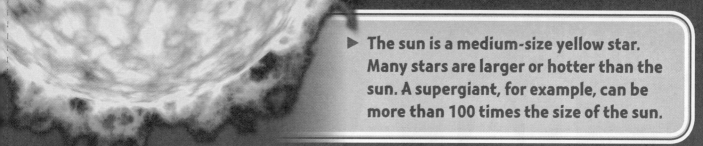

► The sun is a medium-size yellow star. Many stars are larger or hotter than the sun. A supergiant, for example, can be more than 100 times the size of the sun.

A STAR IS BORN

Stars form when gravity causes gas and dust particles found in space to pull together. These particles are squeezed together under great pressure. Eventually, energy stored in the particles is released as heat and light. A star is born.

Stars are classified by their color, temperature, brightness, and size. The color of a star can tell us about its temperature.

For example, blue stars are the hottest. A blue star's average temperature is about 15,000 °C.

Stars have a wide range of sizes. White dwarf stars, for instance, can be as small as a planet. Giant and supergiant stars are many times bigger than the average-size star. The largest stars are also usually the brightest. A star's brightness is related to the amount of visible light it gives off.

Super Hot and Just Hot

Draw a rectangle around the hottest stars in the diagram. Draw a circle around the brightest stars.

GOING GALACTIC

Our solar system is huge. Yet it is only a tiny part of a much larger system in space. Our sun is one star in a group of billions of stars found in the Milky Way galaxy.

Active Reading As you read the next four pages, circle details about the ages of stars in each type of galaxy.

Milky Way Galaxy

YOU ARE HERE

Once, people thought Earth was at the center of the universe. The universe is everything that exists. Now we know that we are not even at the center of our own galaxy!

© Houghton Mifflin Harcourt Publishing Company (b) ©NASA-JPL-Caltech/R. Hurt (SSC); (bkg) ©D. Nunuk/Photo Researchers, Inc.

▶ In the space below, describe the position of the solar system within the Milky Way.

_____

_____

_____

_____

FEATURES OF GALAXIES

A **galaxy** is a group of billions of stars, the objects that orbit the stars, gas, and dust. A galaxy is held together by gravity. There are billions of galaxies in the universe. Galaxies are separated by large distances. On a cloudless night, you might see what looks like a faint band of clouds among the stars. This is a part of our home galaxy, the Milky Way. Most other galaxies can be seen only by using powerful telescopes.

TYPES OF GALAXIES

In the 1920s, astronomer Edwin Hubble was the first to study galaxies. He classified them by shape. Through his telescope, Hubble observed pinwheel-like groups of stars that he called *spiral galaxies*.

Some spiral galaxies, called *barred spiral galaxies*, have a center shaped like a long bar. Recent evidence suggests that the Milky Way is a barred spiral galaxy.

SPIRAL GALAXIES

Spiral galaxies consist of a rotating disk of young stars, gas, and dust and a central bulge made of older stars.

BARRED SPIRAL GALAXIES

Barred spiral galaxies may have two or more spiral arms. Unlike regular spirals, there are young stars at the center of barred spiral galaxies.

MORE TYPES OF GALAXIES

Most of the brightest galaxies in the universe have spiral shapes. But spiral galaxies are not the only type of galaxy. In fact, they make up only about 20 percent of all galaxies. The dimmer *irregular galaxies* and *elliptical galaxies* make up about 80 percent of all galaxies in the universe.

IRREGULAR GALAXIES

Irregular galaxies do not have any particular shape. The stars are randomly scattered. There is lots of gas and dust to form new stars. About 20 percent of all galaxies are irregular. Some astronomers think that gravity from nearby galaxies causes irregular galaxies to form.

ELLIPTICAL GALAXIES

Elliptical galaxies are brightest at their center. About 60 percent of all galaxies in the universe are elliptical. They can be shaped like a perfect sphere or a flattened globe. Large ellipticals are made up of old stars and have too little dust or gas to form new ones.

COSMIC **CRASHES**

Sometimes galaxies collide, or crash together, in space! Why? Gravity pulls galaxies toward each other. Although galaxies may collide, single stars and planets almost never do.

Many things can happen when galaxies collide. Often, large amounts of dust and gas are pressed together. This causes a starburst, or rapid formation of many new stars. Sometimes, a smaller galaxy becomes part of a larger galaxy. A collision of galaxies can also form a large, irregular galaxy. Scientists believe that many irregular galaxies were once spiral or elliptical galaxies that were involved in a cosmic crash.

Galaxies do not stand still. They are always moving. Galaxies can move away from each other or toward each other.

▶ Look at pictures 1–5. Draw a picture to show what you think will happen next to these two galaxies. Write a sentence to describe it.

_____

_____

When you're done, use the answer key to check and revise your work.

The universe is composed of billions of galaxies. Dust, gas, and billions of stars make up a galaxy. The idea web below summarizes information about stars and galaxies. Complete it using the words and phrases from the box.

Types of Galaxies	Elliptical	Temperature
Spiral	Characteristics of Stars	Size
Color	Irregular	

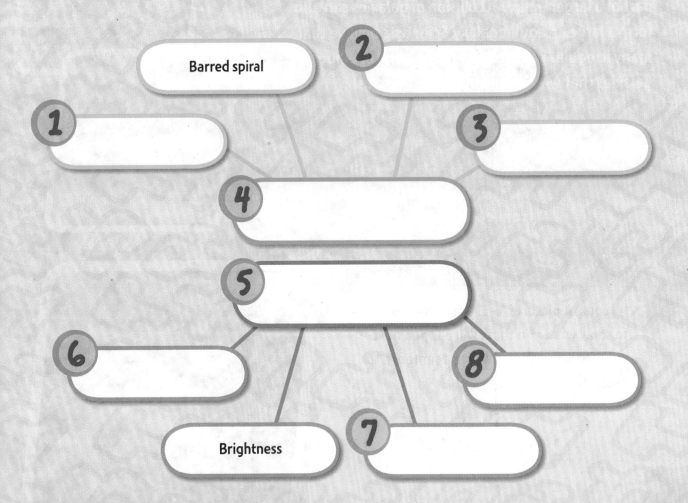

Barred spiral

2

1

3

4

5

6

8

Brightness

7

Answer Key: 1–3 (in any order): Spiral, Elliptical, Irregular. 4. Types of Galaxies. 5. Characteristics of Stars 6–8 (in any order): Color; Size; Temperature

Name _____

Word Play

1 Complete the puzzle. If you need help, use the words in the box below the clues.

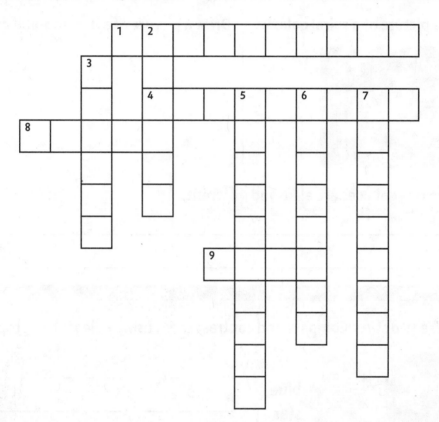

Across

1. A person who studies the universe
4. A galaxy with no particular shape
8. Characteristic that is related to a star's temperature
9. A ball of hot, glowing gases

Down

2. A pinwheel-like galaxy
3. A group of stars, dust, and gases
5. A galaxy shaped like a flattened globe
6. Everything that exists—planets, stars, dust, and gases
7. The study of the objects in space and their properties

spiral	elliptical	astronomy*	irregular	galaxy*	star*
astronomer	color	universe*			

*Key Lesson Vocabulary

Apply Concepts

2 What are some ways in which galaxies differ?

_____

_____

3 Look at this picture of a spiral galaxy. | Draw a picture of a barred spiral galaxy.

Tell how the two galaxies are alike and different.

_____

_____

4 Look at these two stars. Compare and contrast them using at least two properties.

red giant   blue star

_____

_____

_____

5 How do these stars compare to the sun?

_____

_____

Take It Home!

Find out which are the brightest stars that are visible this time of year in your area. With an adult, observe the stars. Make a diagram of the night sky showing where to find the brightest stars.

Tools in Space

An astronaut often has to use screwdrivers or drills to fix things in space. The astronaut's tools are specially designed for a person wearing bulky gloves and floating in orbit. Hand tools must work in the extreme cold vacuum of space and be tethered so they don't float away. A robotic arm helps the astronaut move around outside. However, the astronaut's most important tool is the space suit that maintains an environment in which the astronaut can breathe.

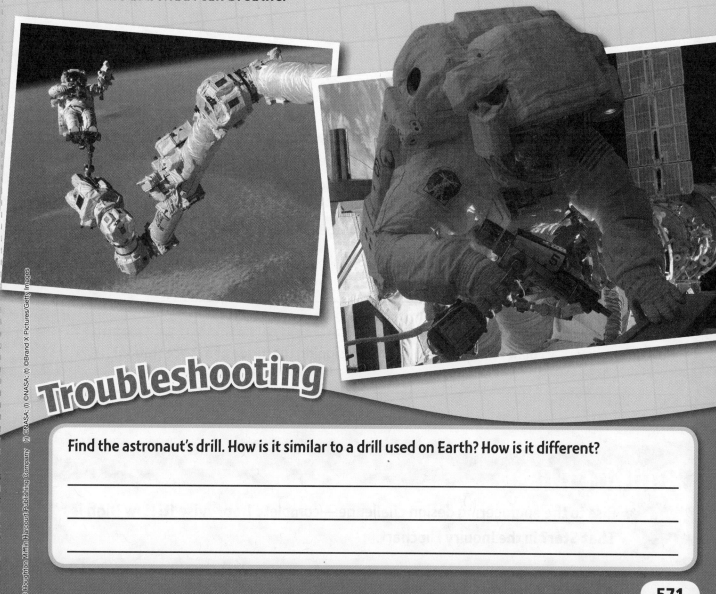

Troubleshooting

Find the astronaut's drill. How is it similar to a drill used on Earth? How is it different?

S.T.E.M.

continued

You are used to doing everything under the pull of Earth's gravity. That's what makes it possible for you feel motions as up, down, and side-to-side. There is no "right side up" in space! It is harder than you might think to work in such an unfamiliar environment.

Turn your book so that the top of this page is closest to you.

Hold your pencil near the eraser. Write your name on the line above so that it reads properly when you turn the page right side up again.

What made this task difficult?

How do engineers account for microgravity when designing the inside of a space station?

Build On It!

Rise to the engineering design challenge—complete **Improvise It: How High is That Star?** in the Inquiry Flipchart.

Unit 12 Review

Vocabulary Review

Use the terms in the box to complete the sentences.

| asteroid |
| comet |
| galaxy |
| solar system |
| star |

1. Together, a star and all the planets and other objects orbiting it

   form a(n) _____.

2. A chunk of rock or iron that is less than 1,000 km (621 mi) in
   diameter and that orbits the sun is called

   a(n) _____.

3. A huge ball of very hot, glowing gases in space that can produce

   its own heat and light is called a(n) _____.

4. A group of solar systems that are held together by gravity and

   classified by shape is called a(n) _____.

5. The picture shows an example of a(n)
   _____.

Science Concepts

Fill in the letter of the choice that best answers the question.

6. Scientists use models to represent or
   explain things in the natural world. Why
   are models useful for the study of the
   solar system?

   (A) because models cannot be proved
       wrong

   (B) because models are always accepted
       by all scientists

   (C) because models describe the way
       things actually are

   (D) because models can be used to
       describe how things work

7. On a clear night, Ram correctly identified
   some clouds among the stars as the Milky
   Way. What part of the Milky Way was
   most visible to Ram?

   (A) asteroids

   (B) dust

   (C) planets

   (D) stars

Science Concepts

Fill in the letter of the choice that best answers the question.

8. Astronomers use the term *brightness* to describe the amount of light a star produces, not how bright a star appears from Earth. The diagram below compares the color, temperature, and brightness of some stars that can be seen from Earth.

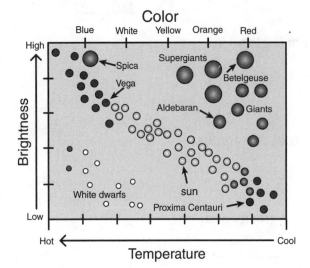

Which of these stars produces the **most** light?

Ⓐ Betelgeuse

Ⓑ Proxima Centauri

Ⓒ our sun

Ⓓ Vega

9. During a school field trip to an observatory, Smita used a telescope to observe stars of different colors. Based on the diagram in Question 8, which factor determines a star's color?

Ⓐ its size

Ⓑ its brightness

Ⓒ its temperature

Ⓓ its distance from Earth

10. Ming is doing a project on planets in other solar systems. She learns about a planet called Planet Z. Planet Z is very large and has a thick atmosphere and a low density. Which planet is Planet Z most similar to?

Ⓐ Earth   Ⓒ Mercury

Ⓑ Mars   Ⓓ Saturn

11. The diagram below shows planets orbiting a star.

What type of group is the diagram illustrating?

Ⓐ a constellation   Ⓒ a solar system

Ⓑ the Milky Way   Ⓓ a universe

12. Some elliptical galaxies appear to be perfect spheres. How are the stars distributed within this kind of galaxy?

Ⓐ The stars are evenly distributed throughout the galaxy.

Ⓑ The center is very dense with many stars, and density decreases farther out.

Ⓒ Most of the stars are near the outside of the sphere with dust clouds in the center.

Ⓓ The stars are spread throughout the sphere in bands that look like the arms of spiral galaxies.

13. There are many types of stars. Each picture below shows two stars of the **same** color. Which picture and statement is true?

Ⓐ

The larger star must be brighter.

Ⓑ

The smaller star must be hotter.

Ⓒ

The smaller star must be closer to Earth.

Ⓓ

Stars that are the same color are usuallly the same size.

14. All the planets in the solar system orbit the sun. What is the main difference between the orbits of the inner and outer planets?

Ⓐ The inner planets and outer planets orbit in different directions.

Ⓑ The inner planets travel a greater distance than the outer planets do.

Ⓒ The outer planets take longer to orbit the sun than the inner planets do.

Ⓓ The outer planets rotate as they orbit the sun, and the inner planets do not.

15. The diagram below shows the orbit of Earth and the orbit of Borrelly.

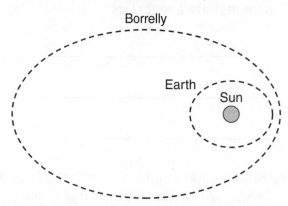

Which of these types of space objects is Borrelly **most** likely to be?

Ⓐ an asteroid

Ⓑ a comet

Ⓒ a moon

Ⓓ a planet

16. When Galileo observed Jupiter, he saw four objects in line with the planet. These four objects moved from night to night and sometimes disappeared in front of or behind the planet. What kind of space object was Galileo observing?

Ⓐ dwarf planets

Ⓑ solar systems

Ⓒ meteoroids

Ⓓ moons

Apply Inquiry and Review the Big Idea

Write the answers to these questions.

17. When Galileo used his telescope to observe the Milky Way, the stars appeared as small points of light. What did Galileo's observations demonstrate about stars?

_____

_____

_____

18. On a cloudless night, a milky band known as the Milky Way is visible from Earth. Explain how the structure of our galaxy and the position of our solar system within our galaxy relate to this observation.

_____

_____

_____

19. Sofia observes an object in the night sky. What questions and observations can she use to determine whether the object is a planet or a star?

Questions _____

_____

Observations _____

_____

20. People have developed models of the universe for thousands of years. Identify two observations that a model of the universe would need to explain in order to be useful.

a. _____

_____

b. _____

_____

Matter

Big Idea

All matter has properties that can be observed, described, and measured.

I Wonder Why

Step right up and try your luck! Why do all the prizes at the carnival booth look so different? *Turn the page to find out.*

HOT
FRESH
DELICIOUS
Pop Corn
HOT
FRESH
DELICIOUS

Here's why Scientists classify matter in many different ways. Color, size, and state are all ways to classify matter.

In this unit, you will explore the Big Idea, the Essential Questions, and the Investigations on the Inquiry Flipchart.

Levels of Inquiry Key ■ DIRECTED ■ GUIDED ■ INDEPENDENT

Big Idea All matter has properties that can be observed, described, and measured.

Essential Questions

Now I Get the Big Idea!

Science Notebook

Before you begin each lesson, be sure to write your thoughts about the Essential Question.

Essential Question

What Are Solids, Liquids, and Gases?

Engage Your Brain!

As you read the lesson, look for the answer to the following question and record it here.

Bottled water and the snow from this snow machine are both water. How are these forms of water different?

_____

_____

_____

_____

_____

Active Reading

Lesson Vocabulary

List the terms. As you learn about each one, make notes in the Interactive Glossary.

_____ _____

_____ _____

_____ _____

Compare and Contrast

Many ideas in this lesson involve comparisons and contrasts—how things are alike and different. Active readers stay focused on comparisons and contrasts when they ask themselves, How are these things alike? How are they different?

What's the Matter?

This book is made of matter, and so are you. You might think that matter can be seen and felt. But did you know that air is matter also? What is matter?

Active Reading As you read these two pages, draw two lines under each main idea.

Breathe in and out. Can you feel air hitting your hand? You can't see air, and you can't grab it. Yet air is **matter** because it has mass and it has volume. Matter cannot be created or destroyed. It might change form, but it is still matter.

Mass is the amount of matter in something. Each of the tiny particles that make up matter has mass, even though the particles are so small you cannot see them. **Volume** is the amount of space something takes up. When air is blown into a balloon, you can see that it has volume.

The large pencil has more matter than the smaller pencils. It has more mass and more volume.

Name That Matter

Look at the matter in this picture.

1. What matter is soft and sticky?

_____

2. What matter is hard and sharp?

_____

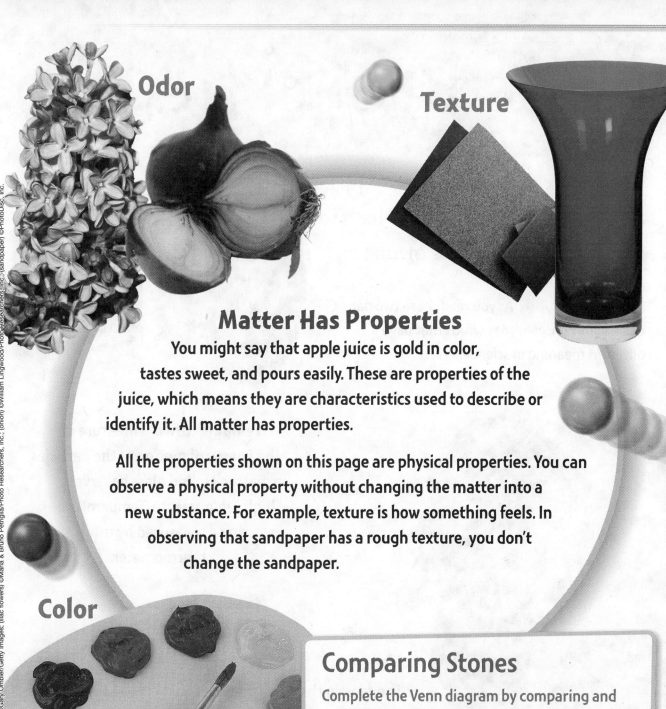

Odor

Texture

Matter Has Properties

You might say that apple juice is gold in color, tastes sweet, and pours easily. These are properties of the juice, which means they are characteristics used to describe or identify it. All matter has properties.

All the properties shown on this page are physical properties. You can observe a physical property without changing the matter into a new substance. For example, texture is how something feels. In observing that sandpaper has a rough texture, you don't change the sandpaper.

Color

Comparing Stones

Complete the Venn diagram by comparing and contrasting the properties of the two stones.

More Properties

Color, texture, and odor are just a few physical properties. What are some other properties of matter?

Active Reading As you read these two pages, circle common, everyday words that have a different meaning in science.

Temperature

Temperature is a measure of the energy of motion of the particles in matter. Melted glass has a very high temperature. Temperature can be measured by using a thermometer.

Volume

The food in the small bowl has less volume than the food in the large bowl because it takes up less space. Many tools can be used to measure volume.

Mass

A bowling ball and a basketball have about the same volume. The bowling ball has a greater mass because it contains more matter. Mass can be measured by using a balance.

Density

Density is found by dividing the mass of an object by its volume. The density of the gas in this balloon is less than the density of the air around it. That is why the balloon "floats" in air.

Do the Math!
Use Division

Use the data to find the density of each of these foods.

Determining Densities of Foods			
Food	Mass (g)	Volume (cm³)	Density (g/cm³)
gelatin	75	100	
pudding	90	100	
whipped cream	50	100	

Liquids

A **liquid** is a substance that has a definite volume but does not have a definite shape. The particles in a liquid move slower than the particles in a gas, and they slide by each other.

States of Matter

Another physical property of matter is its state. Solid, liquid, and gas are the most common states of matter on Earth.

Active Reading As you read these two pages, draw boxes around the names of the three things that are being compared.

Gases

A **gas** is a substance that does not have a definite shape or volume. The particles in a gas move very quickly and are far apart from each other.

Matter is made of tiny particles. The particles in solids, liquids, and gases have different amounts of energy. The amount of energy affects how fast the particles move and how close together they are.

The shape and volume of something depends on its state. Because each particle in a gas is affected little by the other particles, gas particles are free to move throughout their container. Gases take both the shape and the volume of their container.

Particles in a liquid cannot move as freely. A sample of a liquid keeps the same volume no matter what container it is in. However because the particles slide by each other, a liquid takes the shape of its container.

The particles in a solid do not move from place to place, so solids keep the same shape and volume.

Solids

A **solid** is a substance with a definite shape and volume. The particles in a solid are very close to each other. They don't move from place to place. They just vibrate where they are.

The bubbles in the tank are a _____.

The water is an example of a _____.

The castle is a _____.

A Matter of Temperature

On a hot day, an ice cube melts. This change is caused by a change in temperature. When matter changes state, the type of matter is not changed.

Active Reading As you read these two pages, draw one line under a cause. Draw two lines under the effect.

When matter takes in or releases energy, its temperature changes. When enough energy is taken in or released, matter can change state.

When a gas releases energy, its temperature goes down until it *condenses,* or changes to a liquid. When a liquid releases energy, its temperature goes down until it *freezes,* or changes to a solid.

When a solid takes in energy, its temperature rises until it *melts,* or changes to a liquid. When a liquid takes in energy, its temperature rises until it *evaporates,* or changes to a gas. Evaporation and boiling are similar—both turn liquids into gases. Evaporation is slower and happens only at a liquid's surface. Boiling is faster and happens throughout the liquid.

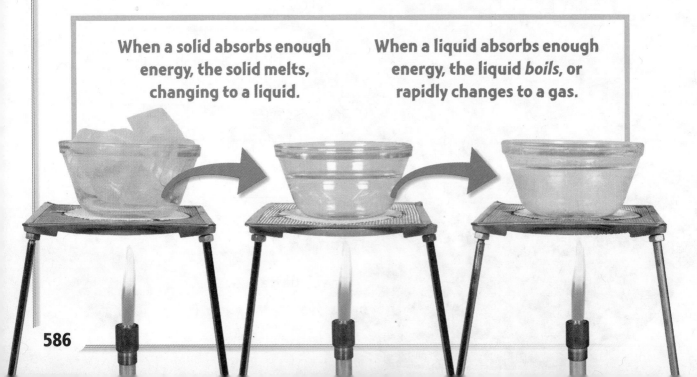

When a solid absorbs enough energy, the solid melts, changing to a liquid.

When a liquid absorbs enough energy, the liquid *boils,* or rapidly changes to a gas.

When a gas releases enough energy, the gas condenses, changing to a liquid. Particles of water vapor condense and form raindrops and dew.

When a liquid releases enough energy, the liquid freezes, changing to a solid. Dripping water that freezes can form icicles.

The temperature at which a certain type of matter freezes or melts is the same. The temperature at which a type of matter condenses or boils is also the same. For water, the melting and freezing points are 0 °C. The condensation and boiling points are 100 °C. Evaporation can happen at temperatures below the boiling point.

Lava is hot, melted rock that erupts from a volcano. Lava releases energy as it cools and becomes solid rock.

▶ Complete this graphic organizer.

As a solid takes in energy, its temperature _____. Eventually, it will _____, changing to a _____.

If the liquid takes in enough _____, it will _____, changing to a _____.

Properties of Solids, Liquids, and Gases

Each different material has its own unique properties. However, properties can change depending on the state of the material.

Active Reading As you read these two pages, find and underline facts about each state of matter.

Each state of matter has different physical properties. Liquids and gases both flow, moving from place to place. Gases can expand, taking up more space, or compress, taking up less space. Solids have definite textures.

Liquid water flows much more quickly than honey.

Liquids
All liquids flow from one place to another. Different liquids may flow at different rates.

Solids

Although clay and a wooden table are both solids, each one feels different. All solids have a shape, but the shape of some solids can be changed easily.

Gases

A lot of gas has been compressed in this tank. It is under high pressure. Compressed gas from the tank expands, filling many balloons.

▶ Complete this main-idea-and-details graphic organizer.

Main Idea
_____

Liquids	Gases	_____
Motor oil and milk _____ at different rates.	When you push on the sides of a balloon, the gas inside is _____.	Glass and sandpaper have different _____.

When you're done, use the answer key to check and revise your work.

Read the summary statements below. Each one is incorrect. Change the part of the summary in blue to make it correct.

1. A property is a characteristic of matter that is used to determine the state of the matter.

_____

2. A sample of ice has a volume of 1.0 cm³ and a mass of 0.9 g. The density of the ice is 1.1 g/cm³.

_____

3. The particles in a solid are close together, but they can slide past each other.

_____

4. A solid changes to a liquid during a process known as freezing.

_____

5. Solids and liquids can be compressed when put under pressure.

_____

6. The mass of an object can be measured by using a measuring cup.

_____

Summarize

Read the properties below. Write S for solid, G for gas, and L for liquid. Some properties may have more than one answer.

7. Has a definite texture and shape _____

8. Can melt _____

9. Can freeze _____

10. Can boil _____

11. Takes the volume of its container _____

12. Can condense _____

13. Can flow _____

14. Takes the shape of its container _____

15. Has a definite volume _____

Word Play

Name _____

1 Use the clues below to fill in the words in the puzzle.

1. To squeeze a gas into a smaller space
2. A physical property that describes how something feels
3. The state of matter that keeps its shape and volume when it is placed in a different container
4. The measure of the energy of motion of particles of matter
5. Anything that has mass and volume
6. What happens to a liquid when it releases enough energy
7. Calculated by dividing mass by volume
8. The state of matter that has particles that slide by each other
9. The amount of space something takes up
10. The state of matter that expands to fill its container

1. ☐☐☐☐☐☐☐☐
2. ☐☐☐☐☐☐☐
3. ☐☐☐☐☐
4. ☐☐☐☐☐☐☐☐☐
5. ☐☐☐☐☐
6. ☐☐☐☐☐☐☐
7. ☐☐☐☐☐☐
8. ☐☐☐☐☐☐☐
9. ☐☐☐☐☐
10. ☐☐☐

Read down the squares with red borders. The word you find will complete the riddle below.

Perry the porcupine's portrait perfectly portrayed his pestering personality and prickly ___ ___ ___ ___ ___ ___ ___ ___ .

Apply Concepts

2 Tell what property each of the following tools is used to measure.

_____   _____   _____

3 Complete these descriptions of the different states of matter.

_____	_____	Solids
_____	Particles are closer together and move past each other.	Particles are very close and vibrate in place.
_____		
Examples: air; helium in balloons; oxygen in a tank	Examples: _____ _____	Examples: _____ _____

4 Fill in the name of the processes (such as freezing) that are represented.

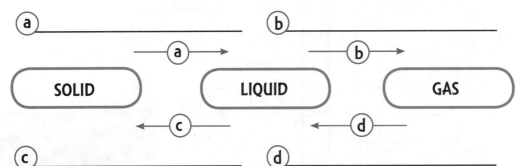

a _____   b _____

c _____   d _____

Take It Home!

Play a game of 20 Questions with members of your family. Have them choose a simple item that you can see in the room. Try to guess what the item is by asking yes/no questions about the item's properties.

Carbon fiber is used to make this bike wheel strong and lightweight.

Strong, Light, or Both?

A bicycle wheel has to be strong to be safe. You also want it to be lightweight so it takes less energy for you to pedal the bike. You could easily bend one of these wheel spokes all by itself, but arranged together they make the wheel strong enough to support your weight and more!

Carbon fiber threads are woven into fabric.

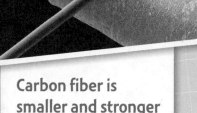

Carbon fiber is smaller and stronger than a human hair!

Spider silk is the strongest, lightest natural material. It is stronger than steel! Carbon fiber is a strong, human-made thread that can be woven into fabric. A single carbon fiber is much finer than a human hair. Carbon fiber is one of the strongest and lightest materials made by people.

Circle a natural material. Put an X on a manufactured material. What are two ways these materials are alike?

_____

_____

S.T.E.M.
continued

Every design has its upside and its downside. When a design for an object is chosen to meet one purpose, other features may not be as good. A quality that a designer must give up in order to get a desired quality is called a design trade-off. A designer needs to think of both the upside and the downside of a particular design.

Look at these shoes. List two examples of the upside and two of the downside for each shoe. Think of another type of shoe. Draw it in the empty space, and explain the trade-offs.

Upside	Downside
_____	_____
_____	_____
_____	_____

Upside	Downside
_____	_____
_____	_____
_____	_____

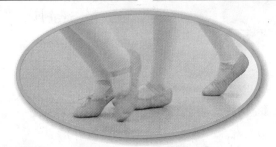

Upside	Downside
_____	_____
_____	_____

Upside	Downside
_____	_____
_____	_____

Build On It!

Rise to the engineering design challenge—complete **Design It: Distillation Device** in the Inquiry Flipchart.

Name _____

Essential Question

How Does Water Change?

Set a Purpose
What can you learn from this experiment?

_____

_____

Think About the Procedure
Why do you dry the bag in step 2?

_____

_____

Where did the moisture on the outside of
the bag come from?

_____

_____

Make a Prediction
Write your prediction from step 3.

_____

_____

_____

_____

Record Your Observations
In the space below, draw a table to record
the masses that you measured.

Draw Conclusions

Was your prediction correct? Explain.

_____

_____

_____

_____

_____

_____

_____

Analyze and Extend

1. Why was the mass of the bag not important in this activity?

_____

_____

_____

2. What properties of water changed during this activity? What properties did not change?

_____

_____

_____

_____

3. What do you predict would happen to the mass if you put the bag from step 5 in the freezer and then found the mass after the water changed back to ice?

_____

_____

_____

4. Suppose you poured the water from step 5 into a container and measured its volume. If you froze the water, would its volume change or stay the same? Explain.

_____

_____

_____

_____

5. What other questions would you like to ask about how water changes during a physical change? What experiments could you do to answer the questions?

_____

_____

_____

_____

_____

596

Essential Question

How Does Matter Change?

🧠 Engage Your Brain!

As you read the lesson, look for the answer to the following question and record it here.

A piece of iron can change in different ways. How is iron bending different from iron rusting?

_____

_____

_____

Active Reading

Lesson Vocabulary

List each term. As you learn about each one, make notes in the Interactive Glossary.

_____

_____

_____

_____

Main Idea and Details

Detail sentences give information about a topic. The information may be examples, features, characteristics, or facts. Active readers stay focused on the topic when they ask, What fact or information does this sentence add to the topic?

Classifying Change

▲ Slicing apples and cracking eggs are physical changes.

When an apple pie cooks, chemical changes occur. Cooked apples do not have the same properties as a raw apple.

Matter has properties, but matter also undergoes changes. How many different ways does matter change?

Active Reading Each visual on these two pages has an empty bubble. Write a *C* if the visual shows a chemical change. Write a *P* if it shows a physical change.

Matter has physical properties that can be observed without changing the type of matter. Matter can also change in ways that do not affect the type of matter. These changes are called **physical changes**.

When you sharpen a pencil, the pencil goes through a physical change. The wood shavings and bits of graphite don't look like a pencil any more. But the wood is still wood, and the graphite is still graphite.

▲ Slicing a pie is another physical change.

▲ The properties of the ash and gases that form when wood burns are different from the properties of wood.

▲ When iron rusts, it undergoes a chemical change.

Matter has other properties that cannot be observed without changing the identity of the matter. These properties are chemical properties. For example, you don't know if a type of matter will burn unless you burn it. When matter burns, it changes identity.

In the same way, **chemical changes** result in a change in the identity of matter. When a strawberry rots, it undergoes chemical change. The rotten strawberry's properties are quite different from those of a fresh strawberry. A chemical **reaction** is the process in which new substances are formed during a chemical change.

◀ When you eat apple pie, chemical changes in your body digest the food.

▶ Place a *P* by each physical change and a *C* by each chemical change.

Change	Type
Bacteria decompose leaves.	
A newspaper turns yellow in sunlight.	
Water evaporates.	
Gasoline burns in a car engine.	

599

Swelling
and Shrinking

Why do you think many car owners use one tire pressure in summer and another one in winter? When temperature differs, volume often differs.

Most matter expands when the temperature goes up and contracts when the temperature goes down. Some kinds of matter expand and contract more than others. People may run hot water over the metal lid of a glass jar. This expands the lid so that it's easier to take off the jar.

One exception is water. It expands when it freezes. Because ice takes up more volume than the same amount of liquid water, ice is less dense than water. That's why ice floats in a glass of water. In winter, ice first forms at the surface of a lake.

Liquid Water
Volume = 1.00 L

Frozen Water
Volume = 1.09 L

One of water's unique properties is that it expands when it freezes.

◀ Sometimes water flows into cracks in rocks and freezes. The expanding water makes the cracks in the rock larger and breaks large rocks into smaller pieces.

Expansion Joints

▶ Explain why bridges have expansion joints in them.

_____

_____

_____

_____

◀ This photo shows the same balloon at two different temperatures. The size of a sample of gas depends on its temperature. The gas in a balloon expands when it is warmed. The gas compresses when it is cooled.

Temperature = –80 °C
Volume = 1.9 L

Temperature = 35 °C
Volume = 3.0 L

Tampering with Temperature

When a burner on a stove is really hot, it glows red. A change in color is just one way temperature can affect matter.

Active Reading As you read this page, underline examples of how temperature affects physical changes in matter.

Some physical changes, such as tearing a piece of paper, are not affected by temperature. Other physical changes happen faster or slower at different temperatures. How quickly a change occurs is called the rate of change.

For example, ice on a lake will melt if the air temperature is above 0 °C. It will melt even faster if the air temperature is warmer. In the same way, water condenses more quickly on the outside of a very cold soft drink can than it does on a cool can.

Hot! Hot! Hot!
As iron is heated, it glows red or yellow.

WOW! This metal rod has been heated to more than 500 °C (932 °F).

OUCH! The filament of a light bulb is made of a metal called tungsten. It is glowing because it is heated to 2,500 °C!

Do the Math!
Graph Data

The data table shows how long it takes identical ice cubes to melt when placed in equal amounts of water at different temperatures. Make a line graph of these data.

Temperature of water (°C)	Melting time of ice (sec)
14	450
19	300
27	170
42	140
48	90
70	25

When grass and the air around it cool at night, water vapor in the air might condense, forming dew. As morning sunlight warms the air, the dew evaporates. In this photograph, the grass in the shade is wet but the grass in the sun has dried.

Adding it Up!

What happens to the mass of substances during physical or chemical changes?

As you read these pages, underline examples of conservation of mass.

75 grams

110 grams

90 grams

During physical and chemical changes, matter may change its appearance or its identity. In either type of change, the total mass of the matter before and after the change remains the same. This is called **conservation of mass**. To *conserve* means "to save."

For example, as water boils, it seems to disappear. However, the total mass of the particles of water vapor in the air equals the mass of the water that boiled away. Suppose you tear a 100-gram cardboard box into pieces. The total mass of all the pieces will also be 100 grams. The mass of the cardboard box stays the same. In this example, however, the volume of the cardboard box changes because tearing it into pieces causes it to lose its shape.

The total mass of the mixed salad is the sum of the masses of the vegetables in it.

▶ **What is the mass of the salad?**

_____

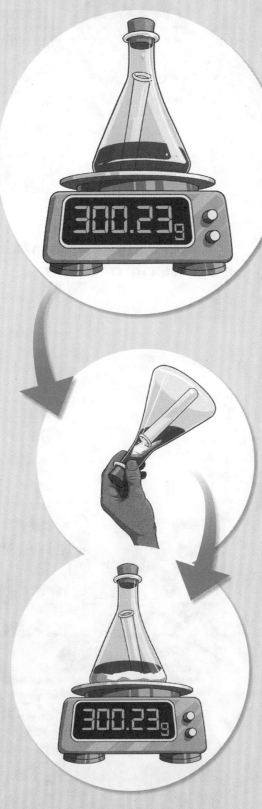

During this chemical reaction, the flask is sealed. Nothing can enter or leave, so the final mass equals the starting mass.

A chemical change turns one kind of matter into another. However, the mass of the matter stays the same. It can be tricky to compare, though. First, you must collect and measure the mass of everything you begin with. Then, you must collect and measure the mass of everything you are left with.

When wood burns, it combines with oxygen from the air. Burning produces ashes, smoke, and other gases. The mass of the wood and oxygen equals the mass of the ashes, smoke, and gases that are produced.

Do the Math!
Solve Problems

In a physical change, sugar is dissolved in water to form sugar water. In a chemical change, iron combines with oxygen to form rust. Fill in the missing values in the table.

Physical Change	Mass (grams)
sugar	125
water	
sugar water	198
Chemical Change	
iron	519
oxygen	23
rust	

Faster or Slower?

Temperature affects the rate at which chemical changes occur, too. Read to find out how.

cold water   warm water

An effervescent antacid tablet reacts more quickly with warm water than it does with cold water.

Active Reading As you read this page, circle two clue words or phrases that signal a detail such as an example or an added fact.

Increasing temperature often speeds up the rate of a chemical change. For example, increasing oven temperature speeds up the chemical changes that occur when a cake bakes or a potato cooks.

Decreasing temperature usually slows down the rate of chemical change. This is why food stays fresh longer when it is kept cool. Also, unused batteries stay charged longer when kept in the refrigerator.

The chemical changes that make food spoil are slowed down by keeping the food in the refrigerator.

Fevers

You feel awful. Your head hurts, and you have a fever. Why might having a fever be a good thing?

When you have a fever, your temperature rises above your normal body temperature (about 37 °C). A low fever is between 38 °C and 39 °C. A high fever is greater than 40 °C. Low fevers help the body fight disease. High fevers can cause severe problems.

Temperature can increase for many reasons. For example, certain bacteria have materials that your brain identifies as harmful. The brain sends out signals that cause an increase in the chemical changes that produce energy. Your temperature increases. Bacteria cannot survive at this higher temperature.

Do the Math!
Use a Number Line

On the number line below, plot the following values in °C.
a. normal body temperature
b. a slight fever
c. a high fever

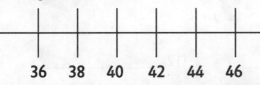

36 38 40 42 44 46

When you're done, use the answer key to check and revise your work.

The outline below is a summary of the lesson. Complete the outline.

I. Matter undergoes changes.

    A. One type of change is a (1) _____.

        1. Matter does not change identity.

        2. Example: (2) _____

    B. (3) _____

        1. Matter changes identity.

        2. Example: (4) _____

II. Temperature affects matter.

    A. When temperature increases,

        1. the speed of a chemical change (5) _____.

        2. the rate of melting and boiling (6) _____.

    B. When temperature decreases,

        1. the speed of a chemical change (7) _____.

        2. the rate of freezing or condensing (8) _____.

III. During physical or chemical changes, the total mass of matter (9) _____.

Tell whether each change is a physical change or a chemical change.

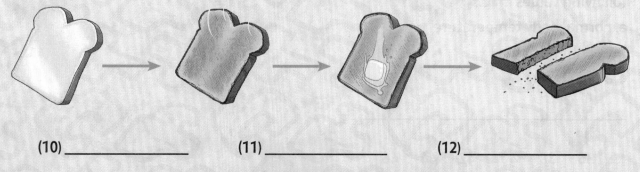

(10) _____ (11) _____ (12) _____

Name _____

Word Play

1 It's easy to get tongue-tied when talking about how matter changes. Look at the statements below. Switch the red words from one sentence to another until each statement makes sense.

A. In a chemical change, the identity of matter does not change.

_____

B. Water will melt faster on a very cold soft drink can than it will on a cool soft drink can.

_____

C. Another name for a chemical change is a chemical property.

_____

D. Ice will condense more slowly in cold water than in warm water.

_____

E. In a physical change, the identity of the matter changes.

_____

F. When water freezes, its mass decreases.

_____

G. A reaction of matter will stay the same during a physical change.

_____

H. When water freezes, it contracts.

_____

Challenge The words in the boxes below are jumbled. Put them in the correct order to make a meaningful sentence.

changes are rusting and chemical burning
_____
_____

is physical and mass changes in chemical conserved
_____
_____

Apply Concepts

2 Each of the pictures shows a change. Write a *P* by the pictures that show physical changes and a *C* by the pictures that show chemical changes.

3 Make a list of physical changes and chemical changes that you observe or see the effects of in your school.

Physical Changes

_____

_____

_____

_____

_____

_____

_____

Chemical Changes

_____

_____

_____

_____

_____

_____

_____

_____

_____

4 What would make each of the following processes happen faster? On each line, write *increase in temperature* or *decrease in temperature*.

> Ice cream melting
>
> _____

> Boiling water to cook potatoes
>
> _____

> Water condensing on
> the outside of a glass
>
> _____

> Water freezing
> overnight on a street
>
> _____

5 Explain what is happening in these pictures. Tell whether the changes are physical or chemical.

_____

_____

_____

_____

_____

6 Why is it important to follow the instructions on this jar of food?

_____

_____

_____

_____

_____

7 Draw a picture of a chemical reaction. Then explain what happens and why mass is conserved during the reaction.

_____

_____

_____

_____

_____

8 Explain why most sidewalks have built-in cracks every few feet.

_____

_____

_____

_____

_____

9 Explain what happens in a campfire.

Wood is made of cellulose, lignin, and other substances.

↓

The wood is set on fire, and a _____ change occurs.

↓

The cellulose and lignin are changed into other substances, including _____ and _____.

Take It Home!

Ask an adult to help you practice taking the temperature of someone in your family. Determine whether any of your family members have a fever. Explain to family members why people get fevers.

Essential Question

What Are Mixtures and Solutions?

Engage Your Brain!

As you read the lesson, look for the answer to the following question and record it here.

How are a smoothie and a salad alike? How are they different?

_____

_____

_____

_____

Active Reading

Lesson Vocabulary

List each term. As you learn about each one, make notes in the Interactive Glossary.

_____

_____

Problem and Solution

Ideas in this lesson may be connected by a problem-solution relationship. Active readers mark a problem with a *P* to help them stay focused on the way information is organized. When multiple solutions are described, they mark each solution with an *S*.

Matter Mix-Up

A box of colored pencils. A basket of footballs, tennis balls, and hockey pucks. A toy box full of toys. All these things are mixtures. But what is a mixture?

Active Reading As you read the next page, draw two lines under the conclusion. Draw one line under each fact that leads to the conclusion.

This fruit salad is a mixture of different pieces of fruit.

Look at the mixtures on these pages. They have a few things in common. First, two or more substances or objects were combined. The fruit salad has several types of fruit. The laundry pile has several types of clothing. Second, each type of matter in a mixture keeps its own identity. The peach in the fruit salad is the same type of matter as it was before it was mixed into the fruit salad. The jeans in the laundry pile are still jeans.

By now, you've probably figured out that a **mixture** is a combination of two or more substances that keep their identities. The parts of a mixture don't undergo a chemical change. Making a mixture is a physical change.

A carbonated beverage is a mixture of water, gases, and other ingredients.

▶ These clothes are all jumbled together. How do you know this pile of laundry is a mixture?

_____

_____

_____

Find a Solution!

In some mixtures, it's easy to see the individual pieces that are mixed together. In other mixtures, small parts are very evenly mixed. What are these special mixtures?

Active Reading As you read these two pages, underline lesson vocabulary words each time they are used.

Each bite of fruit salad contains different combinations of fruit. You can separately taste peaches and different kinds of berries. But what do you notice when you drink a glass of lemonade? Every sip tastes the same. This is because lemonade is a solution. A **solution** is a mixture that has the same composition throughout.

> When food coloring is added to water, the two liquids evenly mix, forming a solution.

A solution forms when one substance *dissolves* in another. When something dissolves, it breaks up into particles so tiny they can't be seen even with a microscope. These particles then evenly mix with the other part of the solution. Not everything dissolves. If you put a rock and salt in water, the rock won't dissolve, but the salt will.

Solutions are commonly liquids, such as the mixture of the different liquids that make up gasoline. But not all solutions are liquids. Air is a solution of different gases. Tiny particles of nitrogen, oxygen, and other gases are evenly mixed in air. Brass is an example of a solid solution formed from solid copper and solid zinc.

A mixture of sand and water forms where waves wash over the sand. Such a mixture is not a solution.

Ocean water itself is a solution. It contains several different dissolved substances.

► What makes a solution different from other mixtures?

_____

_____

Separating Mixtures

Suppose you really don't like olives. How are you going to get them off that deluxe pizza your friend ordered? Sometimes you need to separate the components of a mixture.

Active Reading As you read this page, put brackets [ ] around the sentence that describes the problem and write *P* next to the sentence. Underline the sentence that describes the solution and write *S* next to it.

Mixtures are not always easy to separate. But since mixing is a physical change, each component in a mixture keeps most of its physical properties. Physical properties such as color, size, melting point, boiling point, density, and ability to dissolve can be used to separate mixtures. Separating a mixture can be very simple. Or it can involve several, complex steps when one method is not enough.

Density

Every substance has its own density. A less-dense substance will float on a denser substance. Objects will float in water if they are less dense than water. They will sink if they are denser than water.

▶ What property was used to separate the items on this tray?

_____

When One Isn't Enough

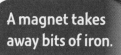

A magnet takes away bits of iron.

sieve/mesh screen

A sieve or mesh screen has holes that matter can pass through. Matter that is smaller than the holes passes through the mesh screen while matter that is larger than the holes stays above the mesh screen.

magnetic force

A magnet attracts matter that contains iron, separating it from the other parts of the mixture.

filtration

A filter works like a mesh screen with very tiny openings, or pores. Only the smallest bits of matter—like water particles and dissolved particles of salt—can pass through the pores.

evaporation/boiling

Boiling is when a liquid rapidly changes to a gas at the boiling point of the liquid. Evaporation also changes a liquid to a gas, but it occurs at temperatures below the boiling point. During these processes, only the liquid particles leave the solution. Dissolved particles stay behind.

Water is added. Then the filter removes the soil.

The water is boiled away. Only salt is left behind.

Proportions and Properties

When you make lemonade, it's important to get the amounts of lemon and sugar right. If it's too sweet or too sour, it doesn't taste right. How do proportions affect the properties of a mixture?

Mixtures of metals are called *alloys*. The properties of the alloy depend on how much of each metal is in the mixture. Chemists first decide on the properties they need their alloy to have. Then they decide how much of which metals will give them those properties.

Steel is an alloy. It is made from iron and other substances. Different substances give steel different properties. For example, adding chromium will make steel shiny. Metals such as nickel and titanium can keep it from rusting. Carbon is often added to steel to make it stronger. Other substances help steel used in tools stay sharp or keep from wearing down.

To make an alloy, metals and other elements are melted together and then allowed to harden.

► For each steel object on this page, list at least two properties that the steel must have.

Kettle

_____
_____
_____

Sculpture

_____
_____
_____

Steel Building Frame

_____
_____
_____

Do the Math!
Use Graphs

Compare and contrast the metals and other substances in stainless steel and tool steel by making two circle graphs.

Substance	Stainless Steel %	Tool Steel %
Iron	74	94
Chromium	18	0
Nickel	8	1
Carbon	0	1
Other	0	4

Sum It Up!

When you're done, use the answer key to check and revise your work.

Write *S* if the photo and caption describe a mixture that is a solution.
Write *M* if they describe a mixture that is NOT a solution.

_____ (1) When you combine ingredients to make a sandwich, each ingredient keeps its identity. You could easily separate them.

_____ (2) Soft drinks are made by dissolving a gas and other ingredients in water. The dissolved particles are much too small to be seen.

_____ (3) The solid bits of orange pulp do not dissolve in the liquid. Because the pulp particles are large, they will eventually settle out.

_____ (4) Particles of several different gases make up air. Air on one side of a room is just like the air on the other side.

Summarize

Fill in the missing words to tell how to separate mixtures.

To sort the items in your junk drawer, you'd use observable (5) _____

such as size, color, shape, and (6) _____ attraction. But how would you separate

table sugar, sand, and pebbles? Because the pebbles are (7) _____

than the grains of sugar and sand, you could remove them using a sieve, or mesh (8) _____.

You could then add water and shake until the sugar (9) _____.

If you poured this mixture through a coffee (10) _____ into a beaker, the

(11) _____ would be left on the filter, but the sugar solution would pass

through. Adding heat would cause the water to (12) _____ , leaving solid sugar

behind.

Name _____

Word Play

1 Complete the crossword puzzle. Use the words in the box if you need help.

Across

1. Another name for a mesh screen
4. Type of change that doesn't involve the formation of a new kind of matter
5. Tool that attracts objects that contain iron
6. What an object that is less dense than water will do when placed in water
7. Object used to separate very small particles from a mixture
8. The amount of matter in a given volume

Down

1. A physical property; for example, round, square, rectangular, or flat
2. Process by which a liquid changes slowly to a gas
3. Kind of mixture that has the same composition throughout
5. A combination of two or more substances that keep their individual identities

| sieve | shape | evaporation | solution* | physical |
| magnet | mixture* | float | filter | density |

Key Lesson Vocabulary

623

Apply Concepts

2 Circle the substances below that are solutions.

brass trumpet   trail mix   shells   sandwich   drink from a mix

3 Make a list of solid mixtures in your classroom.

_____   _____

_____   _____

_____   _____

_____   _____

4 Draw and label a diagram to show how you would separate each mixture.

5 Answer these questions in terms of what you know about mixtures.

a. How would changing the proportions of substances in an alloy change its properties?

_____

_____

_____

b. Why is it possible to use physical properties to separate a mixture?

_____

_____

c. Recycling help us conserve resources. Draw a line connecting each piece of garbage in a mixed bag with the bin it should be thrown in.

milk jug   soup can   envelope   cardboard box

soda can   water bottle   broken pencil

Garbage   Plastic   Aluminum and Tin   Paper

6  Salt seems to disappear when it is poured into water. Use the terms *mixture, solution,* and *dissolve* to explain what happens.

_____

_____

_____

7 Tell how you would use one or more of these tools to separate the mixtures.

Rice from dried soup mix

_____

_____

_____

_____

_____

_____

Salt from saltwater

_____

_____

_____

_____

_____

_____

Nails from gravel

_____

_____

_____

_____

_____

_____

8 Tell what would happen if you stirred each of these cups faster.

_____   _____

_____   _____

Water and Sugar

_____   _____

_____   _____

_____   _____

_____   _____

_____   _____

Water and Sand

Take It Home!

Share what you have learned about mixtures with your family. With a family member, identify examples of mixtures at mealtime, or in places in your home.

Name _____

Essential Question

What Affects the Speed of Dissolving?

Set a Purpose
What will you learn from this experiment?

_____

_____

_____

State Your Hypothesis
Write your hypothesis, or testable statement.

_____

_____

_____

Think About the Procedure
Why do you need to rinse the containers between steps?

_____

_____

_____

Would it affect the conclusions for this activity if two different groups stirred at different rates?

_____

_____

_____

_____

Record Your Data
Record your results in the data table below.

| Time It Takes to Dissolve ||
Treatment	Time (sec)
No Stirring	
Stirring Slowly	
Stirring Quickly	
Coarse Salt	
Table Salt	
Cold Water	
Warm Water	

Draw Conclusions

Make a bar graph to display the data in which you tested how stirring affects the rate of dissolving.

What conclusion can you draw?

_____

_____

_____

_____

Analyze and Extend

1. You're adding sugar to a glass of iced tea. How might you speed up how quickly the sugar dissolves?

_____

_____

_____

_____

2. Minerals dissolve in river water. Would you expect minerals to dissolve faster in a fast-moving river or one that moves slowly? Why?

_____

_____

3. A water softener is a device that uses salts to remove certain substances from water. Most home water softeners use salt pellets or rock salt, both of which are chunks of salt. Why wouldn't you want to use table salt in a softener?

_____

_____

_____

_____

4. Think of other questions you would like to ask about the rate of dissolving a solid in water.

_____

_____

_____

_____

_____

_____

Essential Question

What Is the Atomic Theory?

🧠 Engage Your Brain!

As you read the lesson, look for the answer to the following question and record it here.

This building in Brussels, Belgium, is called the Atomium. Why do you think it was given that name?

_____

_____

_____

Active Reading

Lesson Vocabulary

List the terms. As you learn about each one, make notes in the Interactive Glossary.

_____   _____

_____   _____

_____   _____

Visual Aids

A diagram adds information to the text that appears on the page with it. Active readers pause their reading to review the diagram and decide how the information in it adds to what is provided in the text on the pages.

DEMOCRITUS

→ **Atoms**

Elements

Compounds

A Teeny Tiny Theory

From the time of Democritus, scientists have studied matter and proposed theories about it. What do we now think about what makes up matter?

Active Reading As you read the next page, draw a line from each part of the atom diagram to the sentences that describe it.

Suppose you could break a silver chain into smaller and smaller pieces. The pieces would become so small that you couldn't see them without a microscope. How small could the pieces get before they were no longer silver? The answer— one silver atom. An **atom** is the smallest unit of an element that maintains the properties of that element.

The **atomic theory** is a scientific explanation of the structure of atoms and how they interact with other atoms. Democritus first suggested that the smallest part of matter is an atom. Over the years, theories that scientists made about atoms have changed as scientists learn more about atoms.

Gold is one type of matter.

Gold brick

Flakes of gold

Atoms are the building blocks of all matter.

Current atomic theory states that an atom is mostly empty space. At its center, there is a small, dense core called the nucleus. The nucleus is surrounded by electrons.

Proton

A *proton* is a positively charged particle found in the nucleus of an atom.

Neutron

Neutrons are also particles found in the nucleus, but a neutron has no charge.

Electron

Electrons are negatively charged particles that speed through an area around the nucleus called the electron cloud.

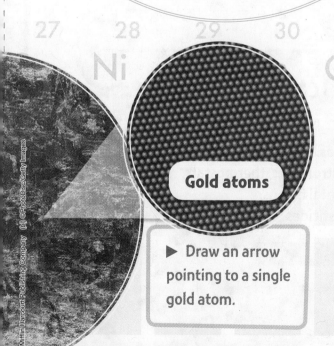

Gold atoms

► Draw an arrow pointing to a single gold atom.

► Use the Venn diagram to compare and contrast electrons and protons.

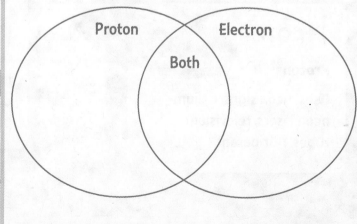

Proton   Electron

Both

110	111	112	113	114	115	116
Mt	Ds	Rg	Uub	Uut	Uuq	Uup	Uuh

In the mid-1800s, I organized all known elements by their properties and increasing mass. Scientists still organize elements based on my work.

MENDELEEV

Atoms

→ Elements

Compounds

Copper, oxygen, and mercury have one thing in common. They are all elements. Exactly what is an element?

Active Reading As you read these two pages, draw a large *E* next to the names of five elements that are described.

There are many kinds of matter. An **element** is the type of matter made of just one kind of atom. All atoms of an element have the same number of protons. For example, boron is an element. Every atom of boron contains exactly five protons. No other element has atoms with exactly five protons.

What's so special about protons? Electrons are far from the nucleus, so they can be gained or lost. Also, different atoms of the same element can contain different numbers of neutrons. Protons stay the same.

Neon

Protons: 10

Uses: neon signs, helium-neon lasers, television tubes, refrigerant

Mercury

Protons: 80

Uses: laboratory instruments, thermostats, dental fillings, pesticides

Elements are substances that can't be broken into simpler substances.

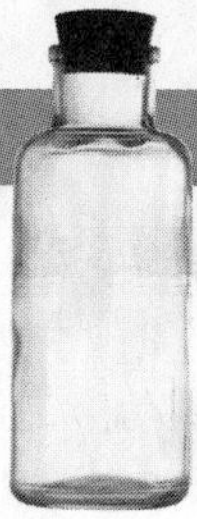

Chlorine

Protons: 17

Uses: disinfecting water; making paper, paints, plastics, and dyes

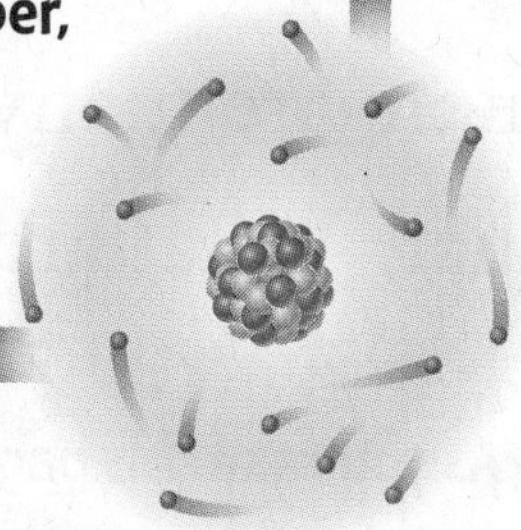

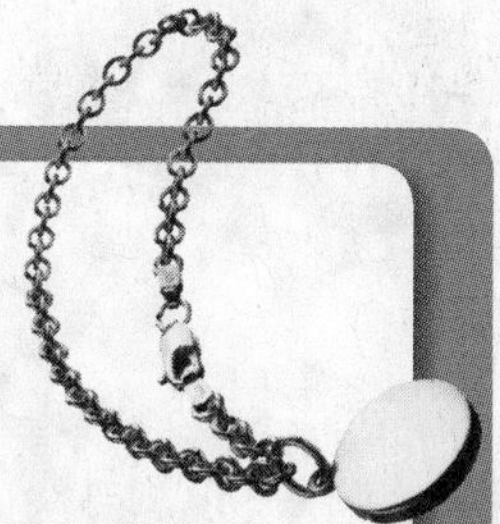

Silver

Protons: 47

Uses: jewelry, silverware, photography, welding solder, mirrors

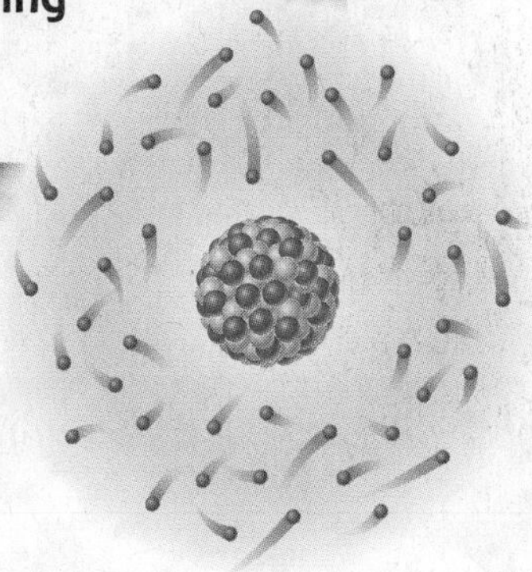

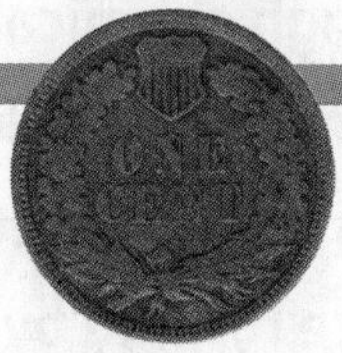

Copper

Protons: 29

Uses: plumbing, coins, electrical wires, making brass and bronze

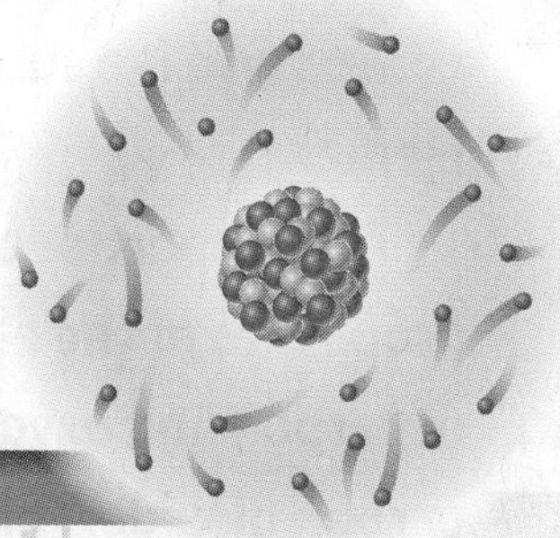

Draw and Label a Carbon Atom

Use the information provided to draw and label a carbon atom.

Protons: 6

Neutrons: 6

Electrons: 6

Part of my atomic theory stated that different types of atoms combine to form chemical compounds.

DALTON

Atoms

Elements

→ Compounds

Putting It All Together

There are more than 100 elements, but you can see that there are many more types of matter than that. What are these other types?

Active Reading As you read this page, draw boxes around the names of the two things that are being compared.

Many atoms go through chemical change with a different type of atom and form molecules. A **molecule** is made up of two or more atoms joined together chemically. A **compound** is a substance formed by atoms from two or more elements.

The properties of a compound are often different from the properties of the elements that form it. For example, atoms of carbon and oxygen will react, forming the compound carbon dioxide. This compound has its own properties that are different than those of carbon and oxygen.

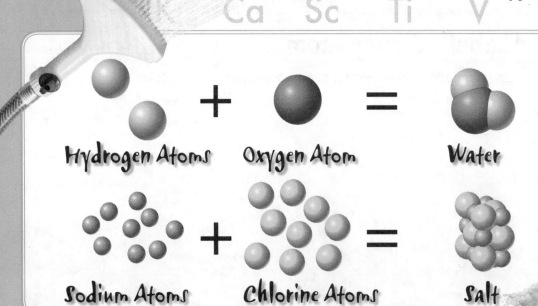

Hydrogen Atoms + Oxygen Atom = Water

Sodium Atoms + Chlorine Atoms = Salt

Firework Colors

Orange
calcium chloride

1 calcium

2 chlorine

Yellow
sodium nitrate

1 sodium

1 nitrogen

3 oxygen

Red
lithium carbonate

2 lithium

1 carbon

3 oxygen

Some of the colors in fireworks come from compounds. For example, calcium chloride, which contains one calcium atom for every two chlorine atoms, results in an orange color.

Fructose is often called fruit sugar. For every 6 atoms of carbon in the compound, there are 12 hydrogen atoms and 6 oxygen atoms.

Corn Syrup

Do the Math!
Use Fractions

Add the total number of atoms in fructose. In lowest terms, what fraction of fructose consists of:

1. carbon atoms? _____

2. hydrogen atoms? _____

3. oxygen atoms? _____

Sum It Up!

When you're done, use the answer key to check and revise your work.

1 **Label the parts of this atom.**

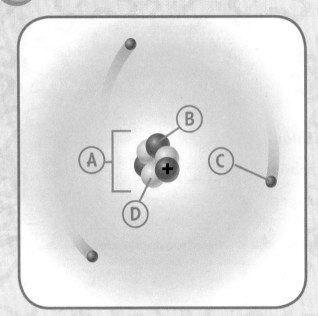

Ⓐ _____

Ⓑ _____

Ⓒ _____

Ⓓ _____

2 **Sequence the following from smallest to largest.**

_____ Ⓐ atom   _____ Ⓑ proton   _____ Ⓒ molecule   _____ Ⓓ nucleus

3

Fill in the blanks.

An atom is the smallest particle of an Ⓐ _____ that has its properties. Our current

Ⓑ _____ is the result of the ideas of many scientists over

many years. Scientists currently theorize that atoms contain a dense core that is called the

Ⓒ _____ . It contains positively charged particles called Ⓓ _____,

and Ⓔ _____ , which have no charge. Particles called Ⓕ _____

move around the center of the atom. The identity of an element is determined by the number of

Ⓖ _____ in one atom of the element. When two or more atoms are joined together,

Ⓗ _____ form.

Answer Key: 1a. nucleus 1b. proton 1c. electron 1d. neutron 2a. 3 2b. 1 2c. 4 2d. 2 3a. element 3b. atomic theory 3c. nucleus 3d. protons 3e. neutrons 3f. electrons 3g. protons 3h. molecules

Name _____

Word Play

1 For each jumbled term, unscramble the letters to form a term from this lesson. Use the clues to help you.

1. tasmo

___ ___ ___ ___ ⊙   The smallest particles of an element

2. ueotnrn

___ ___ ⊙ ___ ___ ___ ___   The particle in an atom that has no charge

3. retelocn

___ ___ ___ ___ ___ ⊙ ___   Moves around the outside of an atom

4. omdocpun

___ ___ ___ ⊙ ___ ___ ___ ___   Formed from at least two types of chemically combined atoms

5. onropt

⊙ ___ ___ ___ ___   The positively charged part of the nucleus

6. mitoca rohety

___ ___ ___ ___ ⊙ ___ ___ ___ ___ ___   Changed through history as scientists learned more about atoms

7. cnluseu

___ ___ ___ ⊙ ___ ___   The dense, central part of an atom

8. nemtele

⊙ ___ ___ ___ ___ ___   Contains only one kind of atom

Riddle Put the circled letters into the riddle in the order they are circled.

What did the chemistry teacher get for her birthday?

the element of ___ ___ ___ ___ ___ ___ ___ ___ ___

Apply Concepts

2 Draw and label a diagram of a nitrogen atom.
It should have 7 protons, 7 neutrons, and 7 electrons.

3 Use the terms *atom* and *element* to explain what makes silver and gold different.

_____

_____

4 Complete the table.

Compound	Atoms	Fraction of each type of atom
methane	5 total: 1 carbon, 4 hydrogen	
propane	11 total: _____	$\frac{3}{11}$ carbon, $\frac{8}{11}$ hydrogen
hydrogen peroxide	4 total: 2 hydrogen, 2 oxygen	
carbon dioxide	3 total: _____	$\frac{1}{3}$ carbon, $\frac{2}{3}$ oxygen

Take It Home!

Check the ingredient lists on labels of several household products.
Find the names of two different compounds. Use reference books or
the Internet to find out what elements are in the compounds.

Meet the Atomic All-Stars

Marie Curie

Marie Curie worked as a scientist in France. She discovered that some elements are radioactive. That means energy radiates, or comes out, of the elements. In 1903, Marie Curie became the first woman ever to win a Nobel Prize. In 1911, she won another. She is one of the most famous female scientists of all time.

In some of Marie Curie's early work on radioactivity, she studied this type of uranium mineral, known as pitchblende.

Inés Triay

Inés Triay is a scientist who works with radioactive materials, too. She works to clean up dangerous wastes that are produced when radioactive elements are used in nuclear power plants. In 2009, President Barack Obama assigned Triay to an important job in the U.S. Department of Energy. She is head of the team that properly disposes of nuclear waste.

RADIOACTIVE

The symbol on this sign warns of radioactivity that could be dangerous to your health.

Complete a Timeline

Fill in the boxes with information about Marie Curie and Inés Triay. For each entry you add, draw a line to the correct location on the timeline.

1898 Marie Curie discovers two new radioactive elements, called radium and plutonium.

1896 Marie Curie's teacher, Henri Becquerel, first discovers radioactivity.

1908 Hans Geiger invents a tool now called the "Geiger counter." It measures radioactivity.

_____
_____
_____
_____

1951 For the first time, electricity is generated using radioactive elements.

1934 Marie Curie dies from a disease caused by radiation. No one knew that radioactivity can be very bad for human health.

1979 Two scientists, Godfrey Hounsfield and Allan McLeod Cormack, win the Nobel Prize in Medicine for the C.T. scan machine. It uses small amounts of radiation and takes pictures of the inside of the human body.

_____
_____
_____
_____

Think About It!

How did Marie Curie's work lead to improved health care?

_____
_____
_____
_____

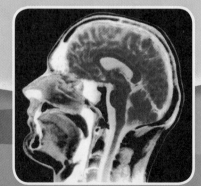

Unit 13 Review

Vocabulary Review

Use the terms in the box to complete the sentences.

> chemical changes
> compound
> element
> gas
> liquid
> molecule
> physical changes
> solution

1. Matter that has a definite volume but no definite shape is

   a(n) _____.

2. A mixture that has the same composition throughout is called

   a(n) _____.

3. Changes in one or more substances that form new and different

   substances are called _____.

4. A single particle of matter made up of two or more atoms joined

   together chemically is called a(n) _____.

5. Changes in which the form or shape of a substance changes
   but the substance still has the same chemical makeup are

   called _____.

6. Matter without a definite volume or shape is called

   a(n) _____.

7. Matter that cannot be broken into a simpler substance is

   a(n) _____.

8. A substance in which at least two types of atoms are chemically

   combined is a(n) _____.

Science Concepts

Fill in the letter of the choice that best answers the question.

9. Which graph shows how the volume of a gas changes as the temperature of the gas increases?

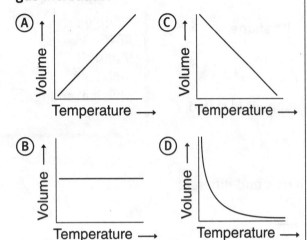

10. Which of the following is a physical property of matter?

Ⓐ the ability to burn

Ⓑ the ability to rust

Ⓒ the ability to decay

Ⓓ the ability to dissolve

11. Which of the following physical changes is **not** an example of a change in state?

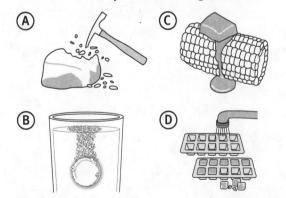

12. This diagram shows what happens when water changes state.

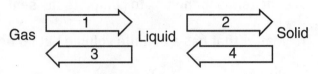

Which statement is **true**?

Ⓐ Temperature increases in Step 1 and Step 2.

Ⓑ The energy of the molecules decreases in Steps 3 and 4.

Ⓒ The mass of the water stays the same between any two steps.

Ⓓ The mass of the water changes between any two steps.

13. Nadia has a mixture of oil and water. She wants to remove most of the oil from the mixture. How can she do this?

Ⓐ use a magnet to attract the oil

Ⓑ pour the mixture through a sieve

Ⓒ stir the mixture until the oil dissolves

Ⓓ let the oil float to the top and skim it off

14. An engineer is making a mixture of metals to make steel for the frame of a building. Which two properties should the steel have?

Ⓐ shiny and easily shaped

Ⓑ strong and slightly flexible

Ⓒ shiny and magnetic

Ⓓ magnetic and resistant to rust

15. The drawing below shows the parts of an atom.

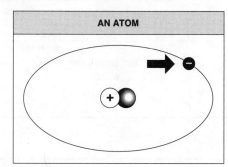

AN ATOM

To which part of the atom is the arrow pointing?

(A) electron   (C) neutron

(B) proton   (D) nucleus

16. Daniel puts water, sugar, and yeast into a balloon. He knows that yeast will react with sugar and water. He measures the mass of the balloon and its contents. He puts the balloon in a warm place for two hours. Then he measures the mass again. He repeats his experiment three times to get more data. Predict how the mass of the balloon will change.

(A) It will increase.

(B) It will decrease.

(C) It will stay the same.

(D) It has no mass.

17. Which of these correctly describes how water changes state?

(A) Liquid water melts to form ice.

(B) Liquid water boils to form water vapor.

(C) Ice condenses to form liquid water.

(D) Water vapor evaporates to form liquid water.

18. Piet has a sample of the element copper. Which statement is **true** about **all** the copper atoms in his sample?

(A) They all have the same number of electrons.

(B) They all have the same number of neutrons.

(C) They all have the same number of protons.

(D) They all can be broken down to make other elements.

19. What does the modern atomic theory state?

(A) All matter is made of atoms.

(B) All matter is made of compounds or molecules.

(C) Atoms of different elements are exactly the same.

(D) Atoms of different kinds combine to form different elements.

20. The rate at which a solid dissolves in a liquid depends on many factors. Which of these properties does **not** affect the rate at which a solid dissolves?

(A) temperature of the liquid

(B) the size of the solid

(C) whether or not the liquid is stirred

(D) the color of the solid

Apply Inquiry and Review the Big Idea

Write the answer to these questions.

21. Kym tested how quickly 10 g of sugar dissolved in 1 L of water at different temperatures. A graph of her results is shown here. What were Kym's variables? Based on her graph, do you think she correctly labeled her beakers of water? Why or why not?

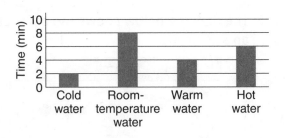

_____

_____

_____

22. Frank was learning about states of matter in science class. He made some drawings but forgot to label them. His drawings are shown below.

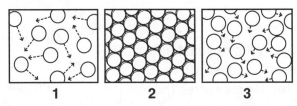

Describe what each of Frank's drawings shows.

_____

_____

_____

23. Mia is having a picnic. She will provide orange juice, unsweetened tea, and sodas. She plans to make peanut butter sandwiches and trail mix. She will also make some gelatin with bananas in it. Which picnic items are mixtures? Which are solutions? Explain your choices.

_____

_____

_____

_____

Light and Sound

Big Idea

Sound and light are forms of energy that are carried in waves.

I Wonder Why

When I watch fireworks from a distance, why do I see the fireworks exploding before I can hear them? Turn the page to find out.

Here's why Sound and light are two forms of energy that your brain detects from its surroundings. The bright light from the fireworks travels faster than the sounds of the explosions. That's why sometimes you will see the burst of distant fireworks before you hear the explosion.

In this unit, you will explore the Big Idea, the Essential Questions, and the Investigations on the Inquiry Flipchart.

Levels of Inquiry Key ■ DIRECTED ■ GUIDED ■ INDEPENDENT

Big Idea Sound and light are forms of energy that are carried in waves.

Essential Questions

Now I Get the Big Idea!

Science Notebook

Before you begin each lesson, be sure to write your thoughts about the Essential Question.

© Houghton Mifflin Harcourt Publishing Company (inse) ©Radius Images/Getty Images; (c) ©Stephen Ortilla/Alamy; (borde) ©NDisc/Age Fotostock

Essential Question

What Is Sound?

🧠 Engage Your Brain!

Find the answer to the following
question in this lesson and record it here.

How does a drummer make music?

_____

_____

_____

Active Reading

Lesson Vocabulary
List the terms. As you learn about each one,
make notes in the Interactive Glossary.

Wave   frequency

pitch   wavelength

volume   Amplitude

Compare and Contrast
In this lesson, you'll read about how
characteristics of sound are alike and
different from one another. Active readers
stay focused on comparisons and contrasts
when they ask themselves, How are these
things alike? How are they different?

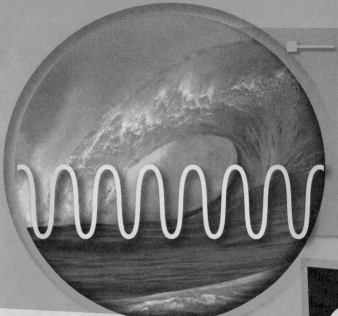

You may have seen water waves that look like this. Water waves move in an up-and-down motion as shown here. No matter how a wave is shaped, it carries energy.

Waves of *SOUND*

Some waves are long and flat. Other waves are tight and tall. But all waves move from place to place in a regular way.

Active Reading As you read these pages, underline the effect of plucking a guitar string.

Water waves carry energy as they move, one after another, across a lake. A **wave** is a disturbance that transmits energy. There are other kinds of waves that you can't see. Sound is a series of vibrations traveling in waves. *Vibrations* are the back-and-forth movements of an object. When you pluck a guitar string, the string vibrates, causing sound waves. The vibrating body of the guitar makes the sound louder.

Musical Vibrations

Use arrows to indicate the parts of the guitar that vibrate.

1 The coils in one area become bunched up, or compressed. They then stretch out, or separate.

2 and **3** These compressions and separations occur along the length of the spring as the wave moves away from it's starting point.

Musical instruments aren't the only things that make sound. Striking the head of a nail with a hammer causes sound vibrations, too. Many animals make sounds by moving a column of air up through the throat and mouth.

All sound vibrations travel in compression waves. As a compression wave moves, molecules of air or other matter are pushed together, or compressed. Then the molecules spread apart. Sound energy moves away from its source as this bunching and spreading of molecules is repeated over and over. Your ears detect sound waves when the waves make parts of your ears vibrate. Your brain interprets these vibrations as sound.

▶ Tell how a compression wave and a water wave are alike and different.

They both travel in waves. Compression waves moves molecules of air.

A bird's song has a high pitch and a high frequency. Its sound waves have many vibrations per second.

This dog's bark has fewer vibrations per second. It has a low pitch and a low frequency.

It Sounds LIKE...

Our world is full of sounds—many of them pleasant, others harsh or annoying.

Active Reading As you read these two pages, underline the definitions of *pitch, frequency,* and *volume.*

People measure characteristics of sound in order to understand, describe, and control how sounds affect our ears. Pitch and volume are two useful ways to measure sound. The highness or lowness of a sound is its **pitch**. A flute produces high-pitched sounds. A tuba produces low-pitched sounds. **Frequency** is the number of vibrations that occur during a unit of time. A sound with a high pitch has a high frequency. Low-pitched sounds have lower frequencies.

The loudness of a sound is its **volume**. Volume is measured in units called *decibels* [DES•uh•buhlz], abbreviated *dB*. The softest sounds that humans can hear are near 0 dB. The humming of a refrigerator is 40 dB. Heavy city traffic is about 85 dB. Any noise at this level can cause hearing loss if a person listens for a long period of time. It's wise to wear earplugs if your ears will be exposed to 15 minutes or more of noise at 100 decibels. No more than one minute of noise at 110 decibels is safe without ear protection.

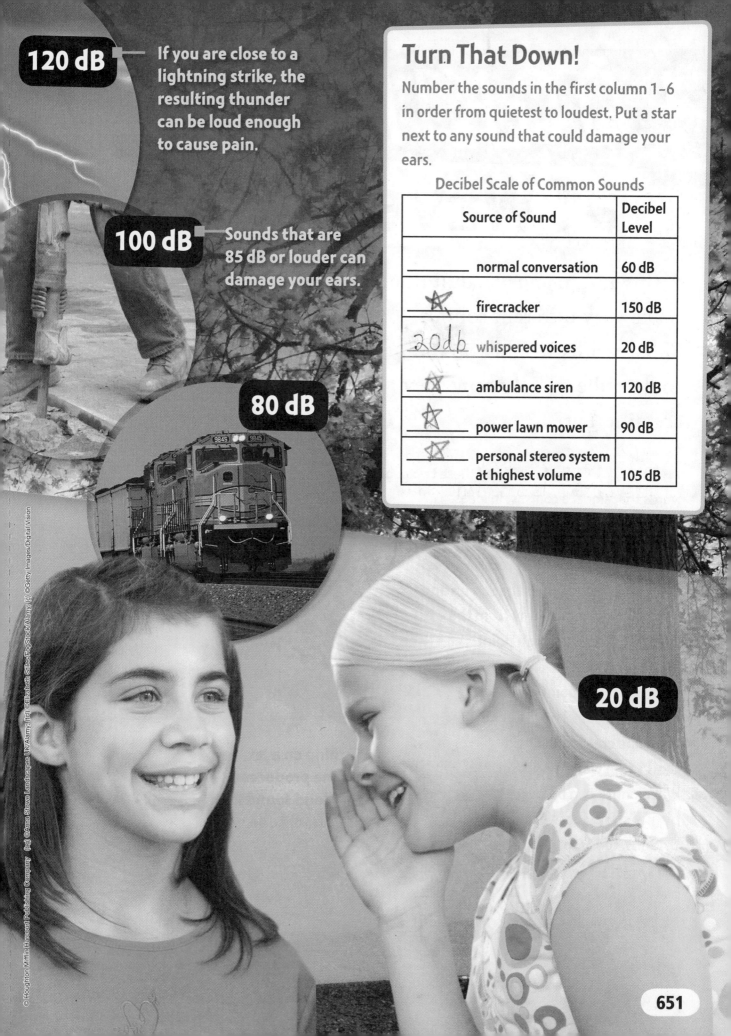

120 dB — If you are close to a lightning strike, the resulting thunder can be loud enough to cause pain.

100 dB — Sounds that are 85 dB or louder can damage your ears.

80 dB

20 dB

Turn That Down!

Number the sounds in the first column 1–6 in order from quietest to loudest. Put a star next to any sound that could damage your ears.

Decibel Scale of Common Sounds

	Source of Sound	Decibel Level
	normal conversation	60 dB
☆	firecracker	150 dB
20db	whispered voices	20 dB
☆	ambulance siren	120 dB
☆	power lawn mower	90 dB
☆	personal stereo system at highest volume	105 dB

LOOKING
at Waves

A tiny kitten and an adult lion make very different sounds. What words would you use to describe exactly how they are different?

Active Reading As you read these two pages, circle words that signal a contrast in ideas.

People don't only use words to describe sound. They use diagrams. Waves consist of curving lines that go up and down as they move away from the sound source. Each high point of a wave is called a *crest*, while each low point is called a *trough* [TRAWF]. The distance from one crest to the next crest is the **wavelength**. Wavelength can be found by measuring between troughs, too.

Turning on a jet engine produces a very loud sound with high amplitude.

amplitude

The taller the wave is from its resting point, the larger the amplitude, and the more energy the wave carries.

Dropping a pin onto a hard surface produces a soft sound with low amplitude.

Size Matters

Look back at the previous two pages. List the objects that produce sounds with high amplitude. How are a wave's amplitude and volume related?

They move up - and down.
Volume move up and down
to.

Amplitude describes the amount of energy in a wave. A jet engine produces a sound wave with an extremely large amplitude. On the other hand, a pin hitting the floor produces a sound wave with a very small amplitude. As you may have guessed, the volume of a sound and the amplitude of its wave are related. Loud sounds have large amplitude, whereas soft sounds have small amplitude. Amplitude is measured by finding the distance from a wave's highest or lowest point to its midline. The midline is a horizontal line drawn straight across the middle of a wave.

The TRAVELS of Sound

Sound can travel through walls, windows, and floors as well as air and water. Does sound travel at the same speed through solids, gases, and liquids?

Active Reading As you read these two pages, **underline** places where solids, liquids, and gases are compared or contrasted.

The sound of this boy's voice moves through gases (air) and a liquid (water) before reaching the other boy's ears underwater.

Sound travels in waves. But sound can only travel if there are particles that the waves can cause to vibrate. Most of the sounds you hear move though the air. Air and other gases have particles that vibrate as sound energy hits them. Liquids and solids are also made of particles, so sound waves can move through these materials, too. However, if there are no particles to move, then sound cannot travel. What would happen if an astronaut dropped a heavy rock on the moon? Would it fall with a thump? Since the moon does not have an atmosphere, there would be nothing for the sound waves to travel through. So, dropping a rock would produce no sound.

Use the information in the table to calculate how long it will take a sound to travel 4,575 m through each type of matter.

Type of Matter	Approximate Speed of Sound (m/s)
Pure water	1,525
Dry air	300
Cast iron	4,575

Pure water: 4,575 ÷ 300

Dry air: 4,575 ÷ 1525

Cast iron: 1525 × 300

4,575 ⟌
300   15 R2   1525
575   × 300
500
750   4575
600   4575   0
750

Sound waves travel through different kinds of matter at different rates. The speed at which sound waves pass through solids, liquids, and gases has to do with how their particles are arranged. Particles in a solid are packed closely together. The particles in gases are far apart. Liquids are in between. For this reason, sound travels through gases more slowly than it travels through liquids and solids.

When you knock on a door, the sound moves through a solid (wood) and through a gas (air) on the other side of the door.

Sound All Around

Understanding the properties of sound allows people to control sound.

Sometimes people want sounds to be softer or to not be heard at all. At other times, people want sounds to be louder or clearer. Engineers design rooms and buildings to reduce outside noise and to make indoor sounds more pleasant.

Sound insulation contains tiny air cells. Sound is absorbed as the cells trap sound waves. This keeps the sound inside the room. Similar technology is used in apartment buildings to help limit the amount of noise you hear from your neighbors!

Engineers use knowledge of sound's properties as they record music, voices, and other sounds in studios. Sound engineers also combine the singer's voice with the background music.

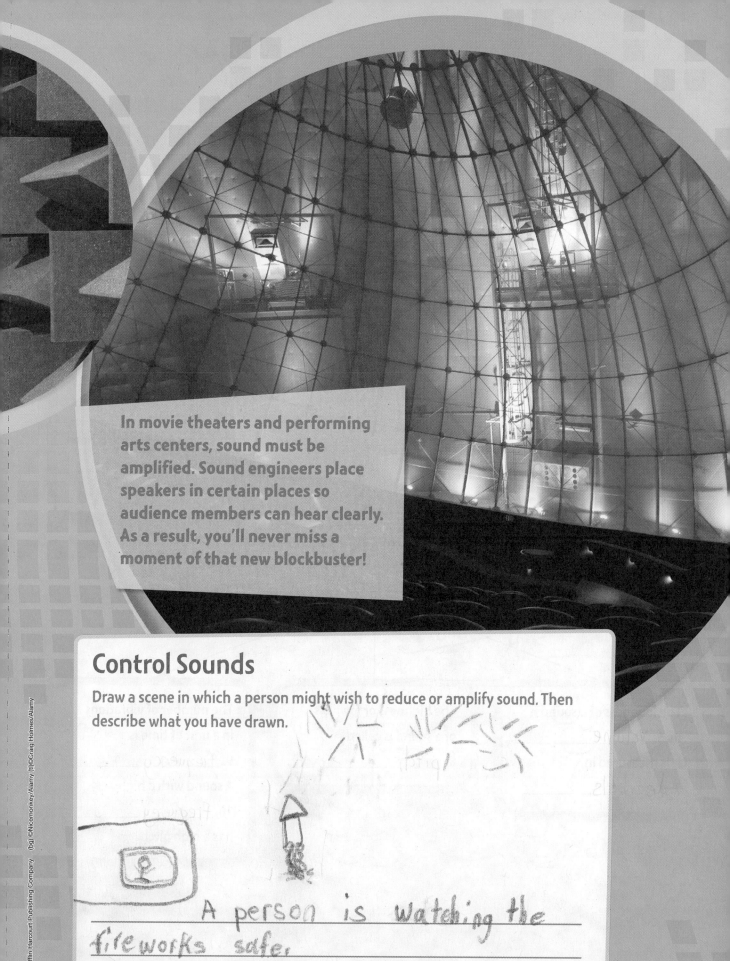

In movie theaters and performing arts centers, sound must be amplified. Sound engineers place speakers in certain places so audience members can hear clearly. As a result, you'll never miss a moment of that new blockbuster!

Control Sounds

Draw a scene in which a person might wish to reduce or amplify sound. Then describe what you have drawn.

A person is watching the fireworks safe.

When you're done, use the answer key to check and revise your work.

Parts of a Wave

The highest part of the wave is the 1. _crest_ . The lowest part is the 2. ~~trough~~ .

(trough)

The distance from one crest to another is 3. _wavelength_ .

The distance from a crest to the midline of a wave is 4. _amplitube_ . This measurement tells how much 5. _energy_ the wave carries.

Characteristics of Sound

The loudness of a sound is its 6. _volume_ . It is measured in 7. _decibels_ .

The highness or lowness of a sound is called 8. _pitch_ .

The number of vibrations in a unit of time is 9. _frequency_ . A sound with a high 10. ~~frequency~~ has a high pitch.

Answer Key: 1. crest 2. trough 3. wavelength 4. amplitude 5. energy 6. volume 7. decibels 8. pitch 9. frequency 10. frequency

Name _____

Word Play

1 Match each picture to a term, and each term to its definition.

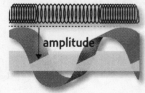

amplitude

decibel · the loudness of a sound

amplitude · disturbances of particles in matter as a sound wave travels forward

pitch · the amount of energy in a wave

vibrations · a disturbance that carries energy

volume · the highness or lowness of a sound

wave · the unit of measure for the volume of sound

Apply Concepts

2 Define *wave*. Then explain how vibrations, waves, and energy are related to sound.

Sound is a series of vibration traving in waves.

3 Label the pictures *1*, *2*, and *3* to indicate the speed at which sound waves travel through each kind of matter. Let *1* be fastest and *3* be slowest.

2   3   1

4 Identify the level of volume and pitch for each sound. Underline your choices.

fire-engine siren
volume: high/low
pitch: high/low

bird chirping
volume: high/low
pitch: high/low

large diesel truck engine
volume: high/low
pitch: high/low

refrigerator hum
volume: high/low
pitch: high/low

falling rain
volume: high/low
pitch: high/low

thunder
volume: high/low
pitch: high/low

660

Name _____

5 Explain how a sound's pitch and frequency are related.

the all are related because they all make sound

6 Explain how volume and decibels are related.

Volume

7 Write a caption for each picture that uses the term *amplitude*.

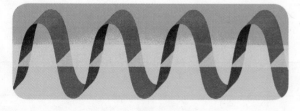 

8 Draw a sound wave that has at least three crests and three troughs.

- Draw an arrow above that shows the direction energy is traveling.
- Below, draw dots to show two areas where air molecules are crowded together and two areas where the molecules are spread apart.
- Use arrows to show areas of compression with parts of the wave.

9 Label the wave. Use *C* for crest, *T* for trough, *W* for an area where you could measure wavelength, and *A* where you could measure amplitude.

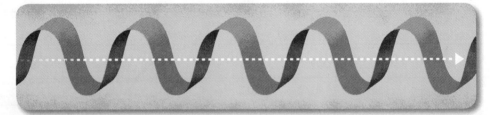

10 List four sounds that could damage your ears. Tell how you could protect your ears from these dangerous sounds.

_____

_____

_____

_____

Take It Home!

Spend time walking slowly from room to room. List and classify the sounds you hear with a family member. For example, you might classify them as *loud* and *soft*, or *electronic, mechanical, human,* or *natural*.

Ask a Sound Designer

Q. What does a sound designer do?

A. The sound designer plans and provides the sounds you hear in a play or movie. They are in charge of making noises and sound effects. They make every sound from the slam of a car door to the roar of a lion.

Q. How do designers come up with the sounds?

A. They start by studying the script. They gather information about the settings of the play or movie, and what sounds a person might hear in those places. They also think about the mood. An audience might not even notice some sounds that provide mood and feelings. Music can give information about a character or a story. It can also help the viewer know when something in a play or movie is about to happen.

Q. What do sound designers need to know about sound?

A. They need to know a lot about the quality of sounds and how they are made. Sound designers have to understand pitch, volume, and how sound travels and lasts.

Did You Hear That?

Can you figure out the sound each object makes?
Read the description of each sound. Write the number
of the sound next to the picture that matches it.

1. This object makes a warning
   sound with a very high volume
   and a high pitch so people are
   sure to hear it.
2. This makes a low-pitched sound
   when you strike it.
3. This makes sounds when you
   strum it.
4. This can make high- or low-
   pitched sounds when you blow
   into it.
5. This object makes a sound with a
   low pitch and a high volume.
6. This organism can make a high-
   volume sound with a high pitch.

Name _____

How Does Sound Travel Through Solids, Liquids, and Gases?

Set a Purpose

What about sound will you understand better after completing this experiment?

_____

_____

_____

Think About the Procedure

What stays the same in all of the trials?

_____

_____

_____

What variable will you change in each trial?

_____

_____

_____

Why will you start by listening to the sound without pressing your ear against any surface?

_____

_____

_____

Record Your Data

Record your observations in the table below.

How do sound waves travel to your ear?	Describe each sound.
Step 1 From the drum through air (gas)	
Step 2	
Step 3	
Step 4	
Step 5	
Step 6	

Draw Conclusions

Why did you place a hand over your free ear in Steps 2–5?

_____

_____

_____

Did the sound change from Step 1 to Step 2? Explain.

_____

_____

_____

_____

Were your descriptions of the sounds in Step 1 and Step 4 different? Why?

_____

_____

_____

_____

_____

Why do you think the sounds produced in Steps 5 and 6 were different?

_____

_____

_____

_____

Analyze and Extend

1. Based on your observations, what statement can you make about how gases, liquids, and solids can change the way we hear a sound?

_____

_____

_____

_____

2. Why might the results you got differ from those of other groups?

_____

_____

_____

_____

3. Most of the sounds you hear travel through air, which is a gas. If you could, how would you change the procedure to better hear sounds transmitted through solids and liquids?

_____

_____

_____

_____

4. What other questions would you like to ask about how sound travels in different types of matter?

_____

_____

_____

Essential Question

What Is Light?

Engage Your Brain!

Find the answer to the following question in this lesson and record it here.

What kind of light is used to produce these hologram images?

_____
_____
_____
_____

Active Reading

Lesson Vocabulary

List the terms. As you learn about each one, make notes in the Interactive Glossary.

Light is a form of energy
that moves. spectrum is a
rang of light waves. Light bld
shines in all diffrent directions

Main Idea and Details

In this lesson, you'll read about light and its uses. A few sentences contain main ideas about light, while others give details that add information to these ideas. Details can include facts, examples, or features of a topic. Active readers remain focused on the topic as they ask, What information does this detail add to the main idea?

LIGHT Energy

Have you ever made shadow figures with your hands? If you have, you have experienced one of the characteristics of light.

Active Reading Draw a box around the main idea of the paragraph. Draw circles around three details that add information about this idea.

Light is a form of energy that moves in waves and can travel through space. Light waves are *transverse waves*. As these waves move forward, energy is carried perpendicular to their forward motion, forming an S shape. Light spreads out in all directions, traveling in straight lines from its source. Light can move through a vacuum because it does not need matter to transmit its energy. This is why light can reach Earth from space. Light travels faster than anything else in the universe. It takes only about 8 minutes for light to travel the more than 149 million km (93 million mi) from the sun to Earth. All life on Earth depends on energy from sunlight.

A wave moving on a rope is an example of a transverse wave. Each part of the rope moves up and down as the wave travels to the right.

Shadows form when a solid object blocks light.

Light naturally spreads outward in all directions as it travels.

Light travels in a straight line until it hits the lampshade.

▶ Draw arrows to show how light travels away from the bare bulb in the photo on the right. Draw arrows to show how a shade affects the path of light in the photo on the left.

Do the Math!
Multiply Whole Numbers

Light travels at a rate of about 300,000 km/s. Calculate how long it would take light to travel from Earth to Mars, a distance of 56 million km.

168,000,000

300,000
56
x
1800000
±150000000

Radio waves can have wavelengths as long as several football fields.

"Night vision" instruments use infrared waves to make objects visible in dark settings.

Low Frequency   RADIO   INFRARED

Long Wavelength   MICROWAVE

Wireless phones transmit and receive microwaves, which have some of the longest wavelengths and lowest frequencies in the electromagnetic spectrum.

Now You SEE IT Now You Don't

You may think of light as the energy that allows your brain, with the help of your eyes, to perceive the world around you. But there's a lot more to light than that! Most of the wavelengths of light are invisible to our eyes.

Active Reading As you read these pages, underline the sentences that tell how light waves differ.

Humans can see **visible light**, which has intermediate wavelengths and frequencies near the middle of the electromagnetic spectrum.

Sunscreen helps protect human skin from the sun's **ultraviolet rays**.

VISIBLE LIGHT   **ULTRAVIOLET**

High Frequency

X-RAYS   **Short Wavelength**

▶ How would you describe the position of visible light in the electromagnetic spectrum?

At one end the spectrum.

X-rays **have very short wavelengths.**

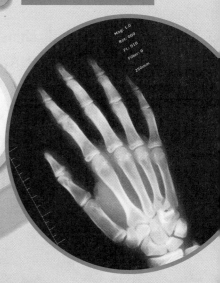

Light waves are all around us, but many of them are invisible. The **electromagnetic spectrum** is a range of light waves organized by frequency and wavelength. At one end of this spectrum, waves have long wavelengths and low frequencies. These include infrared waves, microwaves, and radio waves. At the other end, waves have short wavelengths and high frequencies. These include ultraviolet rays from the sun and X-rays.

The light that our eyes detect is called visible light. Visible light forms one very narrow section in about the middle of the electromagnetic spectrum. Visible light looks white to our eyes, but it is actually made up of many colors. Red light has the longest wavelength in the visible spectrum, and violet has the shortest.

LASER Light

Lasers have many uses in schools, hospitals, stores, and homes. What exactly is a laser? Why are lasers important to people in so many different fields?

Light from a bulb shines in all directions. Laser light is different. A *laser* is a beam of light focused in only one direction. Also, a laser beam contains only one wavelength of light. These features make a beam of laser light very precise and powerful.

Laser scanners read barcodes in stores and libraries.

▶ Write a caption for this photo. Explain how lasers are being used.

lasers are fun for animals or people to play with. It can help to scan people thing if they want to buy or return.

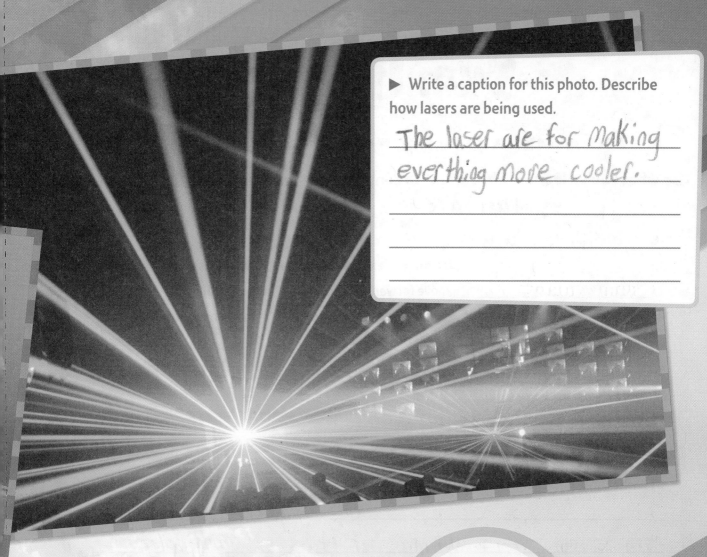

The laser are for making everthing more cooler.

Artists use lasers to make three-dimensional images called holograms. Some doctors use lasers as cutting tools in surgery. Lasers are used to cut steel in factories and metal shops. Laser pointers help teachers in classrooms. Police detectives use lasers to analyze fingerprints at crime scenes. In all of these cases, lasers must be used safely. You should never look into the source of a laser's light, as it can damage your eyes.

Lasers read digital information on compact discs and DVDs.

Sum It Up!

When you're done, use the answer key to check and revise your work.

Use what you've learned about light to complete the following.

Summarize

1. _____Light_____ is a form of energy that travels in waves. As
2. _____light waves_____ move forward, energy moves perpendicular to the forward motion. Infrared waves, ultraviolet waves, microwaves, radio waves, X-rays, and visible light are organized by wavelength and frequency in the 3. _____electromangnetic spectrum_____. The power of
4. _____laser_____ comes from the fact that they contain a single wavelength of light focused in just one direction.

Describe three new things that you learned about light.

It is a range of light waves organized by frequency.
Visible light looks white but it is in many color.
Light travel very fast in the universe.

_____

_____

Name _____

Word Play

1 Use the words in the box to complete the puzzle.

Across 1: light
Down 1: laser
Down 2: transverse
Across 4: shadow
Down 3: ultraviolet
Down 5: visible
Down 6: infrared
Across 7: perpendicular
Across 8: spectrum

Across

1. A form of electromagnetic energy, some of which is visible
4. A dark area where light is blocked by an object
7. The direction energy is carried as a light wave moves forward
8. The range of electromagnetic waves from radio waves to X-rays

Down

1. A beam of light of a single wavelength focused in a single direction
2. A type of wave that forms an S shape
3. A type of wave that comes from the sun and may harm human skin
5. The type of light that helps humans see the world
6. A type of wave that is used in "night vision" equipment

electromagnetic*   infrared   laser   light*   perpendicular

shadow   transverse   ultraviolet   visible

* Key Lesson Vocabulary

2 Explain how light travels. Include as many details as you can.

Light is a form of energy that moves in waves. They are transverse waves.

3 Describe the part of the electromagnetic spectrum that people *can* see. Then name three devices that use electromagnetic waves that people *can't* see.

microwaves and radio. x-ray colors

4 Circle the light that would be best for pointing out details on a map hanging high on a wall. Then explain your choice.

you can hold it and circle it around

5 Explain why light produced by the sun reaches Earth, but sound produced by the sun does not.

The energ from the sun get to the light blud.

Take It Home!

With a family member, go on an electromagnetic wave scavenger hunt. List items that use light waves to function. Organize the objects in your list by the terms *infrared*, *ultraviolet*, and *visible light*.

Essential Question

What Are Some Properties of Light?

Engage Your Brain!

Find the answer to the following question in this lesson and record it here.

Why do lighthouses use lenses?

_____

_____

_____

_____

Active Reading

Lesson Vocabulary

List the terms. As you learn about each one, make notes in the Interactive Glossary.

Opaque   reflection
transparent   refraction
tanslucent   prism

Compare and Contrast

Many ideas in this lesson are connected because they explain comparisons and contrasts—how things are alike and different. Active readers stay focused on comparisons and contrasts when they ask themselves, How are these things alike? How are these things different?

Just Passing Through

Light acts differently when it strikes windows, thin curtains, or brick walls. How does each material affect the light that strikes it?

Active Reading As you read these two pages, underline sentences that provide details about how light acts when it strikes different materials.

Light travels outward in all directions from its source until it strikes something. Light behaves in different ways depending on the kind of matter it meets. Most objects absorb some of the light that hits them. The amount of light absorbed depends on the material the object is made of.

Opaque materials do not let light pass through them. Instead, the material absorbs light—light enters the material but doesn't leave it. When a material absorbs light, the energy from the light is transferred to the material. Many solid objects are opaque because they are made of materials such as metal, wood, and stone that do not allow light to pass through. Objects that are opaque cause shadows to occur because the objects absorb or reflect all of the light that hits them.

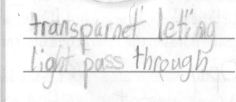

transparnet leting
light pass through

> Write a caption for each picture. Tell whether the light or lampshade is opaque, translucent, or transparent. Explain how light interacts with each material.

opaque it not leting light pass through

translucent can see to material

Materials that let light pass through them are **transparent**. Transparent materials absorb very little of the light that hits them. This makes it easy to see objects through transparent materials. Clear glass, air, and pure liquid water are transparent.

A third kind of material both transmits some light and absorbs some light. These materials are **translucent**. Ice, wax paper, and frosted glass are translucent. You can see through a translucent material, but the image is fuzzy or unclear.

Mirror, Mirror

Did you look at yourself in a mirror as you got ready for school? The properties of light enabled you to see your image.

As you read these two pages, draw boxes around the words or phrases that signal when things are being contrasted.

The bouncing of light off an object is known as **reflection**. When light traveling from an object strikes a smooth, shiny surface, such as a mirror, all of the light hitting the surface from one direction is reflected in a single new direction. Your eyes detect the reflected light, and you see a clear, reversed image of the object—a reflection. In contrast, you can't see an image in something with a rough surface, such as cloth or wood, because the roughness causes light to reflect in many directions.

The smooth surface of the water acts like a mirror. Light rays are reflected back in a way that enables you to see a clear, reversed image.

The backpack appears yellow because its material reflects yellow light and absorbs all other colors of light.

▶ Compare the surfaces of the metal container and the paper bag. The smooth surface reflects light in a single direction back to your eyes. The rough surface reflects light in all directions. Identify the material that would produce the better reflection.

The paper bag is smooth and the rough surface is reflects light

How an object reflects light also determines what colors you see. As light strikes the surface of an object, the object absorbs certain colors of light and reflects others. A ripe strawberry absorbs nearly all colors of light, but it reflects red light. So, your eyes see the strawberry as red. Grass reflects green light while absorbing all other colors.

Black objects absorb all colors of light. They also absorb more of the energy in light. White objects, though, reflect all colors of light and absorb less energy. Because white clothes don't absorb as much energy, wearing white rather than dark clothes on a bright, hot day will keep your body cooler.

▶ When we look at these fruits and vegetables, we see a variety of colors.

Choose one fruit or vegetable. Explain why it's the color it is.

Strawberry color of light so it red

Light Bends

What happened to the straw in the glass? Did someone break it? No! What you are observing is another property of light—refraction.

Active Reading As you read these pages, underline words that identify the cause of refraction. Circle words that identify an effect of refraction.

The bending of light as it passes at an angle from one type of matter into another is called **refraction**. Refraction occurs because the speed of light varies depending on the material through which the light travels. As the light changes speed, it bends. Look at the straw at the top of this page. Light from the top of the straw passes through the air and the glass to your eyes. But light from the bottom part starts out in the water and passes into the glass and then into the air. Each time the light enters a new material, it bends slightly because it changes speed. By the time this light reaches your eyes, it is coming from a different angle than the light from the top of the straw. As a result, the straw appears to be bent or broken.

Refraction produced the illusion that this polar bear's head is separate from its body.

A **prism** is a transparent material that separates white light into its component colors by refraction. When white light enters a prism, the different colors of light bend at different angles. The light moves through the prism and exits it as a rainbow.

Light bends in other ways. *Diffraction* is the bending of light around barriers or through openings. If you look at the edges of a shadow cast in bright sunlight, you may notice that the edges of the shadow are blurry. This blurriness is caused by light bending around the edge of the object. The colors of the sunset are a result of diffraction as sunlight bends around particles in the air.

Do the Math!
Angles of Refraction

The diagram shows how light bends as it enters and then exits a transparent material. Use a protractor to measure the angles formed as the light is refracted.

_____

_____

_____

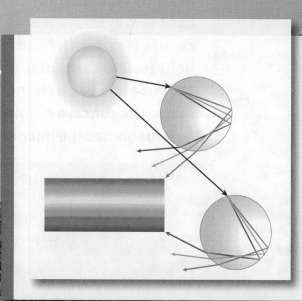

Rainbows are a product of refraction and reflection. Sunlight separates into colors as it passes from the air into a water droplet. The colored light is reflected off the back of the drop, and it is refracted again as it passes into the air. Light from many droplets forms the arcs of color in a rainbow. Red light comes from droplets higher in the air, and violet light comes from lower droplets.

Lenses

Cameras, telescopes, and eyeglasses all contain lenses. Even your eyes have a lens inside each of them! What do lenses do?

Active Reading As you read the next page, put brackets [ ] around the details that describe convex and concave lenses. Draw a line under the main idea that the details help explain.

Lenses are curved transparent objects that refract light. You can find lenses in DVD players, photocopiers, and binoculars. Even the microscope you use in many science activities has a lens. Most lenses are circular and are made of clear glass or plastic. Many devices use a series of lenses to make images clearer. Lenses vary greatly in size. Microscopes use several tiny lenses to magnify small objects. The Yerkes Observatory in Wisconsin has a reflecting telescope with a lens that is over a meter in diameter!

Telescopes use lenses to magnify objects. Incoming light moves through a convex lens, which bends light toward the center of the tube and brings it into focus. The concave eyepiece lens magnifies the image.

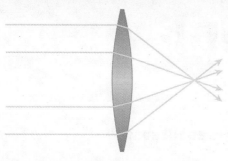

Convex lenses have an outward curve on at least one side. The other side may be curved or flat. These lenses refract light toward a focus, or focal point.

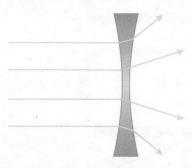

Most concave lenses have an inward curve on both sides. These lenses spread light waves apart.

A *convex lens* is a lens that is thicker at the center and thinner at the edges. Convex lenses are sometimes called positive lenses because they bring light waves together. In other words, a convex lens focuses light. This bending allows an image to form at a point called the focal point.

A *concave lens* is a lens that is thicker at the edges and thinner at the center. Sometimes called negative lenses, concave lenses spread light waves apart from a focal point.

Eyeglasses may have concave or convex lenses, depending on the type of vision correction needed.

Concave, Convex, or Both?

Fill in the Venn diagram to compare and contrast concave and convex lenses.

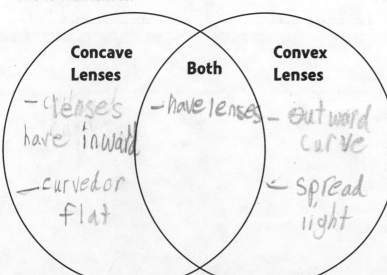

Concave Lenses
- lenses have inward
- curved or flat

Both
- have lenses

Convex Lenses
- outward curve
- spread light

When you're done, use the answer key to check and revise your work.

Use the terms below to fill in the graphic organizers about some properties of light.

| reflection | translucent | diffraction |
| opaque | refraction | transparent |

Descriptions of Ways Different Materials Absorb Light

1. transparent

2. opaque

3. diffraction

The Bouncing or Bending of Light

4. reflection

5. refraction

6. translucent

Answer Key: 1, 2, and 3: transparent, translucent, and opaque in any order 4, 5, and 6: reflection, refraction, and diffraction in any order

Name _____

Word Play

1 Use the clues to help you write the correct word in each row.
Some boxes have already been filled in for you.

a. | d | i | f | F | R | a | c | t | i | o | n |
b. | | r | e | F | R | a | c | t | i | o | n |
c. | | r | e | F | l | e | c | t | i | o | n |
d. | | | | | | p | R | i | s | m |
e. | t | r | A | n | s | p | a | R | e | n | t |
f. | t | r | A | n | s | l | u | c | e | n | t |
g. | o | p | A | q | u | e |

Clues

a. This makes the edges of a shadow look blurred.

b. It's another way of saying "the bending of light."

c. This is the word for the bouncing of light off an object.

d. This object will separate light into the colors of the spectrum.

e. This word describes objects that let light pass through them.

f. This word describes objects that let only some light pass through them.

g. This word describes objects that let little or no light pass through them.

transparent*   reflection*   prism*   diffraction

translucent*   opaque*   refraction*

*Key Lesson Vocabulary

Bonus

The prefix con- means "with." What words with this prefix can you find in the lesson?

transparent

Apply Concepts

2 Which is better: checking your appearance in a regular mirror or checking it in a sheet of crumpled aluminum foil? Explain why one reflective surface is better than the other.

it's surface the appearance

3 Explain why the fisherman is having a hard time catching the fish.

Because of the reflection is diffrent.

4 Circle the image that shows an opaque material.

Take It Home! With a family member, walk through the rooms of your home and identify opaque, transparent, and translucent objects. See how many surfaces you can find in which you can see a reflection.

Play It Again

The hand-cranked Victrola was one of the first machines to play back recorded sound. The grooves on a flat disk send a sound vibration through a needle.

A record player makes sound the same way a Victrola did, but it is powered by electricity.

Instead of coming from physical grooves, the sound on a reel-to-reel player comes from signals recorded on magnetic tape.

An MP3 is a type of computer file. It contains the digital code for recorded sounds. Many devices, from computers to phones to pocket-sized music players, can play back MP3 files.

Cassette tapes are magnetic like reel-to-reels, but they are small and portable. So are cassette players.

Compact discs have grooves like records. But a CD player reads the grooves with a laser beam instead of a needle.

Circle the sound devices that use discs. How are the players alike? How are they different?

_____

_____

Devices that play back recorded sound
have improved over time.

	How is an electric record player an improvement over a hand-cranked Victrola? _____
	How is a cassette tape an improvement over a reel-to-reel tape? _____
	You have to rewind a cassette tape to get back to the beginning after it plays. How is a CD easier to play? _____
	What makes MP3 files the most convenient way to play back recorded sound? _____
	Draw a sound playback device that would be even better. What features might it have? _____

Build On It!

Rise to the engineering design challenge—complete **Design It: Looking Around a Corner** on the Inquiry Flipchart.

Name _____

Essential Question

What Happens When Light Is Reflected?

Set a Purpose
What do you expect to understand about light after you complete this investigation?

_____

_____

_____

Write a statement that tells what you plan to investigate.

_____

_____

_____

Think About the Procedure
Why do you think it is important to tape the mirror so that it stands up straight?

_____

_____

How is the mirror different from all of the other materials in the experiment?

_____

_____

What is the same about the positions of the first two pushpins?

_____

_____

Record Your Data
In the space below, record your measurements of the two angles described in Step 4.

Draw Conclusions

Compare the two angles you measured in Step 4. What do they have in common?

_____

_____

_____

What do the lines you drew show about the path of light?

_____

_____

_____

Analyze and Extend

1. How would a mirror be less useful to people if it did *not* reflect light in a straight line?

_____

_____

_____

2. Suppose you know the angle at which light hits a mirror. Predict the angle at which the light will reflect.

_____

_____

_____

3. Look closely at the word *reflection*. One of the meanings of the Latin prefix *re-* is "again." How does this meaning relate to the reflection you observed in the investigation?

_____

_____

_____

4. What other questions would you like to explore about how light travels when it strikes different surfaces?

_____

_____

_____

Name _____

Vocabulary Review

Use the terms in the box to complete the sentences.

> electromagnetic
>   spectrum
> light
> opaque
> pitch
> refraction
> volume

1. Materials that do not let light pass through them are called

   _____.

2. The highness or lowness of a sound is its

   _____.

3. A form of energy that moves in waves and can travel through

   space is called _____.

4. The loudness of a sound is its _____.

5. A range of light rays organized by frequency and wavelength is

   called the _____.

6. The bending of light as it passes at an angle from one type of

   matter to another is called _____.

Science Concepts

Fill in the letter of the choice that best answers the question.

7. Which of these objects produces a sound with low volume and high pitch?

   Ⓐ an ambulance siren

   Ⓑ an air conditioner

   Ⓒ a chick

   Ⓓ a cow

8. Which of the following can be found in binoculars, photocopiers, cameras, and DVD players?

   Ⓐ a lens

   Ⓑ a laser

   Ⓒ a prism

   Ⓓ a CD

Science Concepts

Fill in the letter of the choice that best answers the question.

9. Helena used a spring to model a wave.

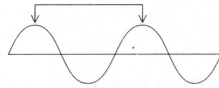

Which of the following **best** describes the part of the wave indicated by the dotted line at the far right?

(A) a vibration in a light wave

(B) a crest in a transverse wave

(C) an area where molecules come together in a compression wave

(D) an area where molecules spread apart in a compression wave

10. Jenna drew a diagram of a wave.

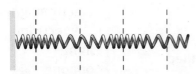

What is the distance indicated by the arrows called?

(A) trough

(B) wavelength

(C) amplitude

(D) volume

11. Julio drew this picture of a light bulb.

What concept **best** describes what Julio is trying to show with his picture?

(A) Light moves in waves that can travel through space.

(B) Visible light travels faster than anything else in the universe.

(C) Visible light forms one section of the electromagnetic spectrum.

(D) Light spreads out in all directions, traveling in straight lines from its source.

12. Look at the illustration below.

Which sentence best summarizes what is happening to light that is hitting the surface of the mirror?

(A) It is reflected in many new directions.

(B) It passes through the surface of the mirror.

(C) It is reflected back in the same direction from which it came.

(D) It changes speed and bends slightly as it moves in a single new direction.

13. Farida drew this diagram of the electromagnetic spectrum.

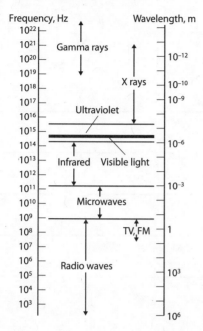

Which statement is the **best** summary of **all** the information shown in a diagram of the electromagnetic spectrum?

(A) It shows the colors of the rainbow arranged by hue.

(B) It shows the wavelengths of visible light in relation to those of radio waves.

(C) It shows a range of light waves arranged by wavelength and frequency.

(D) It shows a range of objects and devices arranged by the decibel level of the sounds they produce.

14. Which features make laser light different from light from a light bulb?

(A) Laser light contains only long infrared waves.

(B) Laser light contains an infinite number of wavelengths.

(C) Laser light shines in all directions and contains ultraviolet rays.

(D) Laser light contains one wavelength and is focused in one direction.

15. While swimming underwater in a pool, Hamid hears the honking of a truck's horn. What happened as the sound waves traveled from the horn to Hamid's ears?

(A) The waves stopped when they reached the water.

(B) The waves sped up when they passed from the air to the water.

(C) The waves slowed down when they passed from the air to the water.

(D) The waves did not change speed as they passed from the air to the water.

16. Look at this picture.

Which word **best** describes the material used to make the lamp shade?

(A) opaque

(B) ultraviolet

(C) transparent

(D) translucent

Apply Inquiry and Review the Big Idea

Write the answers to these questions.

17. This picture shows Dak doing homework at his desk. There are several sounds being produced nearby. Using details about how sound waves travel, explain why Dak may have a hard time concentrating, and what he might do to improve the situation.

_____

_____

_____

_____

_____

18. The diagrams below show two types of lenses.

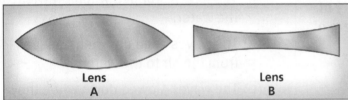

Lens
A

Lens
B

Identify the two types of lenses shown, and tell how each bends light.

Lens A: _____

_____

Lens B: _____

_____

19. If you place a straw in a clear glass of water, how will the straw look? Give a description of the straw and the water and explain why it has this appearance.

_____

_____

_____

Forces and Motion

Big Idea

Forces interact with objects to produce motion. Motion can be observed, measured, and described.

I Wonder Why

Why does a pit crew need to replace the racecar's tires several times during the race? *Turn the page to find out.*

Here's why Friction gives the racecar traction and allows it to grip the track, but it also produces a lot of heat. The high speed and forceful turns of a race wear tires out quickly.

In this unit, you will explore the Big Idea, the Essential Questions, and the Investigations on the Inquiry Flipchart.

Levels of Inquiry Key ■ DIRECTED ■ GUIDED ■ INDEPENDENT

Track Your Progress

Big Idea Forces interact with objects to produce motion. Motion can be observed, measured, and described.

Essential Questions

Now I Get the Big Idea!

Science Notebook

Before you begin each lesson, be sure to write your thoughts about the Essential Question.

Essential Question

What Are Forces?

Engage Your Brain!

As you read the lesson, figure out the answer to the following question. Write the answer here.

What forces are acting on this cyclist? Are all the forces balanced?

Yes and no because
the person does not
have the same balanced
and force.

Active Reading

Lesson Vocabulary

List the terms. As you learn about each one, make notes in the Interactive Glossary.

force   Balanced force
Gavity   unbalanced
friction   Forces

Cause and Effect

Some ideas in this lesson are connected by a cause-and-effect relationship. Why something happens is a cause. What happens as a result of something else is an effect. Active readers look for effects by asking themselves, What happened? They look for causes by asking, Why did it happen?

PUSHING
and Pulling

You pull on a door to open it. You lift up a backpack. You push on the pedals of a bike to go faster. What is the relationship between force and motion?

Active Reading As you read this page, underline the effects a force can have on an object.

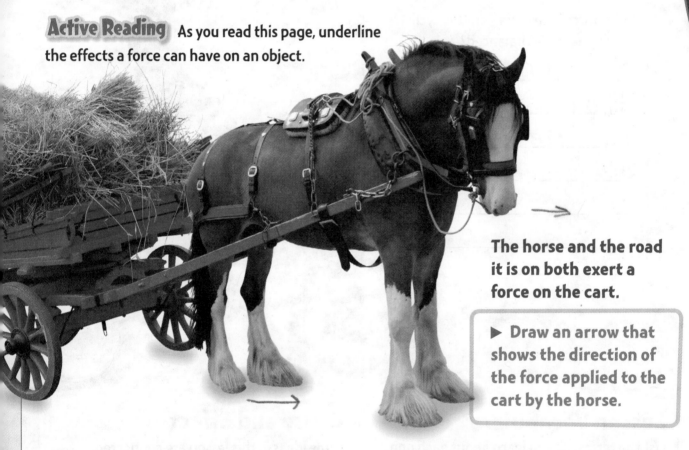

The horse and the road it is on both exert a force on the cart.

► Draw an arrow that shows the direction of the force applied to the cart by the horse.

Changes in motion all have one thing in common. They require a **force**, which is a push or a pull. Forces can cause an object at rest to move. They can cause a moving object to speed up, slow down, change direction, or stop. Forces can also change an object's shape.

Forces are measured with a spring scale in units called newtons (N). The larger the force, the greater the change it can cause to the motion of an object. Smaller forces cause smaller changes. Sometimes more than one force can act together in a way that does not cause a change in motion.

700

When the rowers pull back on the oars, the oars push against the water.

▶ Weight is a measure of the force that gravity exerts on an object. You can measure weight with a spring scale. Record the weight shown on each spring scale in the spaces below.

0.5

2.2

The water pushes back against the oars. This force causes the boat to move.

When the ball hits the floor, the force of the floor makes the ball stop and change its direction of movement. When the ball hits the player's hand, the same thing happens.

TWO COMMON Forces

What do the skydivers and some of the flower petals have in common? They are both falling! What causes this?

▶ Draw an arrow showing the direction of the gravitational force between Earth and the falling flower petals.

→ Gravity

Gravity is a force of attraction between two objects. The size of this force increases as the mass of the objects increases. It decreases as the distance between the objects increases. Gravity acts on objects even if they are not touching.

Large objects such as Earth cause smaller objects, such as the skydivers, to accelerate quickly. We expect to see things fall toward Earth. However, the force of attraction is the same on both objects. If you place two objects with the same mass in outer space, they will move toward one another. If one object is "above" the other, the bottom object will appear to "fall up" as the other "falls down"!

702

© Houghton Mifflin Harcourt Publishing Company (t) ©blickwinkel/Alamy; (b) ©Peter Casolino/Alamy

Friction changes the energy of motion into thermal energy. When you use sandpaper to smooth wood, you can feel the temperature rise.

→ Friction

Is it easier to ride your bike on a smooth road or on a muddy trail? Why?

Friction is a force that opposes motion. Friction acts between two objects that are touching, such as the bike tires and the road. Friction can also exist between air and a moving object. This is called air resistance.

It is easy to slide across smooth ice because it doesn't have much friction. Pulling something across rough sandpaper is a lot harder because there is lots of friction.

Dec

An air hockey table blows air upward. This layer of air reduces the surface friction, so the pieces move quickly.

▶ In the pictures on this page, circle the places where there is friction between two objects. In the small boxes, write *Inc* if the object is designed to increase friction and *Dec* if the object is designed to decrease friction.

Inc

The tires on this bike are designed to keep the rider from slipping. You have to pedal harder on a rough surface to overcome the force of friction.

BALANCED or Unbalanced?

The tug-of-war teams are both applying forces. So why isn't anyone moving?

Active Reading Draw a circle around a sentence that explains why objects don't always move when a force is applied.

When you sit on a chair, the force of gravity pulls you down. The chair pushes you up. You stay in one place because the forces on you are balanced. **Balanced forces** are forces on an object that are equal in size and opposite in direction. They cancel each other out.

The tug-of-war teams in the picture don't move because the forces are balanced. Friction keeps them from sliding. They won't move until one side exerts a larger force. Then, the forces are no longer balanced. **Unbalanced forces** are forces that cause a change in motion. A force must also overcome the force of friction before an object will move.

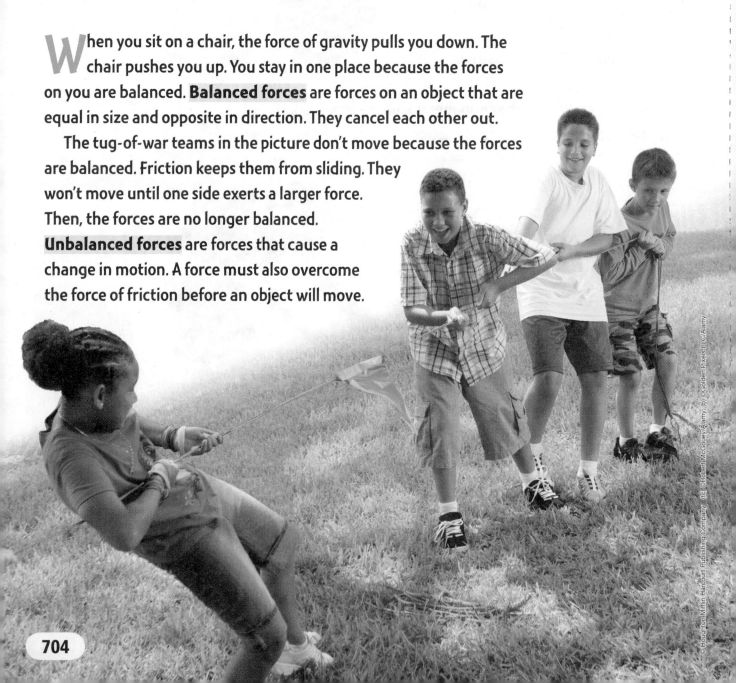

The push on the first domino was a(n) **Unbalanced** force that caused it to fall into the next domino. As each domino fell, it transferred the force to the next domino.

When a plane flies at a constant velocity, all the forces on the plane are balanced. If they weren't, the plane would speed up, slow down, or gain or lose altitude.

The force exerted on this domino by the falling dominoes is balanced by the force of the box. Because the forces are **balanced**, the domino doesn't fall.

▶ Are there any forces acting on the dominoes that have fallen? If so, are they balanced or unbalanced? How do you know?

I think it is both because the first one is the first one to fall and same as the last one. All the dominoes are fall together.

The forces on the dominoes are **Balanced** when they are standing upright. When a falling domino hits them, the forces become **Unbalanced** and they fall.

PULL (or Push) Harder!

Would you expect a bunt in baseball to go out of the park? Why or why not?

Active Reading As you read, circle the sentences that explain the relationship between the size of a force and motion.

▶ Use forces to explain why the boy can't ring the bell.

He dosen't have lots of force

When the man swings the hammer, he exerts a force on a plate. The plate transfers the force to a piece of metal that rises up the column and rings the bell.

The boy swings the same kind of hammer at the same kind of machine. Why doesn't the metal hit the bell?

TEST YOUR STRENGTH

TEST YOUR STRENGTH

If you want to make the cue ball knock another ball into a pocket, you hit the cue ball with a lot of force. This large force makes the cue ball change its velocity, or accelerate, quickly. It has lots of energy to transfer to the other ball. The energy causes the other ball to accelerate.

The greater the force applied to the cue ball, the more force it can transfer to the other ball. A large force will cause a large change in the motion of the other ball. A small force will cause little change. Changes in velocity can also include changes in direction.

Do the Math!
Display Data in a Graph

Use the data in the table to make a graph that shows the relationship between the force applied to an object and its acceleration.

Force (N)	Acceleration (m/sec²)
1	0.5
2	1.0
5	2.5
8	4.0
10	5.0

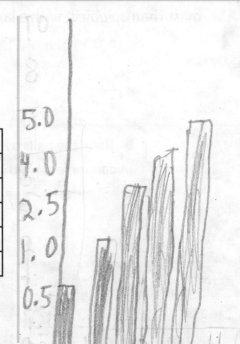

I'M NOT Moving!

It's easy to lift your empty backpack off the ground. Could you use the same force to lift it when it's full of books?

Active Reading As you read these pages, circle cause-and-effect signal words, such as *because*, *so*, or *therefore*.

The springs in the pictures all exert the same force on the balls, causing them to roll across the page. The ball with the least mass accelerates the fastest. Therefore, it travels the farthest. The same force has a greater effect on an object with a small mass than an object with a larger mass.

▶ Rank the balls by writing *greatest*, *middle*, or *least* in the six blanks.

Foam Ball

mass: <u>less</u>

acceleration: <u>more</u>

Baseball

mass: <u>middle</u>

acceleration: <u>Middle</u>

▶ Both drivers began to brake at the same time. The brakes applied the same force to the trucks. Why did one truck take longer to stop?

One truck has more stuff but the other one has nothing.

An object's acceleration depends on the object's mass and the force applied to it. The larger the force, the greater is the acceleration. Suppose you push a wagon gently. The wagon speeds up slowly. If you use more strength to push, then the wagon's speed changes quickly.

The less an object's mass is, the less force is needed to change its motion. It's easier to push an empty shopping cart than a full one. Light cars are used in drag races because a car with less mass speeds up faster than a car with more mass.

If you want to slide a heavy box across the floor faster, you have two options. You could take some items out of the box, which decreases its mass. Or you could have a friend help you, which increases the force you apply.

Steel Ball

mass: *More*

acceleration: *less*

How did I get to Mars?

LET'S GO to Mars!

How did an understanding of forces help to send a rover to Mars and safely land it there?

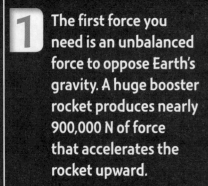

1 The first force you need is an unbalanced force to oppose Earth's gravity. A huge booster rocket produces nearly 900,000 N of force that accelerates the rocket upward.

2 After the booster rocket falls away, smaller rockets in the second stage fire. The rockets change the direction of the vehicle's motion and put it in orbit around Earth.

3 The third-stage rocket firing produces enough force to reach "escape velocity." Earth's gravity can no longer pull it back down. We're on our way!

▶ What forces act on the rocket while it's at rest on Earth's surface? Are they balanced or unbalanced?

balanced because

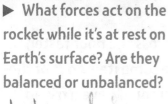

Balanced

▶ At what points during the Rover's trip to Mars are the forces on it balanced?

when it is in space it get ride of rocket gester so the weight is balanced

Unbalanced

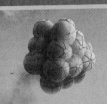

▶ What unbalanced forces are acting on the Rover as it lands on Mars?

when the rover land on Mars it bounces around. It makes it unbalanced.

Gravity

▶ Use forces to explain why the Rover required a parachute and "air bags."

Oder to land ther Rover there has to be Gravity.

During much of the time it takes the spacecraft to travel to Mars, it travels at a constant velocity. The forces acting on the spacecraft are balanced, so its motion does not change.

Tiny rockets occasionally fire to keep the spacecraft on course. During these times, the forces are unbalanced.

As the spacecraft approaches Mars, gravitational attraction begins to accelerate it toward the surface. Like a person jumping from a plane, the Rover detaches from the spacecraft. Parachutes open to slow its fall. Then a big ball inflates around the Rover. When the Rover hits the surface of Mars, it bounces around until it comes safely to rest.

Mars Rover air bag testing

When you're done, use the answer key to check and revise your work.

Change the part of the summary in blue to make it correct.

1. Forces are pushes and pulls that increase the speed of objects.

   change the motion or shape objects

2. Gravity is the force of attraction between a planet and another object.

   any two object

3. An object moving through the air slows down because it is affected by the force of gravity.

   force of friction

4. When balanced forces act on an object, the object falls.

   Dosen't change motion

5. In order for an object to change its speed or direction, someone has to push it.

   unbalanced force act on it

Answer Key: 1. can change the motion or shape of objects 2. any two objects 3. the force of friction 4. doesn't change its motion 5. an unbalanced force must act on it

Name _____

Word Play

1 A foreign-language teacher placed words from other languages into the following sentences. For each sentence, write the English word that means the same as the foreign word. Then use the circled letters to complete the riddle.

1.
   Italian

   A push is an example of a forza. Another example is a pull.

   f (o) r (c) e
     11   3

2.
   French

   The force of attraction between Earth and objects on its surface is pesanteur.

   (g) r a v i t y
     8

3.
   Russian

   The force between two moving objects that are touching is Трение.

   (f) r i c t i (o) n
    4   7

4.
   German

   Two forces that are equal in size but opposite in direction are ausgeglichene Kräfte.

   b a l a n (c) e d   f o (r) (c) e (s)
          10   5   9

5.
   Portuguese

   Two forces that are not equal in size are Forças desequilibradas.

   (u) n b a l a n c e d   f o r (c) e s
    2   6

6.
   Chinese

   A 弹簧秤 is a tool that can be used to measure the size of a force.

   (f) o r c e s   (s) k a l (e)
    1   12   13

Riddle: What conclusion did the student draw?

The f o u r c e of the f o r c e is the h o r s e, of c o u r s e.
 1 2 3   4 5 6   7 8 9   10 11   12 13

Try saying that five times fast!

Apply Concepts

2 Draw pictures of two activities that you might do. In the first, draw a pushing force. In the second, draw a pulling force.

pushing force

pulling force

3 The golfer applied a force when he hit the ball. Describe at least two forces acting on the ball as it rolls. Draw arrows to show the forces.

Gravity and friction because the ball goes up and the ball will stop.

4 Two students are using a catapult to try and hit a target. The catapult has only one setting. The first time they tried, they used Rock B. Which of the remaining rocks is likely to come closer to the target? Why?

B or C because if it was A it will go far and d it will not go far but B and C because the size.

5 Use the words *balanced* and *unbalanced* as you name and describe the forces acting in each of these pictures.

a.

accelerating

It is balanced
because it has
4 wheels to make
it balanced.

b.

This is balanced
because there
are two hands
to balanced it.

c.

This is unbalanced
because there
is noting to
balanced.

6 Draw what will happen to a ball that you throw straight up into the air. Explain why this happens.

What would happen
is it will come
down with lots of
force and there is
no gravity to hold the
ball.

7 Explain why it is easy to slip on a floor that is wet.

It is easy to slip
because there is
no friction on the
floor because it's
is wet.

8 Look at the drawings to the right. Mary measured the distance each ball traveled. Draw lines to match the ball with the distance it traveled.

Explain why each ball traveled a different distance.

Traveled different distance
because the springs are
diffrent.

25 cm

15 cm

20 cm

9 Give an example of each of the following.

a. A force is applied but nothing happens.

Inertia

b. A force causes an object to change shape.

balanced

c. A force causes an object to change position.

force

d. A force causes an object to stop moving.

friction

10 Circle the object(s) whose velocities are not changing. Draw an up arrow next to the object(s) whose speeds are increasing. Draw a down arrow next to the object(s) whose speeds are decreasing.

A car travels 35 miles per hour around a bend in the road. ↑

A car comes to a stop when a traffic light turns red. ↓

A race car accelerates when a race begins. ↑

A car is driving 45 miles per hour down a straight road. ↑

Take It Home! Discuss with your family what you've learned about forces. Together, identify five forces that you use to change the motion of objects in your everyday life. Consider forces that weren't discussed in the lesson.

S.T.E.M.
Engineering Technology

Football Safety Gear

Football is a rough sport. In order to protect players from injury, designers have developed protective gear.

The first helmets were custom made out of leather by horse harness makers. Later, ear holes and padding were added. These helmets had little padding and no face guards.

Hard plastic shells, fitted foam linings, and metal facemasks now make helmets more protective. Some helmets even contain sensors that transmit signals to warn if a player's head has been hit hard enough to cause a serious injury.

Critical Thinking

How do modern materials make it possible to build a better helmet than one made of just leather?

_____

_____

S.T.E.M.
continued

When engineers develop new materials, it can spark new and improved designs of all sorts of familiar objects.

Choose two pieces of safety gear from your favorite sport or activity. Draw each piece of gear. Do research to find out what material makes up each piece. Label the materials. Explain how one material's properties made it a good design choice.

_____   _____

List three features of this bicycle helmet. Underline the features that are for safety. Circle the features that are for comfort.

_____

_____

_____

_____

Build On It!

Rise to the engineering design challenge — complete **Design It: Balloon Racer** in the Inquiry Flipchart.

Name _____

Essential Question

How Do Forces Affect Motion?

Set a Purpose
What will you learn from this experiment?

_____

_____

_____

State Your Hypothesis
Write your hypothesis, or testable statement.

_____

_____

_____

_____

Think About the Procedure
Why do you use a rubber band to start the toy truck rather than your hand?

_____

_____

_____

Why do you add bolts to the truck?

_____

_____

_____

_____

Record Your Data
In the table below, record the data you gathered.

How Forces Affect Motion			
Part I:	Distance rubber band was stretched		
	1 cm	3 cm	5 cm
Distance traveled (cm)			
Part II:	Rubber band stretched to 3 cm		
	Empty truck	Truck with 4 bolts	Truck with 8 bolts
Distance traveled (cm) Trial 1			
Distance traveled (cm) Trial 2			
Distance traveled (cm) Trial 3			

Draw Conclusions

Each time you changed a variable and launched the truck, you ran three trials. Calculate the average distance traveled by the truck in each experimental setting.

Experimental settings	Average distance traveled (cm)
Rubber band at 1 cm	
Rubber band at 3 cm	
Rubber band at 5 cm	
Truck with 0 bolts	
Truck with 4 bolts	
Truck with 8 bolts	

Draw two bar graphs to display your data.

Analyze and Extend

1. Interpret your data. How is an object's mass related to its change in motion when acted on by a force?

_____

_____

_____

2. How does the size of the force applied to an object affect its motion?

_____

_____

_____

3. Why is it important to repeat an experiment several times or to have several people perform the same experiment?

_____

_____

_____

_____

4. Write another question you could ask about using forces and motion. What experiment could you do to answer your question?

_____

_____

_____

_____

_____

_____

Name _____

What Are Balanced and Unbalanced Forces?

Set a Purpose

What will you learn from this investigation?

_____

_____

_____

_____

Think About the Procedure

What forces are acting on the blocks when they are sitting on the table?

_____

_____

_____

Why will you pull the block across several different surfaces?

_____

_____

_____

Record Your Data

Record your measurements in this table.

Forces Investigation	
Action	**Force (N)**
Lift one block	
Lift two blocks	
Lift three blocks	
Pull block on sandpaper	
Pull block on waxed paper	
Pull block on oiled paper	

Draw Conclusions

What is required to start an object moving?

_____

_____

_____

Analyze and Extend

1. The block below is being pulled to the right. Draw arrows to show the forces acting on the object. Label each arrow.

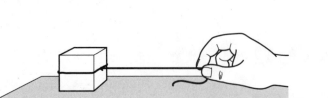

2. At what point during this activity were the forces on the block balanced? Draw the block, and show the forces as arrows.

3. How is an object's mass related to the upward force needed to overcome the pull of gravity?

_____

_____

_____

_____

4. What forces acted on the block as you tried to pull it horizontally? Were the forces balanced or unbalanced?

_____

_____

_____

_____

_____

5. Why did the blocks require a different force to begin moving on the three different surfaces?

_____

_____

_____

_____

6. What other questions would you like to ask about balanced and unbalanced forces? What investigations could you do to answer the questions?

_____

_____

_____

_____

_____

What Are Newton's Laws?

 **Engage Your Brain!**

Look for the answer to the following question in this lesson and record it here.

How does a baseball obey Newton's laws?

_____

_____

_____

_____

Active Reading

Lesson Vocabulary

List each term. As you learn about each one, make notes in the Interactive Glossary.

_____

_____

_____

Cause and Effect

Many ideas in this lesson about Newton's laws of motion are related by cause and effect. A cause is the reason something happens. An effect is what happens as a result of a cause. Active readers look for effects by asking themselves, What happened? They look for causes by asking, Why did it happen?

Hi, I'm Isaac Newton!

Newton's First Law of Motion

In the 1600s, Isaac Newton discovered some laws that still apply to the things you do, see, and feel every day.

Active Reading As you read the next page, **circle** words that identify what Newton said caused an object to accelerate.

Newton did experiments to understand how objects behave in nature. He wanted to know more about what causes an object to start moving or to change the way it moves.

Well, this proves that I can set these bowling pins in motion!

In 1687, Newton published a book about how objects move in the physical world. The English scientist summed up his ideas in three rules, or laws. *Newton's first law of motion* states that no acceleration can happen without an unbalanced force. Here, *acceleration* means "change in motion" and *force* means "a push or a pull." Another way to say Newton's first law is this: Objects at rest don't move unless an unbalanced force acts on them. Objects in motion don't slow down, speed up, stop, or turn unless a force makes them do so.

Newton's first law describes inertia. **Inertia** is the tendency of objects to resist a change in motion. Think of riding in a car. If the car turns sharply in one direction, your body feels pulled to the other side of the car. Your body is attempting to continue moving in the same direction as it was before the car turned. When the car stops, your seat belt and friction from the seat provide the unbalanced force needed to keep you in your seat.

When a car makes a sudden stop or turn, a seat belt helps keep your body from continuing its previous motion.

Describing Inertia

Inertia applies both to objects that are moving and objects that are at rest. Explain each situation, using examples.

_____

_____

_____

_____

_____

_____

_____

_____

Newton's
Second Law of Motion

Newton's first law talks about objects, forces, and motion. Newton's second law is more specific. It also considers, How big of an object? How much force? How much motion?

Newton's *second law of motion* states that an object's acceleration depends on two factors— the amount of force applied to the object, and the object's mass. Think about how kicking a ball harder makes it move faster. In other words, the greater the applied force, the greater the acceleration. A harder kick is a greater force.

I think I know why these dogs are not equally easy to move!

I have a big personality, but my mass is small!

My mass is large, so I have a big interest in resting!

Do the Math!
Solve Word Problems

F means *force*, *m* means *mass*, and *a* means *acceleration*.

Use Newton's second law ($F = m \times a$) to find the missing values in the equations below. Recall that the standard unit of force is the newton (N).

If a mass has a value of 1 and its acceleration is a value of 3, what is the value of the force acting on the mass?

_____

A ball has a mass of 6 units. Its acceleration is 8 units. What is the value of the force that set the ball in motion?

_____

The mass of an object affects how, or if, the object moves when a force is applied to it. Think of an empty shopping cart at a grocery store. How much force does it take to start it moving? Not much, right? Now imagine the cart filled with groceries. If you used the same amount of force as before, would the full cart move? Probably not. Newton's second law explains why you must use more force to move an object with a greater mass. The second law of motion can be written as an equation: Force = mass × acceleration.

The amount of force needed to turn the pinwheel would not be enough to move the blades of the wind turbine.

Newton's Third Law of Motion

Objects are acted upon by more than one force at a time. Newton's third law of motion describes the way different forces relate to each other.

Active Reading As you read this page, **underline** words that identify the effect that happens when one object applies a force to another object.

Whenever one object applies a force to a second object, the second object applies an equal, opposite force to the first object. This is *Newton's third law of motion.* To say this law more simply, forces always act in pairs.

My hand applies a force to this board. The board applies an equal, opposite force to my hand. Ouch!

To better understand Newton's third law, picture two objects—your body and a wall. As you lean against the wall, your body applies a force to the wall. The wall doesn't move because it applies the same amount of force to you. Sometimes scientists use the terms *action force* and *reaction force* to refer to a pair of forces.

Now think about the two adjectives that Newton used to describe a pair of forces. How are action and reaction forces *equal* and *opposite*? The two forces described above are equal in size, and they are opposite in direction.

During takeoff, the rocket's thrusters push the exhaust gases downward as the gases push the rocket upward with an equal force.

Forces in Action

Look carefully at the diagrams of the apple and the table. Draw arrows to show the forces between apple and table. Make longer lines to show stronger forces.

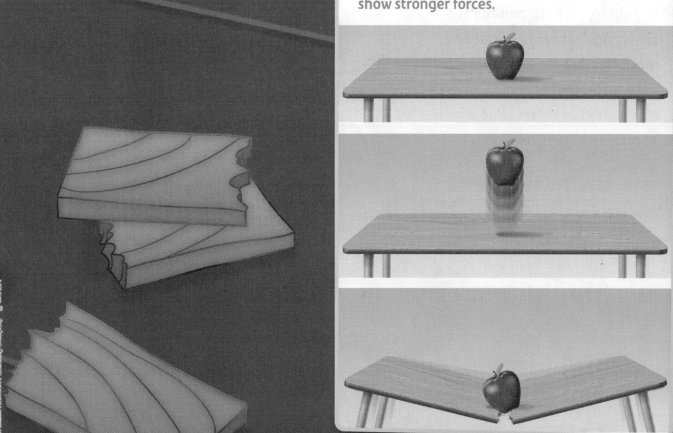

Motion in Space

You've probably seen pictures of astronauts floating with other objects inside a spacecraft. The astronauts, the objects, and the spacecraft are all in motion, and Newton's laws still apply.

Active Reading As you read the next page, **circle** the main idea. **Underline** details that add important information about the main idea.

Astronauts in orbit appear to be weightless. To understand the motion of objects in space, it's important to remember the difference between weight and mass. Remember, *mass* refers to how much matter is in an object. *Weight* refers to how much force is applied to an object by gravity.

Perhaps if I push off the wall with a little more force, I can snag this apple!

As a person swings an object in a circular motion, you can see an example of how objects orbit Earth. The string acts like gravity, constantly pulling the object toward the center of the circular path. If the person lets go, inertia takes over; the object keeps traveling, but in a straight line. The *International Space Station (ISS)* shows how Newton's first law works in space. Because of inertia, the *ISS* moves forward at a contant speed. At the same time, gravity pulls the *ISS* toward Earth, so that the *ISS* constantly changes direction. As a result of these two motions, the *ISS* follows the curve of Earth's surface. What would happen if Earth's gravity did not constantly pull on the *ISS*? Inertia would cause the station to fly off into space in a straight line!

▶ Explain what two forces are acting on Isaac Newton as he floats in the *ISS*.

_____

_____

_____

_____

Newton's laws of motion apply to objects in space, because the laws involve mass, not weight. The mass of an object is the same on Earth and in space. An object's weight can change because it is related to the force of gravity at a particular location. Astronauts feel and look weightless because of microgravity. Often mistakenly called "zero gravity," *microgravity* occurs because Earth's gravity causes the space station to fall toward Earth at a constant rate. Everything inside the space station falls at the same rate. Because the astronauts are also in free fall, they appear to float.

Sum It Up!

When you're done, use the answer key to check and revise your work.

For each of the following questions about Newton's laws of motion, circle the correct answer to complete the sentence.

1. Newton's first law states that no [acceleration / inertia] can happen without a force.

2. When a raindrop strikes a brick wall, the force the raindrop applies to the brick wall is [greater than / equal to / less than] the force the brick wall applies to the raindrop.

3. Two identical boxes are placed on the ground next to each other. One is empty, and one is filled with sand. It would take [more force / the same amount of force / less force] to pull the empty box than the box with sand.

4. When a hammer strikes a nail, the direction of the force the hammer applies to the nail is [the same as / opposite from] the direction of the force the nail applies to the hammer.

5. Two powerful forces that can overcome inertia are [mass / friction] and gravity.

Answer Key: 1. acceleration, 2. equal to, 3. less force, 4. opposite from, 5. friction, 6. microgravity

Name _____

Word Play

1 Unscramble the scrambled words in each sentence. Write the unscrambled word after the sentence. The first one is done for you.

a. The two forces in a pair are *poseptio* in direction.	o p p o s i t e
b. An object's acceleration depends in part on the *sasm* of the object.	_ _ _ _
c. Newton's first law gives a good description of *etirian*.	_ _ _ _ _ _ _
d. In science, *neteocacrila* is a term for a change in speed or direction.	_ _ _ _ _ _ _ _ _ _ _ _
e. Objects do not change their motion unless some *creof* makes them change.	_ _ _ _ _
f. In space, *virmrciroygat* causes an astronaut to feel weightless.	_ _ _ _ _ _ _ _ _ _ _ _

Bonus

In a pair of forces, the first force is sometimes called an _ _ _ _ _ _ force, and

the second force is sometimes called a _ _ _ _ _ _ _ _ force.

acceleration	action	force	inertia*
mass	microgravity	opposite	reaction

* Key Lesson Vocabulary

Apply Concepts

2 Look at the illustrations of two shopping carts. Circle the cart that would be harder to move. Explain why this is so.

_____

_____

3 Explain how a person taking a nap on a grassy meadow is an example of inertia.

_____

_____

_____

_____

_____

_____

_____

4 Make three drawings to illustrate Newton's three laws of motion. Label your drawings with the name of the law and other important words.

Take It Home! Share with your family what you have learned about Newton's laws of motion. With one or more family members, design and perform a demonstration of inertia.

① A safety engineer helps design and test devices to make them safer.

② Safety engineers make changes to designs to avoid possible dangers.

③ I'm a crash test dummy. Some safety engineers use me as a model.

10
THINGS TO KNOW ABOUT
Safety Engineers

④ Safety engineers can make machines, such as cars, safer to use.

⑤ Safety engineers make cars safer with inventions such as seat belts and air bags.

⑥ Some safety engineers focus on stopping specific dangers, such as fires.

⑦ Safety engineers help society have fewer injuries and illnesses.

⑧ Some keep germs from spreading into our food and making us sick.

⑨ They may focus on protecting workers from getting hurt on the job.

⑩ To do their jobs, safety engineers need to study physics, chemistry, math, and human behavior.

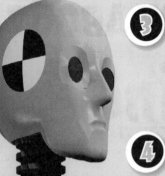

Now You Be the Engineer!

1 What do you think is the best thing about being a safety engineer?

2 How do safety engineers help society?

3 What safety features in cars have safety engineers helped to develop?

4 What question would you like to ask a safety engineer?

1 _____
_____
_____
_____

2 _____
_____
_____
_____
_____

3 _____
_____
_____

4 _____
_____
_____
_____

Name _____

Vocabulary Review

Use the terms in the box to complete the sentences.

balanced forces
force
friction
gravity
inertia
unbalanced forces

1. Forces that cause a change in motion are

   _____.

2. A force of attraction between two objects, even if they are not

   touching, is _____.

3. The tendency of objects to resist a change in motion

   is _____.

4. A push or a pull, which causes movement or change in an

   object's movement or shape, is a(n) _____.

5. Forces on an object that are equal in size and opposite in

   direction are _____.

6. A force that opposes motion and acts between two objects that

   are touching is _____.

Science Concepts

Fill in the letter of the choice that best answers the question.

7. This table shows the masses of several different objects.

Object	Metal washer	Plastic disk	Rock	Wooden block
Mass (g)	1.5	34	16	22

Which object will require the most force to toss it 2 meters?

(A) rock

(B) plastic disk

(C) metal washer

(D) wooden block

8. Which of these is an example of a force being applied?

(A) watching TV

(B) reading a book

(C) pulling a wagon

(D) standing at the top of a hill

Science Concepts

Fill in the letter of the choice that best answers the question.

9. Suri places magnets on three identical toy cars, as shown below. Then she measures how far each car rolls when she launches it from the same starting point using the same stretched rubber band.

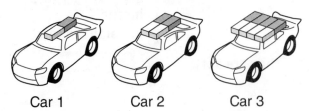

Car 1   Car 2   Car 3

How will the force of the rubber band affect the cars?

Ⓐ Car 3 will travel the longest distance.

Ⓑ Car 1 will travel the shortest distance.

Ⓒ Car 1 will be the least affected by the force acting upon it.

Ⓓ Car 3 will be the least affected by the force acting upon it.

10. When you coast down a hill on a bicycle, you move faster and faster. When you coast on a level surface, you eventually stop moving. How do Newton's laws of motion explain what causes you to stop?

Ⓐ Newton's Second Law explains that no force is acting on your bike on the level surface, so it stops moving.

Ⓑ Newton's First Law explains that after you reach the bottom of the hill, you run out of energy, so you stop moving.

Ⓒ Newton's Third Law explains that friction between the tires and the ground is an unbalanced force that changes your motion.

Ⓓ Newton's First Law explains that gravity affects you when you move downhill, but does not affect you when you move on a level surface.

11. Katja pushes a bowling ball away from her with a lot of force. Then she repeats the same procedure with a soccer ball. How do Newton's laws explain the difference between the movements of the two balls?

Ⓐ Newton's Second Law of Motion explains that the soccer ball moves a greater distance because it has less mass.

Ⓑ Newton's Third Law of Motion explains that the soccer ball moves a greater distance because more force is acting on it.

Ⓒ Newton's Second Law of Motion explains that the bowling ball moves a greater distance because it has more mass.

Ⓓ Newton's First Law of Motion explains that the bowling ball moves a shorter distance because less force is acting on it.

12. A spring scale measures force.

What is the force that causes the reading on the spring scale shown in the illustration?

Ⓐ mass

Ⓑ weight

Ⓒ gravity

Ⓓ friction

© Houghton Mifflin Harcourt Publishing Company

13. Four forces are acting on the block shown in the following illustration:

- *F* is the applied force.
- F_f is friction.
- F_g is the gravitational force.
- F_n is the normal force—the upward push of the table on the block.

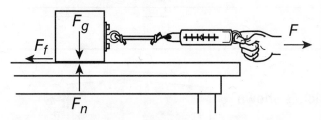

The block is not moving. Which of the following statements is **true**?

Ⓐ *F* and F_f are equal.

Ⓑ *F* and F_g are equal.

Ⓒ F_f is greater than *F*.

Ⓓ F_g is greater than *F*.

14. An object is traveling in a straight line in space. No forces are affecting it. Because of inertia, what will happen to the object's motion?

Ⓐ It will move faster and faster because there is no force to stop it.

Ⓑ It will stop gradually because there is no force to keep it moving.

Ⓒ It will stop immediately when the force that started its motion goes away.

Ⓓ Its motion will not change and it will continue in the same direction at the same speed.

15. This table shows the masses of four blocks and the forces that are being applied to each one.

Block color	Mass (g)	Pushing force (N)	Friction (N)
Red	50	24	6
Green	100	24	6
Blue	40	24	6
Yellow	75	24	6

According to Newton's laws of motion, which block will have the greatest change in motion?

Ⓐ red block

Ⓑ blue block

Ⓒ green block

Ⓓ yellow block

16. The following illustration shows the forces that are acting on a box.

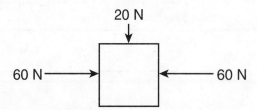

What type of motion will the forces cause?

Ⓐ The box will remain in its current position.

Ⓑ The box will move downward in a straight line.

Ⓒ The box will move to the right in a straight line.

Ⓓ The box will move back and forth from the left to the right.

Apply Inquiry and Review the Big Idea

Write the answers to these questions.

17. Jermaine wondered if a heavy ball rolls down a ramp faster than a light ball. Use the space below to describe an investigation he could conduct in order to find out.

_____

_____

_____

_____

18. This worker is pushing a box with a force, which is shown by the arrow. The box does not move.

What keeps the box from moving even though the worker is pushing on it?

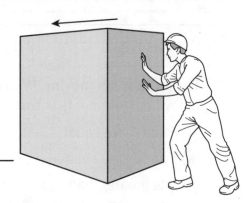

_____

19. Explain why Newton's Laws of Motion apply to objects in space, even though objects in space can look and feel weightless.

_____

_____

_____

_____

20. The spring scale shown has a weight attached to it. When the weight was attached, the pointer on the scale moved downward.

What will happen if a second weight is added to the spring scale? Explain your answer.

_____

_____

Interactive Glossary

As you learn about each term, add notes, drawings, or sentences in the extra space. This will help you remember what the terms mean. Here are some examples.

Fungi [FUHN•jeye] A kingdom of organisms that have a nucleus and get nutrients by decomposing other organisms

A mushroom is from the kingdom Fungi.

physical change [FIHZ•i•kuhl CHAYNJ] Change in the size, shape, or state of matter with no new substance being formed

When I cut paper, the paper has a physical change.

Glossary Pronunciation Key

With every glossary term, there is also a phonetic respelling. A phonetic respelling writes the word the way it sounds, which can help you pronounce new or unfamiliar words. Use this key to help you understand the respellings.

Sound	As in	Phonetic Respelling	Sound	As in	Phonetic Respelling
a	bat	(BAT)	oh	over	(OH•ver)
ah	lock	(LAHK)	oo	pool	(POOL)
air	rare	(RAIR)	ow	out	(OWT)
ar	argue	(AR•gyoo)	oy	foil	(FOYL)
aw	law	(LAW)	s	cell	(SEL)
ay	face	(FAYS)		sit	(SIT)
ch	chapel	(CHAP•uhl)	sh	sheep	(SHEEP)
e	test	(TEST)	th	that	(THAT)
	metric	(MEH•trik)		thin	(THIN)
ee	eat	(EET)	u	pull	(PUL)
	feet	(FEET)	uh	medal	(MED•uhl)
	ski	(SKEE)		talent	(TAL•uhnt)
er	paper	(PAY•per)		pencil	(PEN•suhl)
	fern	(FERN)		onion	(UHN•yuhn)
eye	idea	(eye•DEE•uh)		playful	(PLAY•fuhl)
i	bit	(BIT)		dull	(DUHL)
ing	going	(GOH•ing)	y	yes	(YES)
k	card	(KARD)		ripe	(RYP)
	kite	(KYT)	z	bags	(BAGZ)
ngk	bank	(BANGK)	zh	treasure	(TREZH•er)

Interactive Glossary

A

abyssal plain [uh•BIS•uhl PLAYN] The vast floor of the deep ocean (p. 496)

accurate [AK•yuh•ruht] In measurements, very close to the actual size or value (p. 49)

adaptation [ad•uhp•TAY•shuhn] A trait or characteristic that helps an organism survive (p. 226)

amplitude [AM•pluh•tood] A measure of the amount of energy in a wave (p. 653)

angiosperm [AN•jee•oh•sperm] A flowering vascular plant whose seeds are surrounded by a fruit (p. 197)

asteroid [AS•tuh•royd] A chunk of rock or iron less than 1,000 km (621 mi) in diameter that orbits the sun (p. 548)

astronomy [uh•STRAHN•uh•mee] The study of objects in space and their properties (p. 562)

atom [AT•uhm] The smallest unit into which an element can be divided and still retain all the properties of that element (p. 630)

atomic theory [uh•TAHM•ik THEE•uh•ree]
A scientific explanation of the structure of atoms and how they interact with other atoms (p. 630)

biotechnology [by•oh•tek•NAHL•uh•jee]
A product of technology used to benefit organisms and the environment (p.89)

B

balance [BAL•uhns] A tool used to measure the amount of matter in an object, which is the object's mass (p. 46)

bladder [BLAD•er] Organ in the excretory system that stores and releases urine (p. 159)

balanced forces [BAL•uhnst FAWRS•iz] Forces that cancel each other out because they are equal in size and opposite in direction (p. 704)

bones [BOHNZ] Hard organs that have a spongy layer inside and that may help support the body or protect other organs (p. 140)

bioengineering [by•oh•en•juh•NIR•ing] The application of the engineering design process to living things (p. 88)

brain [BRAYN] The organ in the human body that processes information (p. 128)

Interactive Glossary

C

cast [KAST] A model of an organism, formed when sediment fills a mold and hardens (p. 455)

cell [SEL] The basic unit of structure and function in all living things (p. 104)

cell membrane [SEL MEM•brayn] The thin covering that surrounds every cell (p. 106)

chemical changes [KEM•ih•kuhl CHAYNJ•ez] Changes in one or more substances, caused by a reaction, that form new and different substances (p. 599)

chlorophyll [KLAWR•uh•fil] A green pigment in plants that allows a plant cell to use light to make food (p. 293)

classification [klas•uh•fih•KAY•shuhn] The sorting of things into groups of similar items (p. 176)

comet [KAHM•it] A chunk of frozen gases, rock, ice, and dust orbiting the sun (p. 549)

community [kuh•MYOO•nih•tee] A group of organisms that live in the same area and interact with each other (p. 250)

complete metamorphosis [kuhm•PLEET met•uh•MAWR•fuh•sis] A complex change that most insects undergo that includes larva and pupa stages (p. 217)

consumer [kuhn•SOOM•er] A living thing that cannot make its own food and must eat other living things (p. 295)

compound [KAHM•pownd] A substance made of two or more types of atoms that are chemically combined (p. 634)

continental shelf [kahnt•uhn•ENT•uhl SHELF] A gradually sloping portion of the ocean floor that is made of continental crust (p. 496)

conservation [kahn•ser•VAY•shuhn] The process of preserving and protecting an ecosystem or a resource (p. 344)

continental slope [kahnt•uhn•ENT•uhl SLOHP] The part of the ocean floor that slopes steeply (p. 496)

conservation of mass [kahn•ser•VAY•shuhn uhv MAS] A law that states that matter cannot be made or destroyed; however, matter can be changed into a new form (p. 604)

control [kuhn•TROHL] The experimental setup to which you will compare all other setups (p. 29)

Interactive Glossary

coral reef [KAWR•uhl REEF] Branch-like structures formed by the skeletons of colonies of coral polyps (p. 523)

current [KER•uhnt] A continuous flow of water in a regular pattern in the ocean. (p. 508)

core [KAWR] The layer of Earth extending from Earth's center to the bottom of the mantle. It is mostly metallic iron and nickel (p. 389)

D

decomposer [dee•kuhm•POHZ•er] A living thing that gets energy by breaking down dead organisms and animal wastes into simpler substances (p. 299)

criteria [kry•TEER•ee•uh] The standards for measuring success (p. 70)

deposition [dep•uh•ZISH•uhn] The dropping or settling of eroded materials (p. 368)

crust [KRUHST] The thin outer layer of Earth, including dry land and the ocean floor (p. 389)

dichotomous key [dy•KAHT•uh•muhs KEE] A tool used to identify organisms based on contrasting pairs of characteristics (p. 177)

domain [doh•MAYN] The broadest level of classification of organisms (p. 179)

ecosystem [EE•koh•sis•tuhm] A community of organisms and the environment in which they live (p. 249)

dominant trait [DAHM•ih•nuhnt TRAYT] A trait that appears if an organism has one factor for that trait (p. 115)

electromagnetic spectrum [ee•lek•troh•mag•NET•ik SPEK•truhm] All energy waves that travel at the speed of light in a vacuum; includes radio, infrared, visible, ultraviolet, x-rays, and gamma rays (p. 671)

dwarf planet [DWORF PLAN•it] A nearly round body, slightly smaller than a planet, whose orbit crosses the orbit of another body (p. 548)

element [EL•uh•muhnt] Matter that is made of only one kind of atom (p. 632)

E

earthquake [ERTH•kwayk] A shaking of Earth's surface that can cause land to rise and fall (p. 394)

energy pyramid [EN•er•jee PIR•uh•mid] A diagram that shows that energy is lost at each level in a food chain (p. 312)

Interactive Glossary

engineering [en•juh•NEER•ing] The use of science and math for practical uses such as the design of structures, machines, and systems (p. 65)

evidence [EV•uh•duhns] Information collected during a scientific investigation (p. 6)

environment [en•VEYE•ruhn•muhnt] All the living and nonliving things that surround and affect an organism (p. 248)

experiment [ik•SPAIR•uh•muhnt] An investigation in which all the conditions are controlled to test a hypothesis (p. 23)

epicenter [EP•ih•sent•er] The point on Earth's surface directly above the focus of an earthquake (p. 394)

extinction [ek•STINGKT•shuhn] A plant or an animal species that is no longer living or existing (p. 274)

erosion [uh•ROH•zhuhn] The process of moving sediment from one place to another (p. 368)

F

fault [FAWLT] A break in Earth's crust where rock on one side moves in relation to rock on the other side (p. 394)

food chain [FOOD CHAYN] The transfer of food energy between organisms in an ecosystem (p. 309)

fossil fuel [FAHS•uhl FYOO•uhl] Fuel formed from the remains of once-living things. Coal, oil, and natural gas are fossil fuels. (p. 456)

food web [FOOD WEB] A group of food chains that overlap (p. 310)

frequency [FREE•kwuhn•see] A measure of the number of waves that pass a point in a second (p. 650)

force [FAWRS] A push or pull, which may cause a change in an object's motion (p. 700)

friction [FRIK•shuhn] A force that acts between two touching objects and that opposes motion (p. 703)

fossil [FAHS•uhl] The remains or traces of a plant or an animal that lived long ago (p. 454)

G

galaxy [GAL•uhk•see] A group containing billions of stars, objects that orbit those stars, gas, and dust (p. 565)

Interactive Glossary

gas [GAS] The state of matter in which a substance does not have a definite shape or volume (p. 584)

gymnosperm [JIM•noh•sperm] A vascular plant that produces seeds that are not surrounded by a fruit (p. 196)

genus [JEE•nuhs] In the classification of organisms, a subdivision of a family (p. 179)

H

habitat [HAB•ih•tat] The place where an organism lives and can find everything it needs to survive (p. 252)

germinate [JER•muh•nayt] To begin to grow (a seed, spore, or bud) (p. 200)

heart [HART] The muscular organ that pumps blood through the rest of the circulatory system (p. 148)

gravity [GRAV•ih•tee] The force of attraction between objects, such as the attraction between Earth and objects on it (p. 702)

© Houghton Mifflin Harcourt Publishing Company   HMH Credits

igneous rock [IG•nee•uhs RAHK] A type of rock that forms from melted rock that cools and hardens (p. 429)

incomplete metamorphosis [in•kuhm•PLEET met•uh•MAWR•fuh•sis] Developmental change in some insects in which a nymph hatches from an egg and gradually develops into an adult (p. 218)

index fossil [IN•deks FAHS•uhl] A fossil of a type of organism that lived in many places during a relatively short time span (p. 469)

inertia [ih•NUR•shuh] The tendency for an object to resist change in motion (p. 725)

inherited trait [in•HAIR•it•ed TRAYT] A characteristic passed from parents to their offspring (p. 112)

instinct [IN•stinkt] Behavior that an organism inherits and knows how to do without being taught (p. 232)

intertidal zone [in•ter•TYD•uhl ZOHN] The area between the land and the ocean that is covered by water at high tide and uncovered at low tide (p. 521)

invertebrate [in•VER•tuh•brit] An animal without a backbone (p. 212)

Interactive Glossary

investigation [in•ves•tuh•GAY•shuhn] A procedure carried out to carefully observe, study, or test something in order to learn more about it (p. 4)

J

jetty [JET•ee] A wall-like structure that sticks out into the ocean to prevent sand from being carried away (p. 513)

K

kidneys [KID•neez] Organs in the human excretory system that remove waste materials from the blood (p. 159)

L

life cycle [LYF SEYE•kuhl] The stages that a living thing passes through as it grows and changes (p. 216)

light [LYT] A form of energy that can travel through space and lies partly within the visible range (p. 668)

liquid [LIK•wid] The state of matter in which a substance has a definite volume but no definite shape (p. 584)

liver [LIV•er] A large organ that makes a digestive juice called bile (p. 155)

© Houghton Mifflin Harcourt Publishing Company HMH Credits

lungs [LUNGZ] The large organs in the respiratory system that bring oxygen from the air into the body and release carbon dioxide (p. 144)

meiosis [my•OH•sis] The process that produces reproductive cells (p. 111)

M

mantle [MAN•tuhl] The thick layer of Earth beneath the crust (p. 389)

metamorphic rock [met•uh•MAWR•fik RAHK] A type of rock that forms when heat or pressure changes an existing rock (p. 432)

mass extinction [MAS ek•STINGK•shuhn] A period in which a large number of species become extinct (p. 475)

microscopic [my•kruh•SKAHP•ik] Too small to be seen without using a microscope (p. 43)

matter [MAT•er] Anything that has mass and takes up space (p. 580)

mineral [MIN•er•uhl] A nonliving solid that has a crystal form (p. 414)

Interactive Glossary

mitosis [my•TOH•sis] The process by which most cells divide (p. 110)

muscles [MUHS•uhlz] Organs made of bundles of long fibers that can contract to produce movement in living things (p. 142)

mixture [MIKS•cher] A combination of two or more different substances in which the substances keep their identities (p. 615)

N

natural resource [NACH•er•uhl REE•sawrs] Anything from nature that people can use (p. 330)

mold [MOHLD] An impression of an organism, formed when sediment hardens around the organism (p. 455)

niche [NICH] The role a plant or an animal plays in its habitat (p. 252)

molecule [MAHL•ih•kyool] A single particle of matter made up of two or more atoms joined together chemically (p. 634)

nonrenewable resource [nahn•rih•NOO•uh•buhl REE•sawrs] A resource that, once used, cannot be replaced in a reasonable amount of time (p. 331)

© Houghton Mifflin Harcourt Publishing Company   HMH Credits

nonvascular plant [nahn•VAS•kyuh•ler PLANT] A plant that lacks tissues for carrying water, food, and nutrients (p. 192)

organ [AWR•guhn] A group of tissues that work together to perform a certain function (p. 126)

nucleus [NOO•klee•uhs] The control center of a cell that directs the cell's activities (p. 106)

organ system [AWR•guhn SIS•tuhm] A group of organs that work together to do a job for the body (p. 126)

O

opaque [oh•PAYK] Not allowing light to pass through (p. 678)

organism [AWR•guh•niz•uhm] A living thing (p. 104)

P

opinion [uh•PIN•yuhn] A personal belief or judgment based on what a person thinks or feels but not necessarily based on evidence (p. 9)

pancreas [PAN•kree•uhs] An organ in the body that makes a digestive juice as well as insulin (p. 155)

Interactive Glossary

photosynthesis [foh•toh•SIN•thuh•sis]
The process that plants use to make sugar
(p. 293)

plate tectonics [PLAYT tek•TAHN•iks] The
theory that Earth's crust is divided into plates
that are always moving (p. 390)

physical changes [FIZ•i•kuhl CHAYNJ•ez]
Changes in which the form or shape of a
substance changes but the substance still has
the same chemical makeup (p. 598)

plankton [PLANK•tuhn] Small organisms that
float, or drift, in great numbers in bodies of
salt water or fresh water (p. 526)

pitch [PICH] The highness or lowness of a
sound (p. 650)

pollution [puh•LOO•shuhn] Any waste
product or contamination that harms or
dirties an ecosystem and harms organisms
(p. 337)

planet [PLAN•it] A large, round body that
revolves around a star (p. 540)

population [pahp•yuh•LAY•shuhn] All the
organisms of the same kind that live together
in an ecosystem (p. 250)

prism [PRIZ•uhm] A transparent object that separates white light into the colors of the rainbow (p. 683)

recessive trait [ree•SES•iv TRAYT] A trait that appears only if an organism has two factors for that trait (p. 115)

producer [pruh•DOOS•er] A living thing, such as a plant, that can make its own food (p. 294)

reflection [rih•FLEHK•shuhn] The bouncing of light waves when they encounter an obstacle (p. 680)

prototype [PROH•tuh•typ] The original or test model on which a product is based (p. 68)

refraction [rih•FRAK•shuhn] The bending of light waves as they pass from one material to another (p. 682)

R

reaction [ree•AK•shuhn] The process through which new substances are formed during a chemical change (p. 599)

renewable resource [rih•NOO•uh•buhl REE•sawrs] A resource that can be replaced within a reasonable amount of time (p. 330)

Interactive Glossary

rock [RAHK] A naturally formed solid made of one or more minerals (p. 428)

sediment [SED•uh•ment] Sand, bits of rock, fossils, and other matter carried and deposited by water, wind, or ice (p. 369)

S

salinity [suh•LIN•uh•tee] The saltiness of water (p. 495)

sedimentary rock [sed•uh•MEN•tuh•ree RAHK] A type of rock that forms when layers of sediment are pressed together (p. 430)

science [SY•uhns] The study of the natural world through observation and investigation (p. 5)

shore [SHAWR] The area where the ocean and the land meet and interact (p. 513)

scientific methods [SY•uhn•TIF•ik METH•uhds] The different ways that scientists perform investigations and collect reliable data (p. 22)

skin [SKIN] The human body's largest organ, covering the outside of the body (p. 134)

solar system [SOH•ler SIS•tuhm] A star and all the planets and other bodies that revolve around it (p. 540)

spore [SPAWR] A reproductive structure made by some plants, including mosses and ferns, that can grow into a new plant (p. 194)

solid [SAHL•id] The state of matter in which a substance has a definite shape and a definite volume (p. 585)

spring scale [SPRING SKAYL] A tool used to measure force (p. 47)

solution [suh•LOO•shuhn] A mixture that has the same composition throughout because all its parts are mixed evenly (p. 616)

stars [STARZ] Huge balls of very hot, glowing gases in space that produce their own light and heat (p. 562)

species [SPEE•sheez] In the classification of organisms, the smallest group of closely related individuals (p. 179)

stomach [STUHM•uhk] A baglike organ in which food is mixed with digestive juices and squeezed by muscles (p. 154)

Interactive Glossary

succession [suhk•SESH•uhn] A gradual change in the kinds of organisms in an ecosystem (p. 266)

tissue [TISH•oo] A group of similar cells that work together, such as muscle tissue and stomach tissue (p. 126)

T

technology [tek•NAHL•uh•jee] The use of scientific knowledge to solve practical problems (p. 66)

translucent [trahns•LOO•suhnt] Allows only some light to pass through (p. 679)

temperature [TEM•per•uh•cher] The measure of the energy of motion of particles of matter, which we feel as how hot or cold something is (p. 582)

transparent [trahns•PAIR•uhnt] Allows light to pass through (p. 679)

U

tide [TYD] The regular rise and fall of the ocean's surface, caused mostly by the moon's gravitational pull on Earth's oceans (p. 511)

unbalanced forces [uhn•BAL•uhnst FAWRS•iz] Forces that cause a change in an object's motion because they don't cancel each other out (p. 704)

universe [YOO•nuh•vers] Everything that exists, including galaxies and everything in them (p. 564)

volcano [vahl•KAY•noh] A place where hot gases, smoke, and melted rock come out of the ground onto Earth's surface (p. 398)

V

variable [VAIR•ee•uh•buhl] Any condition that can be changed in an experiment (p. 29)

volume [VAHL•yoom] The amount of space something takes up (p. 580)

vascular plant [VAS•kyuh•ler PLANT] A plant that has transport tissues for carrying water, food, and nutrients to its cells (p. 193)

volume [VAHL•yoom] The loudness of a sound (p. 651)

W

vertebrate [VER•tuh•brit] An animal with a backbone (p. 210)

water pressure [WAW•ter PRESH•er] The downward push of water (p. 495)

Interactive Glossary

wave [WAYV] The up-and-down movement of surface water (p. 506)

wavelength [WAYV•length] The distance between a point on one wave and the identical point on the next wave (p. 652)

wave [WAYV] A disturbance that carries energy, such as sound or light, through matter or space (p. 648)

weathering [WETH•er•ing] The breaking down of rocks on Earth's surface into smaller pieces (p. 367)

© Houghton Mifflin Harcourt Publishing Company   HMH Credits

Index

N

native species, 270–271
natural gas, 457
natural resources, 330–337
  conserving, 344–345, 350–351
  fossil fuels, 331
  at home, 334–335
  pollution and, 336–337
  soil, 346–347
  transportation of, 332–333
  water, 348–349
neap tides, 511
neon, 632
Neptune, 545
nerves, 128, 135
nerve tissue, 126–127
neutrons, 631
newton (N), 49, 700
Newton, Isaac, 724–725
Newton's Laws, 724–731
  first law of motion, 724–725
  second law of motion,
    726–727
  third law of motion, 728–729
niches, 252–253
nocturnal animals, 232
nonrenewable resources, 331
  See also natural resources
nonvascular plants, 192
nose, 130–131
nucleus, 106–107
numbers, 44
nutrition labels, 156–157
nymph, 219

O

observations, 4–5, 25–27
oceanic ridge, 496–497

oceanic trench, 496–497
oceanographers, 531–532
oceans, 492–499, 617
  coral reefs, 499, 522–523
  currents, 508–509
  energy pyramid, 312–313
  floor of, 496–497
  intertidal zone, 520–521
  locations and areas of,
    492–493
  open-ocean zone, 524–525
  plankton in, 526–527
  shores, 512–513
  tides, 510–511
  underwater exploration,
    494–495
  volcanic islands in, 498–499
  waves, 506–507
  weathering and, 375
oil, 332–333, 341–342, 457
Old Faithful, 26
olfactory bulb, 130–131
omnivores, 297
opaque materials, 678
open-ocean zone, 524–525
opinions, 9
ordering, 13
orders (classification), 178–179
organisms, 104
organs, 126–127
organ systems, 126
ovaries, 198
ovules, 196
oxygen, 292–293

P

paleontologists, 4–5, 458, 481
Paleozoic Era, 468
pan balance, 48
pancreas, 155, 161

paramecium, 183
Paricutín, 399
peat, 456
penicillin, 237
people, environment and,
  272–273, 346–347
People in Science
  Alexander, Claudia, 557–558
  Alvarez, Luis, 481
  Alvarez, Walter, 481
  Bascom, Florence, 423
  Chawla, Kalpana, 557–558
  Chin, Karen, 481
  Clark, Eugenie, 531
  Curie, Marie, 639–640
  Forde, Evan B., 531
  Grant, Peter, 305–306
  Grant, Rosemary, 305–306
  Gray, Asa, 165
  Gray, Henry, 165
  Hubbard, Bernard, 423
  Juniper, Jane, 259
  Stevens, Lisa, 223
  Sukumar, Raman, 223
  Triay, Inés, 639–640
  Zavaleta, Erika, 305–306
petrified wood, 455
phloem, 193
photosynthesis, 293, 526
phylum, 178
physical adaptations, 228–231
physical changes, 598, 604
physical properties, 581
phytoplankton, 312
pinecones, 196
pipette, 45
pitch, 650
pituitary gland, 160–161
pivot joint, 141
planets, 540–547
  dwarf, 548